The Incised Drawings from Early Phrygian Gordion

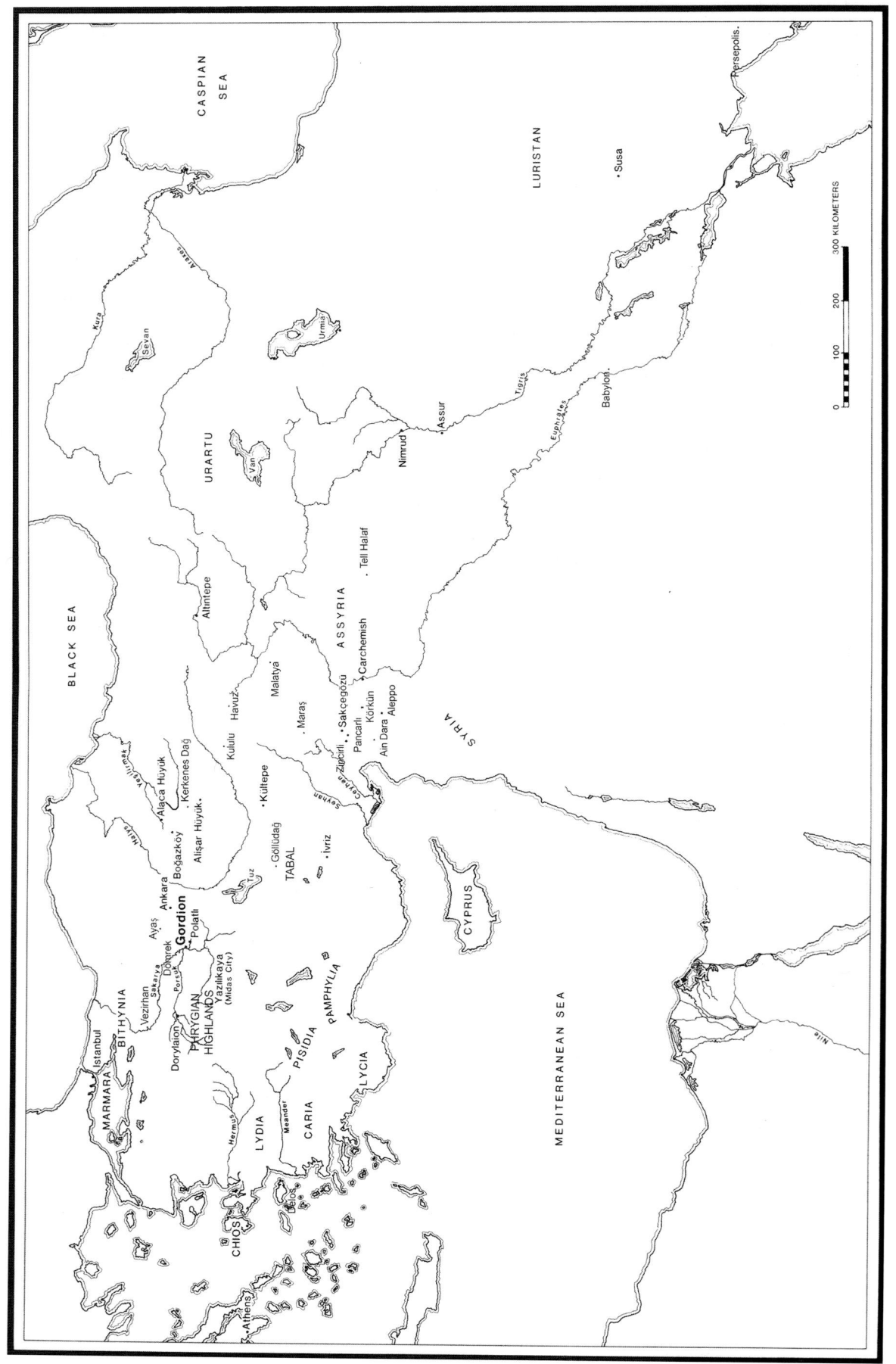

Frontispiece. Anatolia, showing the location of Gordion and sites mentioned in the text.

MUSEUM MONOGRAPH 130

GORDION SPECIAL STUDIES IV

The Incised Drawings from Early Phrygian Gordion

Lynn E. Roller

UNIVERSITY OF PENNSYLVANIA MUSEUM OF ARCHAEOLOGY AND ANTHROPOLOGY
PHILADELPHIA

Lynn E. Roller is Professor of Art History at the University of California, Davis. She received her A.B. and M.A. degrees from Bryn Mawr College and her Ph.D. from the University of Pennsylvania. A member of the Gordion Excavation Project since 1979, her research interests include Phrygian art, epigraphy, and religion, and the relationships between ancient Anatolian civilizations and the Greek world. She is the author of *Gordion Special Studies I: The Non-Verbal Graffiti, Dipinti, and Stamps* and *In Search of God the Mother: The Cult of Anatolian Cybele.*

The publication of this volume was made possible by a generous grant from the Division of Humanities, Arts, and Cultural Studies, College of Letters and Science, and the Office of Research, University of California, Davis, and by a generous grant from an anonymous donor.

Figures 1–18, 66, 70–72, 74–76 are taken from photographs and plans in the Gordion Archives. All other photographs and all drawings were done by the author.

CIP data is available from the Library of Congress.

ISBN-13: 978-1-934536-14-8 (cloth)
ISBN-10: 1-934536-14-8 (cloth)

© 2009 by the University of Pennsylvania Museum of Archaeology and Anthropology
Philadelphia, PA
All rights reserved. Published 2009

Published for the University of Pennsylvania Museum of Archaeology and Anthropology by the University of Pennsylvania Press.

Printed in the United States of America on acid-free paper.

Dedicated to the memory of Ellen Kohler, Keith DeVries, and Rodney S. Young.

Contents

List of Illustrations	ix
Preface and Acknowledgments	xi
I. Commentary on the Incised Drawings from Early Phrygian Gordion	1
Introduction	1
1. Excavation of the Incised Stones	3
2. Technique and Subject Matter of the Drawings	9
3. Subject Matter of the Incised Drawings: Sources and Possible Meanings	19
4. Origin of the Drawings and Their Placement on Megaron 2	39
5. Conclusion: Contribution of the Drawings to an Assessment of Early Phrygian Cultural Development	47
II. Catalogue of Stones 1–105 with Incised Drawings	51
III. Figures, Including Photographs of Stones 1–105	101
IV. Concordances	159
1. Catalogue Number to Gordion Inventory Number	159
2. Gordion Inventory Number to Catalogue Number	161
3. Incised Stone Drawings: Subjects	163
4. Subjects Found in the Incised Stone Drawings	167
Bibliography	169
Index	175

Illustrations

Frontispiece. Map of Anatolia showing the location of Gordion and sites mentioned in the text

FIGURES

1. General view of Gordion settlement showing location of Citadel Mound
2. Plan of the Early Phrygian Pre-Terrace Level, Gordion
3. Plan of the Early Phrygian Destruction Level, Gordion
4. Megaron 2 and enclosure wall to its west; Megaron 1 and Early Phrygian Gate Complex in the background
5. Plan of Megarons 1 and 2 by J. S. Last, in 1956
6. Plan of Megarons 1 and 2 by J. S. Last, in 1957
7. Megaron 2 from north
8. Drawing of the pebble mosaic in the main room, Megaron 2, by J. S. Last
9. Actual state photograph of two piers of incised stones from the southeast corner of Megaron 2
10. Drawing of two piers of incised stones from the southeast corner of Megaron 2, by Dorothy H. Cox, 1956
11. Houses X and Y, behind Megaron 2
12. General view of rear or south wall of Megaron 2, showing stone piers with incised drawings in situ
13. Detail of incised blocks in situ, from south wall of Megaron 2
14. Drawing of incised stone piers from the south wall of Megaron 2, by J. S. Last
15. Incised stones in situ on west wall of Megaron 2
16. Photograph and drawing of poros akroterion found above Megaron 2
17. Poros lion found above Megaron 2
18. Poros lions found above Megaron 2
19. Comparison: **48** and lion from Yılantaş monument
20. Comparison: **80** and lion from Arslantaş monument
21–123. Stones **1–105**

Preface and Acknowledgments

This study continues the practice of earlier volumes in the *Gordion Special Studies* monograph series of publishing the material from Gordion uncovered in the excavations carried out at the site from 1950 to 1973 under the directorship of Rodney S. Young. The present body of material, the incised drawings from Early Phrygian Gordion, makes a good subject for the Special Studies series, since all of the material was uncovered in a single context, the Citadel area of the Early Phrygian settlement, with the majority of it coming from one building, Megaron 2. Megaron 2 was excavated in 1956 and 1957, and the original excavator, Rodney Young, recognized the potential value of the stones with incised drawings. Because of his interest in the material, many of the incised stones were catalogued and kept in a depot in the excavation house compound to await further study. Rubbings were made of the incised surface of every stone, and drawings were then developed from the rubbings. A selection of these drawings appeared in Young's presentation of the incised stones in preliminary publications of the Gordion excavations (a fuller discussion of these circumstances is given in the Introduction). There were, however, a number of problems with the initial recording and publication of the incised stones. The quality and accuracy of the drawings made during the 1950s were very uneven, and several of the early excavation drawings show significant variance from the actual marks incised on the Phrygian stones, often to the point where these drawings form a misleading basis for study. The presentation of the stones in the preliminary publications is also fraught with problems. As discussed in the Introduction, Young initially interpreted the incised drawings as doodles made by casual loiterers in the Early Phrygian city, and he never wavered from this interpretation in subsequent publications. The incised stones that Young chose to illustrate in his published discussions of the material represent only a small sample of the total corpus of material, and these examples seem to have been selected for publication in part because they supported Young's interpretation.

In the years since the original excavation of the incised stones, Young's interpretation and the preliminary drawings of the stones have received considerable attention from scholars interested in the Anatolian Iron Age and in Phrygian culture, and several have offered alternative interpretive hypotheses.[1] Inevitably, though, the discussions of other scholars were limited to the material published by Young and their interpretations were constrained by Young's choice of drawings. As the Catalogue and Commentary presented here show, the subject matter that appears on the stones is much wider than Young's publications imply and several classes of material never appeared in the Gordion preliminary reports. This circumstance, coupled with the questionable accuracy of several of the original pencil drawings that appeared in preliminary publications, renders previous scholarly analysis of the stones and the meaning of the drawings problematic, since these analyses have inevitably been based on incomplete and inaccurate data. In addition, the discovery of a stone in the Early Phrygian Gate complex incised with a variety of subjects similar to those found in the Megaron 2 drawings suggests that such drawings may have been more widespread than originally thought and their meaning may be unrelated to the function of Megaron 2. For all these reasons, it was decided to start afresh with a new set of drawings of the incised stones and publish the whole corpus of the Early Phrygian incised stones together in one volume.

I first became acquainted with the potential value of the Early Phrygian incised stones while I was working on my study of the non-verbal graffiti from

---

1. See especially Mellink 1983, Prayon 1987 and 2004.

Gordion,[2] since I recognized that several of the patterns occurring on the incised stones offered good parallels to the non-verbal graffiti found on Gordion pottery. I began my study of the Early Phrygian incised stones in 1992, and I completed the majority of my drawings of the stones in 1992 and 1993. Various events, including the preparation of my book on the cult of the Phrygian Mother Goddess,[3] resulted in a protracted delay before I was able to complete my work on the incised stones. The delay has been fruitful, however, since the intervening fifteen years have seen major strides in our understanding of Early Phrygian Gordion and more generally of the Anatolian Iron Age and Iron Age chronology. In particular, the major redating of the Early Phrygian Citadel through carbon 14 analysis of plant samples from this level of the site has considerably altered our picture of the cultural development of the Early Phrygian levels at Gordion and their relationship to contemporary cultures of western Asia during the early Iron Age.[4] It is my hope that the full presentation of the Early Phrygian incised stone drawings will contribute to furthering the scholarly dialogue on this fascinating period in a constructive way.

Archaeology, and the publication of archaeological data, is by its very nature a group activity, and so it is a special pleasure to record my thanks to many friends and colleagues who have contributed to my study of this material. The Gordion Excavation has long enjoyed the support of the General Directorate of Antiquities and Museums of Turkey, and the Directorate's representatives at the site during the summer seasons of my work on the incised stones have aided significantly in its completion. At Gordion I owe an immeasurable debt to the Excavation Director, G. Kenneth Sams, and to many Gordion colleagues, including Brendan Burke, Gareth Darbyshire, Matthew Glendinning, Andrew Goldman, Mark Goodman (now deceased), Robert Henrickson, Richard Liebhart, Naomi Miller, William Remsen, Elizabeth Simpson, Maya Vassileva, Mary Voigt, and Cuyler Young (now deceased), all of whom helped critique my interpretive ideas in their formative stages. Preliminary reports on the incised stone drawings were presented at several colloquia on the Anatolian Iron Ages, in Van, Mersin, Eskişehir, and Izmir. These colloquia, arranged at regular intervals by Professor Altan Çilingiroğlu, professor of Anatolian Archaeology at Aegean University in Izmir, have proved to be a fertile and rewarding forum for discussion of a wide variety of problems on the Anatolian Iron Ages, and I owe a special debt of gratitude to Professor Çilingiroğlu and the many scholars who attended them and gave me the benefit of their criticisms there. I would also like to thank other colleagues for helpful comments: Dietrich Berndt, Susanne Berndt-Ersöz, Toni Cross, Crawford H. Greenewalt, Jr., Peter Kuniholm, Taciser Sivas, and Caillouette Thorman. In Davis I owe generous thanks to my student research assistants Anna Kazdaglis Trent, Stephanie Norris, and Melanie Saeck. I am also very grateful to Megan Lancaster and Judit Sawangwan for their help in completing my pencil drawings of the stones. Mediaworks, the center for instructional technology at the University of California, Davis, provided valuable technical assistance in preparing the drawings for publication and improving the photographs to the best quality possible.

My work at Gordion during the preparation of this manuscript has been supported by several faculty research grants from the Office of Research, University of California, Davis, for which I am very grateful. I am also pleased to acknowledge a generous and much appreciated grant from the Dean of Humanities, Arts, and Cultural Studies and the Office of Research at University of California, Davis, to support the preparation and publication of this volume; I owe further thanks to an anonymous donor for additional publication support. Throughout my work on this project, the Gordion Archives Office at the University of Pennsylvania Museum has offered unfailing support in providing access to the records of the Gordion Excavation; I would especially like to acknowledge the help of Gareth Darbyshire, Walda Metcalf, and Jennifer Quick. G. Kenneth Sams read an earlier draft of this manuscript and made numerous suggestions for its improvement; I am grateful to him and to the two anonymous readers for their many helpful comments and corrections. All of the above have helped improve this study immensely; the faults that remain are mine alone.

Finally, I would like to emphasize the special debts I owe to three key members of the Gordion Excavation team, none of whom lived to see my study of the Early Phrygian incised stones brought to completion.

---

2. Roller 1987.
3. Roller 1999b.
4. DeVries, Kuniholm, Sams and Voigt 2003; DeVries 2007.

PREFACE AND ACKNOWLEDGMENTS

The careful records kept by Ellen Kohler, Registrar of the Gordion Excavation during the period of Rodney Young's tenure as Excavation Director, are essential to the study of every aspect of the early Gordion excavations, and her many years of work at the site gave her an unparalleled wealth of knowledge about the Gordion excavations that contributed greatly to making my study of the incised stones possible. My special thanks go to my former teacher and mentor, Keith DeVries, who first invited me to participate in the Gordion project and always encouraged my work at the site and my interest in the Early Phrygian incised stones. My greatest debt is to Rodney Young, who had the wisdom and the foresight to recognize the value of this material and to save it for posterity, even if he did not always read it aright. This volume is dedicated to the memory of these three pioneering scholars of ancient Phrygia.

DECEMBER 2008

I

Commentary on the Incised Drawings from Early Phrygian Gordion

Introduction

This study presents for publication a series of stone blocks with incised drawings recovered from the Early Phrygian Destruction Level at Gordion. The great majority of the incised stones come from a single building in the Destruction Level, Megaron 2. Most were recovered from Megaron 2 itself, either blocks still in place in the walls at the time of the megaron's excavation or blocks found lying nearby, where they had fallen from the building's walls. A few incised blocks found in the clay fill above Megaron 2 probably also came from this building. Two incised blocks formed part of the walls of House Y, one of a pair of small storage buildings behind Megaron 2. Two additional examples of incised drawings occur on stones built into the Early Phrygian Citadel Gateway complex.

The incised stones from Megaron 2 were first uncovered during the building's excavation in 1956 and 1957. They were described in the excavation reports for those years and a sample of the stones were illustrated, both photographs of the actual stones and drawings of them.[5] Rodney Young, their excavator, was fond of them; he included references to the incised stones in two general reviews of the Gordion excavations that appeared in the 1960s and devoted a special study to them in the journal *Archaeology* in 1969.[6] Other than that, the incised stones have received comparatively little attention from scholars. It is not surprising that this should be so. The years 1956 and 1957 were exceptionally productive ones for the Gordion Excavation: two of the most spectacular Phrygian burial tumuli, Tumulus P and Tumulus MM, were opened during those seasons, both with their contents well preserved,[7] and extensive excavation in the occupation levels on the Gordion Citadel mound during the same period was beginning to reveal the potential richness of the Early Phrygian Destruction Level. Compared with such striking material, a series of simple, rather crudely drawn pictures might seem to be of minimal interest. Another factor that surely contributed to the lack of interest in this material, however, is Young's evaluation of the incised stones. He felt that the drawings were casual graffiti scratched onto Megaron 2 by a broad cross-section of the Phrygian population at Gordion, who scribbled onto the walls of the building to pass the time while waiting to conduct business in the Citadel quarter.[8] Young formulated this explanatory hypothesis during the initial phase of the stones' excavation; indeed, both this explanation and his nickname for the incised drawings, "doodles," appear

---

5. Young 1956b:263–64; Young 1957:323, figs. 10–12; Young 1958:142–43, fig. 3.
6. Young 1963:353; Young 1965a:482, fig. 3. For the *Archaeology* article, see Young 1969a.
7. Young 1981.
8. Young was unaware of the incised drawings on the Early Phrygian Citadel Gateway; these have never been discussed in print.

in the excavation notebook entry for the day when the first examples were uncovered. The term "doodles" was used to describe the incised stones in the excavation reports for those years and in virtually every subsequent mention of the stones. As a result, Young's explanatory hypothesis was rarely examined by others.[9] Indeed, Young's characterization of the drawings as "doodles" tended to imply that the information to be gained from them was limited and discouraged further attention to them.

At first glance, Young's label seems appropriate. The drawings on the stones have a very informal, even humorous character that is readily apparent. Many of the drawings are quite simplistic, almost crude, and were clearly not done by a skilled artist. In several cases it appears that one drawing was placed on top of another without any regard for the appearance of the final scene; stones **8**, **10**, **14**, **71**, and **82** offer representative examples. Other examples can be termed "drawings" only in a very loose sense of that term, since they seem to be little more than random lines and formless marks scratched onto the stones. Yet a closer analysis reveals that this material is of considerable interest. The drawings, while not of a high skill level, provide us with some of the earliest examples of representational art in Early Phrygian culture, including depictions of human figures (always rare in Phrygian art), animals, both wild and domestic, and architectural structures. Several of the drawings contain complex pictorial scenes that hint at a narrative function. In addition, at least some of the drawings appear to be imitating a more complex and sophisticated visual model. Some of the scenes show close affinities with contemporary examples of the art of Neo-Hittite cities in southeastern Anatolia and northern Syria, while others provide some of the earliest examples of patterns and symbols that are found in Phrygian religious iconography and Phrygian writing. Moreover, the circumstances under which the drawings were made need to be re-evaluated. Young's hypothesis explaining their origin, as sketches made directly onto the standing walls of Megaron 2, does not stand up to closer inspection, and there is good reason to think that at least some of the drawings may have been incised onto the stones used in the Megaron 2 walls before the building's construction. In addition, two drawings, **104** and **105**, have more recently been noted on blocks from the Early Phrygian Citadel Gateway complex, one on the interior surface of the north court building and one on the wall of the south tower that formed the entrance to the Early Phrygian Citadel. Drawing **104** in the north gate court contains subject matter that is very similar to some of the drawings found on the Megaron 2 blocks, suggesting that the occurrence of the incised drawings may not be related to the function of Megaron 2.[10]

Other circumstances need to be taken into account in an evaluation of the incised drawings. The revised chronology for the Early Phrygian Destruction Level and a greater understanding of the relationship of this level to previous and subsequent occupation levels at Gordion shed a new perspective on the drawings and the information they can contribute to our understanding of Early Phrygian society. The drawings also offer information that helps us place Gordion within the context of other Anatolian cultures during the early Iron Age. For all of these reasons, it seems appropriate to present the incised stones in greater detail and offer an analysis of the drawings on them.

---

9. One exception is Mellink 1983; here Mellink offered the hypothesis that the incised drawings were connected with the cult of the Phrygian Mother goddess. While I disagree with Mellink's interpretation, her study is noteworthy in being the first to recognize that the drawings were more than just casual graffiti.

10. There may have been more than the two examples of incised drawings on the Early Phrygian Citadel Gateway included in the catalogue here. Careful examination of the gate stones in 2004 revealed several additional stones with traces of incised lines that may be ancient. In each case, however, the incised marks were so faint that their nature could not be determined with certainty, and so I have decided to omit them from the catalogue.

1

Excavation of the Incised Stones

In 1956 the excavations conducted by Rodney S. Young on the Citadel Mound at Gordion began to clear an area of individual buildings forming part of a large architectural complex that lay underneath a thick layer of clay several meters deep. This level, marked by extensive signs of burned debris, would later be called the Early Phrygian Destruction Level[11] (Fig. 3). Excavation in the Destruction Level during previous seasons (1953–1955) had revealed significant architectural remains of an elaborate gate complex and a small courtyard inside the gate. As Young continued to clear the area inside the gate complex, a series of individual buildings began to emerge. The first to be uncovered was named the Burnt Phrygian Building, and the one next to it was called the West Phrygian House.[12] Each had a roughly similar plan, a long narrow structure with two rectangular rooms, a smaller room in front and a larger room behind it; entrance was through a door in the center of the front room, forming an interior line of sight through the front room into the larger room beyond it that emphasized the long axis of the building. This building type was called a megaron, a term borrowed from the language of the Homeric epics and also used to describe a similar arrangement of rooms forming the throne room complex found in several Mycenaean palaces on mainland Greece. Subsequent excavation of this area revealed that these buildings were only two of a whole series of similar structures that comprised the central architectural complex of the Early Phrygian Citadel. Because they were the first two megarons uncovered by Young's excavation, the Burnt Phrygian Building was renamed Megaron 1 and the West Phrygian House was called Megaron 2.[13]

In the space between Megarons 1 and 2 were found a number of architectural blocks lying on the ground. Several of these blocks had pictures "scratched" (to use Young's word) onto them, providing the first examples of stones with incised Phrygian drawings, or "doodle stones," as they were informally called. Further clearing in the area revealed that other blocks with similar incised pictures were still in situ in the east wall of Megaron 2, the left wall as one faces the building.[14] When the megaron was completely exposed in 1957, further examples of blocks with incised pictures were found in the upper part of the south, or back, wall of the building, and other examples were also noted in the west wall. In addition to these, incised stones were found on the walls of House Y, one of a pair of storage sheds behind Mega-

---

11. The Early Phrygian Destruction Level corresponds to Voigt's YHSS Level 6A; see Voigt 1994 and Voigt 2005. A good description of the Early Phrygian Destruction Level is given by Sams 1994a:2–7, although Sams' chronology for the destruction should be revised in light of more recent information on the chronology of the Early Phrygian period.

12. Young 1957:322–23, pls. 88–89, figs. 7–12. The West Phrygian House, later Megaron 2, was also called the Mosaic Building in some preliminary reports, e.g., Young 1963:352–54, because of the well-preserved pebble mosaics found inside it. This should not be confused with another building that was also designated the Mosaic Building, a structure of the 4th century BCE; Young 1953:11–14.

13. The term Megaron 2 (abbreviated M 2) first appears on the plans of the Destruction Level published in DeVries 1990: figs. 4 and 7.

14. As can be seen on the plan of the Destruction Level, Figure 3, Megaron 2, like all the buildings on the east side of the courtyard in the Early Phrygian Citadel, was oriented with its front towards the northeast. Thus the wall that I here call the east wall actually extends from northeast to southwest; similarly, the south, or back, wall of the building extends from southeast to northwest, and the southeast corner is actually oriented to the south. This circumstance, however, creates very cumbersome language in the description of the building, and thus I have simplified the description by calling the left side of the building, as one faces its front, the east side; the back wall then becomes the south side, and the right side becomes the west wall. In doing so, I am following the same system of nomenclature used by R. S. Young in his publications.

ron 2, and at least three examples were recovered in the fill above the megaron. Thus, the great majority of the stones with incised drawings were associated with Megaron 2.

While the architecture of the Gordion Destruction Level will receive fuller publication and analysis elsewhere, the construction of Megaron 2 and the circumstances of its destruction have important bearing on our understanding of the incised stones, and so it will be useful to examine the building's construction and period of use in some detail here. Megaron 2 is a standard megaron, approximately 19 x 13 m[15] (Figs. 5, 6). There are two principal rooms, a smaller front room, approximately 3 m deep, which opened onto the courtyard and an interior room behind this, 10.85 x 9.74 m, clearly the main room because of its larger size. Access to the main room was only through the front room. In the space between the front room and the main room of the building there were two small rooms that were entered through doorways on either side of a short passageway connecting the two principal rooms. These seem too small to be useful living spaces, and may have been used as storage areas, or closets.

Megaron 2 did not have a stone front wall; instead the building's front foundation was marked by a wooden beam, on which stood the base of a brick wall ca. 0.32 m wide, the width of a single brick. This suggests that the front wall was a light wall, perhaps one made of mud brick, or a wooden screen set into a mud brick base; alternatively the front room of the megaron could have been an open porch. In contrast, the two side walls and the rear wall of the building are quite substantial, over a meter thick, and were constructed from a combination of stone and timber (Figs. 4, 7). The outer and inner surfaces of these three walls were built of cut stone blocks inserted into a timber framework, with a rubble core in between. A soft off-white limestone, also known as poros, was used. The exposed faces of the blocks forming the exterior and interior surfaces of the building were smooth finished; the tops, bottoms, and ends of the blocks, i.e., the surfaces in contact with adjoining stones, were roughly finished; and the inner faces in contact with the rubble core were not finished at all. On many blocks even the exposed exterior surface is very uneven, with chisel marks still visible. Examples of complete or nearly complete blocks found in situ, such as the surviving stone courses in the south wall and southeast corner (Figs. 9, 12), indicate that while the stone blocks were all rectangular in shape, no standard size block was used.[16] Instead, the blocks were of quite uneven dimensions, and many appear to have been cut as needed to fill the space available. The interior wall surfaces of the two main rooms were covered with thick lime plaster, but there is no evidence that the exterior walls were covered with plaster or any other finishing.

In addition to stone, timber was extensively used in the megaron's construction. Both the outer and inner wall faces were set on horizontal timber beds, and horizontal beams were placed in each wall at varying heights throughout the wall's elevation; these were joined to vertical timbers placed at irregular intervals along the full length of each wall. The stone blocks were set in vertical piers between the timbers. This technique can be seen in the south/back wall of the megaron, the best preserved wall in the structure (Fig. 12). Here a horizontal wooden timber was set approximately 0.75 m above the building's timber foundation. Below this, vertical timbers divided the stone wall into vertical piers with three or four stones in one horizontal course of each pier. Above the horizontal timber, the vertical timbers were placed more frequently, and the stone piers in between them are only the width of a single block. The extensive use of timber in the building's construction contributed substantially to its destruction by fire, as will be discussed in greater detail below.

When Megaron 2 was originally built, it was a free-standing building (Fig. 2). To its east stood Megaron 1 and to its west was a large enclosure wall that separated Megarons 1 and 2 and the courtyard in front of them from the inner section of the Citadel, in which stood Megaron 3 and several other buildings. At some point after the construction of Mega-

---

15. No complete plan of Megaron 2 was ever made, nor were the full external dimensions of the building recorded. The plan and dimensions of the building can be ascertained from the two site plans of the Destruction Level drawn by J. S. Last in 1956 and 1957, here Figures 5 and 6.

16. The longest extant block, **59**, is 0.76 m in length. Other blocks of which the full length is preserved range in size from 0.45 to 0.61 m. The height and thickness of the blocks are similarly variable.

ron 2, two small free-standing rectangular structures of timber and mud brick were built behind it (Fig. 11). Called Houses X and Y in the preliminary reports, these evidently served as storage sheds for the megaron.[17] They were cleaned out and dismantled to their foundation level when a major new construction project forming the complex known as the Terrace Buildings to the southwest of Megaron 2 was started (Fig. 3).[18] The units of the Terrace Buildings stood at a higher level than Megarons 1 and 2 and were supported by a large rubble fill that formed the terrace on which they stood (hence the name). The terrace extended up to the south (i.e., back) wall of Megaron 2 and along its west wall; here part of the enclosure wall between Megarons 2 and 3 was demolished to accommodate it, and the south and west walls of Megaron 2 were used as retaining walls for the terrace. At the same time, another wall was constructed extending from the southeast corner of Megaron 2 and running behind Megaron 1 to the southeast; this also served as a retaining wall for the Terrace Buildings. In addition, the space between Megarons 1 and 2 was partitioned into a series of small storage and work rooms, and a stone bench, ca. 0.70 m high and 0.80 m deep, was constructed along the east side of Megaron 2.[19] The effect of these changes was to block off any access to the back of Megaron 2. The extensive changes to the area around Megaron 2 imply that the building remained in use over a period of several years, although the exact chronology of each phase of activity remains unknown.

It is clear that Megaron 2 played some important role in the elite Phrygian community. It was one of the largest freestanding buildings in the pre-Terrace phase of the Gordion Citadel, exceeded in size only by Megaron 3. The exterior walls of rectangular poros blocks would have created an impressive appearance, particularly in comparison with the mud brick and timber construction used in the neighboring Megaron 1. In addition, the building may well have had architectural sculpture: a stone akroterion and two sculpted lion protomes (Figs. 16–18) found in the fill above Megaron 2 were probably attached to the building, and the presence of these and potentially other sculptural ornaments would have added to the building's imposing appearance.[20] The building's interior had received special treatment also; the floor surfaces of both rooms were covered with mosaics made of brightly colored pebbles.[21] The mosaic in the outer room was badly damaged, but the floor of the main room was much better preserved. Here the entire floor, apart from a central circular space for a hearth and a small, slightly sunken rectangular space at the southeast corner, was covered with a pebble mosaic consisting of irregularly distributed geometric designs (Figs. 7, 8). Taken together, these features of construction and decoration indicate usage for a special purpose. What that purpose was, however, remains unknown. Little information can be gained from the contents of the building, since it was largely empty at the time of its destruction. A few pottery vessels were found inside: a fragment of a coarse storage jar, a large trefoil jug containing nearly three hundred astragals, and a large storage jar found in the sunken area in the southeast corner.[22] Two iron shovels were also found in the hearth in the main room.[23] These circumstances suggest that the building was only in occasional use, perhaps as an audience or reception hall for a ruler, or perhaps for dining and the entertainment that often accompanies a banquet. Some have suggested that Megaron 2 was a temple, but this seems unlikely. The building's plan and the interior arrangement of its rooms are similar to those of most of the other megara in the Gordion Destruction Level, and no cult installations or objects were found in the building

---

17. Young 1958:143; Young 1969a:270–71.
18. The Terrace Buildings functioned as space for storage and for concentrated activities involving food preparation and textile production; see the discussion in Sams 1994a:2–3, and Burke 2005.
19. Sams 1994a:3.
20. Young 1956a: pl. 92, figs. 42, 43 (lions); Young 1956a: pl. 93, fig. 41; Sams 1994b: fig. 20.2, 20.3.4 (akroterion); Mellink 1983:357.
21. Young 1957:322; Young 1965b:10–12; Salzmann 1982:6-7, nos. 47–48, pls. 2/2, 3/1, 4–5.
22. Sams 1994a:3. The coarseware jar, Sams 1994a: no. 1009; the trefoil jug, Sams 1994a: no. 741; the storage jar, Sams 1994a: no. 987. Two other vessels were found nearby, a spouted jar (Sams 1994a: no. 415) from the pavement in front of the building, and a body sherd of another closed vessel (Sams 1994a: no. 1015), found behind the building. Compared to the large quantities of vessels found in the storage rooms behind Megaron 1, Megarons 3 and 4, and the Terrace and CC Buildings, the contents of Megaron 2 were extremely minimal.
23. Gordion inventory number ILS 235, unpublished. I owe this information to Gareth Darbyshire.

that would support identification as a cult structure.[24] The lack of a sturdy front wall to enclose the building clearly implies that Megaron 2 was not used for any purpose in which security was an issue, but beyond that, its role in the Citadel complex is uncertain.

Megaron 2 was destroyed by a major fire that devastated all the buildings on the western side of the Gordion Citadel complex, including Megarons 1 through 4 and the Terrace Building complex. The fire seems not to have crossed the courtyard in front of the megarons, and so the buildings on the east side of the Citadel complex were not damaged. The source of the fire is not clear. At the time of first discovery of the Destruction Level, Young suggested that the destruction was caused by a nomadic group, the Kimmerians, whose activities in central Anatolia are attested by Assyrian sources and by numerous references in Greek literature. According to Strabo, the Kimmerians captured Gordion, whereupon its ruler Midas (of Greek myth fame) committed suicide by drinking bull's blood.[25] The death of Midas was placed by the early Christian chronographers Julius Africanus and Eusebios in 676 or 696 BCE, respectively.[26] From this association a date in the early 7th century BCE for the Destruction Level fire became widely accepted, and the cause of the destruction was assumed to be hostile enemy action, namely from the Kimmerians.

This hypothetical sequence of events is problematic for a number of reasons. The hypothesis relies on a literal reading of highly mythologized accounts of the Kimmerian destruction and the suicide of Midas that were written many centuries after the events they describe. Moreover, the character of the damage to the Early Phrygian Citadel is inconsistent with destruction caused by enemy action: no evidence for weapons was found, nor were there any human skeletal remains in the destruction debris. Recent investigations in the Middle Phrygian settlement levels indicate that rebuilding in the Citadel area was begun within the space of one to two years after the Destruction Level fire; the Middle Phrygian Citadel buildings were constructed following a plan extremely similar to that of the Early Phrygian Citadel and were set into the thick layer of clay brought in to cover the debris from the fire.[27] This circumstance strongly suggests that no major disruption or political dislocation separated the Early and Middle Phrygian Levels. Taken together, these circumstances indicate that the fire was not the result of hostile outside agency against Gordion, although the actual cause of the destruction still remains unclear.

Young's proposed early 7th century BCE date for the Early Phrygian destruction is also questionable, since the date was determined by the tenuous link with the Kimmerian invasion and the later accounts of the suicide of Midas. A more accurate date is suggested by the results derived from C14 testing of organic matter (grain and wood) from the Destruction Level; these indicate a chronological range of 830–805 BCE for the destruction.[28] Since Megaron 2 was one of the buildings destroyed, this provides a reasonably certain terminus ante quem for the end of the building's use. The complex history of the building and its surroundings suggests that Megaron 2 may have been in use for 50–80 years, yielding a date in the early to mid 9th century BCE for the building's construction.[29]

As noted above, stones with incised drawings were found on the exterior surface of the east, south, and west walls of Megaron 2. A large number of incised stones were found lying on the ground in the space between Megarons 1 and 2; these probably had fallen from the east wall when it collapsed as a result of the fire. Here the relationship of one block to another could not be ascertained. Near the southeast corner, where the east wall was supported by the rubble fill of the Terrace Building construction, the wall remained

---

24. Suggested identification as a temple, see Mellink 1983:357–59; Sams 1995:1156–57; Sams 1997:241; Prayon 2004:612. Mellink, Sams, and Prayon all cite the existence of the "doodles," the incised drawings, as evidence for the temple interpretation, but as the discussion in this volume will make clear, the drawings represent a variety of styles and purposes and cannot by themselves be used to support a cult function.

25. On Midas and the Kimmerian destruction, see Strabo 1.3.21. For a discussion of other ancient sources on Midas, see Roller 1983.

26. The ancient sources on the chronology of Midas are analyzed by Berndt-Ersöz 2008.

27. Voigt 1994:274–75; Voigt 2005:32–35; Voigt 2007.

28. DeVries, Kuniholm, Sams, and Voigt 2003; DeVries, Sams, and Voigt 2005; DeVries 2007.

29. Young (1969a:271–72) estimated two generations or sixty years of use for Megaron 2 and Houses X and Y. Any estimate of the exact length of time when Megaron 2 was in use, however, should be considered a plausible guess.

standing to a height of approximately 1.8 m. The position of the blocks in the standing wall was recorded, demonstrating that this portion of the wall consisted of four horizontal courses in the lower wall, then a horizontal wooden timber, and an unknown number of stone courses above the timber (Figs. 9, 10).[30] On this section of the wall, incised drawings can be found on virtually every block. The fill of the Terrace Building complex also preserved the south/back wall of Megaron 2. Here the entire width of the back wall was found standing to a height of ca. 1.5 m. When initially excavated, the wall was partially obscured by the two storage sheds, Houses X and Y, but the removal of the sheds revealed that there were no incised drawings on the stones below the large horizontal timber set into the back wall of the megaron.[31] Above the horizontal timber, about three or four courses of stone in each of the vertical piers survived, and all of them were covered with incised drawings. Here too the position of the stone courses and the placement of the incised drawings on them were recorded in situ (Figs. 13, 14). This drawing furnishes our best evidence for the appearance of the incised drawings on the standing walls of the building.

The west wall of Megaron 2, in contrast, is the most poorly preserved section of the building; here the wall had been extensively plundered and the surfaces of the surviving blocks were extensively cracked and flaked.[32] Several of the blocks found in the courses at ground level had incised drawings on them. Although these were mentioned in the notebooks at the time of excavation, and a few were photographed (Fig. 15 offers an example), none was saved or inventoried. In addition, two blocks with incised drawings were recovered from House Y, one of the storage sheds behind Megaron 2.[33]

The circumstances under which the stones of Megaron 2 were incised will receive fuller discussion in Section 4. We can note here, however, that the evidence strongly suggests that the drawings were already present on the exterior surface of the megaron during the earliest phase of its use, before the construction of Houses X and Y. The back wall of the building would have been blocked off by these two storage sheds, and the back and west side walls would have been blocked by the fill of the Terrace Buildings. At the same time we should note that not every part of the megaron's exterior surface had incised marks; the east wall was extensively covered with incised drawings, while the west wall had fewer, and the south wall had none on the lower part of its surface, although many on the upper part.

Over ninety incised stones from Megaron 2 were lifted from the east and south walls of the building and from House Y, the storage shed, and brought to the Gordion depot for inventory.[34] These are the stones whose drawings form the major portion of the catalogue here. The current state of preservation of the incised stones, however, is quite uneven. The collapse of the east wall caused the stones to fall outward, and many incised stones from this wall were found jumbled together in a heap at the base of the wall. Several

---

30. The incised drawings on the stone courses in the southeast corner of Megaron 2 were photographed (see Fig. 9) and then recorded in a drawing by D. H. Cox; see Young 1958: pl. 21, fig. 3; Young 1969a:271; Prayon 1987:172, fig. 27a; Prayon 2004:619, fig. 1; here Figure 10. All but two of the incised blocks in Cox's drawing, 50 and 53, are no longer extant. There are significant problems with Cox's drawing: the surviving part of the incised face of 50, the upper left block below the horizontal beam, exhibits significant differences from this drawing, and the photographs of the incised stones taken in 1957 also reveal numerous details that are inconsistent with the Cox drawing. These circumstances indicate that Cox's reconstruction of this group of incised stones is not fully reliable. This situation is discussed further in the Catalogue in conjunction with entries **50–57**, where updated descriptions and drawings based on the excavation photographs are given.

31. For the excavation of the south/back wall of Megaron 2, see Young 1958:142–43; 1962:160. Young (1958:143) reports that the position of this horizontal timber was approximately 0.75 m above ground level.

32. Young 1958:143. More recent investigation has shown that this was true of many of the Destruction Level buildings; in rebuilding the Citadel area, the standard practice seems to have been to leave two stone courses standing and pile the rest of the stone into the center of the building; see Voigt 1994:272.

33. A comment by R. S. Young (1969a:271), "the walls of the sheds themselves became space for more doodles," implies that several stones on both storage sheds had incised drawings, but apart from **99** and **100**, none was recorded or preserved.

34. Most of the incised stones from the east wall were removed at the time of their excavation, in 1956 or 1957. The stones from the south wall of the building were removed in 1961, four years after they were first excavated; see Young 1962:160. The final inventoried stone to be removed was **50**, from the southeast corner; this was brought to the Gordion storage depot in 1983. At that point its condition had deteriorated noticeably from the time of its finding.

of these must have fallen with their faces down, since this section includes a number of blocks that are nearly intact with the incised face well preserved. Others, however, suffered markedly in the fire; the blocks were fractured into small pieces and their surfaces were cracked. Often the surface of a block is pitted with holes where salts in the stone exploded as a result of the fire's heat. The two vertical piers in the southeast corner wall, **50–57** in the catalogue, were in good condition at the time of their excavation, but apart from two examples, **50** and **53**, none was saved. The fate of the stones in the upper part of the south wall is also quite uneven. As the drawing of the stone piers illustrates (Fig. 14), many of these blocks had intact surfaces with visible drawings at the time of their discovery and these were recorded. The impact of the fire, however, caused several of the stones in Figure 14 to deteriorate to the point where they disintegrated when they were lifted from the wall; thus several blocks recorded in this drawing either do not survive or are in markedly poorer condition, with much of the incised face now gone. This includes stones **93–98**; these were not inventoried at the time of their discovery, but they can be identified from excavation photographs as part of the south wall of the megaron and are included here. None of the incised blocks from the west wall were inventoried and so their fate is unknown. In addition, a number of small fragments of soft white poros stone with incised drawings were brought to the excavation depot but not inventoried. Most of these have no identifying labels; they may come from Megaron 2 but since this is not certain they have not been included in the present study. Thus it should be noted that the material presented here lays no claim to completeness.

In addition to the stones removed to the Gordion depot, the excavators' daybooks comment on the presence of incised stones that were not removed from Megaron 2, but were left in place in the building. In order to investigate this, during the summer of 2004 I cleared the backfilled earth from the exterior faces of the east and west walls, the two side walls of the megaron, to determine if any incised stones were still visible in situ. The rear, or south wall of the building was not opened, since it was deeply buried by backfilled rubble supporting the Terrace Building; moreover, the excavators' notebooks and the published excavation reports stated clearly that all incised blocks were removed before the area was backfilled.[35] One well preserved example, **48**, a block with a drawing of two lions, was found in 2004 in the lowest course of the east wall; this block, which likely was overlooked in the original excavation of Megaron 2, is included in the catalogue. No other incised drawings were found on the surviving in situ blocks of the east or west walls.

Three stones (**101**, **102**, **103**) found in the fill above Megaron 2 are also included in the present discussion. All appear to be the same soft poros stone that was used in the construction of Megaron 2, and are likely to be fragments of the stone from the megaron that were churned up in the destruction or subsequent cleaning and rebuilding in the area. Two of them, **101** and **102**, bear drawings on the finished outer surface of the block and were probably incised under circumstances very similar to those of the other drawings found on actual building blocks (as discussed in Section 4). The third, **103**, is a smaller fragment and its incised surface is quite rough and blackened; this suggests that the drawing was incised on the stone after the destruction of Megaron 2, during the process of clearing out the rubble.

A few remarks are in order about the two incised stones in the Early Phrygian Citadel Gateway. One is located on the interior east wall of the north courtyard room of the Gateway complex, approximately ten courses above current ground level. The drawings on this block include several subjects, among them a bird, a horse, a maze pattern, and random scratches, that are very similar to those found on some of the Megaron 2 blocks, suggesting that these drawings were part of the same effort. The other incised block is located on the third course above present ground level of the south tower of the Early Phrygian Citadel Gateway, facing the ramp that forms the entrance into the Citadel. The drawing on this block, a series of irregular zigzag lines, could have been done during the construction of the gate tower or at some point afterwards, before the destruction of the Early Phrygian Citadel Gateway.

---

35. Young 1962:160.

2

Technique and Subject Matter of the Drawings

Technical Features of the Drawings

Let us turn our attention now to the character of the drawings on the incised stones. The drawings were incised directly onto the poros blocks, a fairly soft stone that can be scratched with just about any type of sharp tool. The placement of the drawings on the blocks is quite irregular: no effort was made to center the drawings on the blocks or frame them in any way. In some cases (examples include **1, 5, 8, 10, 12, 29, 59, 67, 82, 93, 94, 99, 104**) the incision work covers the whole front surface of the block, while in others (note **4, 6, 21, 27, 31, 36, 48, 53, 80, 95, 102**) incision marks were made only on a portion of the front surface, leaving the remaining area blank.[36] Where two or more adjoining blocks survived in situ (see Figs. 9, 12, 13), we can see that no drawing extends over the edge of one block onto the next, suggesting that each drawing is self-contained on a single block.

I use the word "drawing" to describe the material, but in fact several different techniques can be observed. Some drawings were scratched lightly into the stone, while others were cut more deeply. In a few instances the area around the incised scene was deeply carved and stone was partially cut away from the outline of the figure; examples include **31, 33, 59, 74, 95, 98, and 102**. Drawing **98**, which depicts a man and a lion, furnishes a particularly notable example; here the stone around the lion is deeply cut back in what appears to have been a preliminary attempt at relief sculpture.

The treatments of the individual scenes are equally variable. Some of the drawings show efforts to do careful, precise work. Others, however, are of quite amateurish character, little more than stick figures, and several consist merely of formless lines and shapes scratched onto the stones. On a number of stones one figure overlaps with another on the same block. In some cases such overdrawing seems to be the result of experimentation in the composition of the picture. For example, in drawing **1** we appear to see three drafts of a lion's head in various poses; the lighter lines may form preliminary sketches for the subject and the more deeply incised lines create the final picture.[37] Drawing **10** has the beginning of a sketch of a lion's face above a complete lion's head. Drawing **71** contains two attempts at drawing a human head with a helmet in addition to the final version showing both human head and body. Drawing **53** shows a lion with two tails; the inciser originally made the drawing with the tail extending down between the lion's hind legs and later changed it to curve up and over the animal's back. In other cases it appears that several different artists were at work, intentionally placing multiple subjects on top of another. In **9a** the elevation of a

---

36. For the majority of the stones, the original edges are not preserved so it is no longer possible to determine what percentage of the stone face was incised.

37. Drawing **1** was originally identified as a dog by Rodney Young (1969a:273, lower right); Young assumed that the band around the animal's neck was a spiked collar, such as is worn by many sheep dogs in rural Anatolia today. While it is true that the animal in **1** has the long slender muzzle characteristic of a hound, the drawing was almost certainly intended to depict a lion. The double line and rounded points at the animal's neck fit with the standard schema for depicting a lion's neck ruff and cheek piece, and the animal is shown with the open mouth, sharp teeth, and the sharp angular tongue typical of the Gordion lions. The drawing may have been made by someone who had never seen a lion but was familiar with the domesticated hound. Similarly **4** was also identified by Young as a dog (1969a:274, upper left), but this animal too is more likely to be a lion; it has the neck ruff and cheek piece and long sharp curving claws found on many other Gordion lions.

building was placed over a bird. In **14**, a bird shown in left profile was drawn on top of two warriors who face each other with drawn swords, while the warrior at right was drawn over a lion striding right. Drawing **98** depicts a male figure drawn over a lion; the lion is deeply cut as if for relief sculpture, but the male figure is much more lightly incised and appears to have been added later. Drawing **8** illustrates a particularly complex example. Here the head of a bird drawn in right profile shares a common line with the body of another bird; both are overlain by a lion facing right, which then merges into the outstretched wingspread of a bird in flight, with random lines across the whole. Drawing **82** also displays a complex mixture of geometric patterns and animal figures, with several birds overlapping a lion and a horse.

A large number of drawings contain random lines and arcs interspersed around a more complex subject. In at least a few cases, a pictorial scene appears to have been intentionally obscured by lines or scratches after its completion, as if someone was trying to deliberately erase the scene; examples include **13**, **44**, **58**, **81**, and **83**.

Subject Matter of the Drawings

The unequal nature of the drawing styles and techniques initially gives the impression that the drawings were a completely haphazard series of scenes. A closer review of the material, however, reveals that certain subjects recur regularly, the most common being human figures, animals, and geometric motifs. These tend to fall into patterns that suggest a limited set of sources of the drawings, a circumstance which has interesting implications for their meanings.

This discussion of the subject matter of the drawings will begin with scenes of human figures. As is true of the corpus of drawings as a whole, the drawing styles used to depict human figures vary greatly. A few have an almost cartoon-like quality, such as a pair of stick figures who engage their outstretched hands as if about to fight (**81**), and a small beak-headed man who holds a disproportionately large spear (**74**). In many instances, however, the figure is more carefully drawn and a great deal of detail can be detected. In every case where indications of gender are visible the figure is male, although in some cases the figures are so schematically rendered that the gender cannot be determined, e.g., **49**, **52**, **54**. In most instances the figure was drawn with head in profile, shoulders and upper torso full front, and lower torso and legs in profile (**1**, **2**, **5**, **8**, **14**, **31**, **44**, **46**, **52**, **54**, **59**, **88**, **98**). Two figures are shown with both head and torso fully frontal (**49**, **101**), and a few are in full profile (**50**, **71**, **77**, **94**). In one example (**33**), the drawing's creator apparently started to make a full front figure, and then changed to a profile figure; this drawing is so poorly executed, though, that it is difficult to be certain.

Most of the human figures are shown clothed, and the costumes depicted fall into regular patterns. In the most common costume, the male figure wears a short kilt, sometimes with a visible pattern in the fabric (**2**, **44**, **46**, perhaps also **81**) and/or belt (**5**, **44**, **59**, **101**). This seems to be the costume of a warrior, since in several cases a weapon is also present; this can be a short sword, worn at the side (**5**, **31**, **44**, **46**, **59**, **101**) or extended in use (**14**), a mace (**44**, **98**), a spear (**74**), or a bow and arrow (**33**, **37**). One pair of warriors (**14**) is shown with helmets, on one of which a crest is indicated. On all these figures there is no indication of clothing on the upper torso; this may be due to the simple nature of the drawing and the lack of internal detail, since one would assume that a warrior would wear some form of protection on his upper torso.

Other costumes are quite different. One, found in **71**, **77**, and **94**, is a long gown that appears to cover the whole body and is fastened at the waist with a wide belt and belt buckle. The figures in this costume also wear a type of cylindrical headdress that also occasionally appears on a figure wearing the short kilt, e.g., **46** (both costume and headdress are described in greater detail below). On one example, **88**, a figure wears a long gown that follows the contours of the body but is not belted.

When a hairstyle is visible on a human figure, e.g., **1**, **8**, **14**, **44**, **98**, and perhaps **88**, the style normally shown is with hair pulled to the back of the head and curling up slightly in a pigtail at the nape of the neck. In one example, **101**, the figure's hair appears to be parted in the middle, with braids hanging down on each side of the face; this is also a rare example of a figure shown in a frontal pose. None of the figures who wear the short kilt appears to have a beard, but on some of the figures who wear the long gown, **71**, **77** and **94**, depictions of the chin area appears to merge into the costume, suggesting that the figure may be bearded.

Several drawings merely depict a standing male figure, not obviously connected through costume or pose with a clear identity or activity. These are **1**, one man walking left, the other walking right; **8**, a small male figure facing right; **47**, a crudely drawn figure facing right; **97**, the lower torso of a rather squarish figure facing right; **52** and **54**, both of which show a figure in right profile. Drawing **49** is the simplest figure of all; the drawing depicts a crudely drawn head and columnar body with outstretched arms, with no internal details to suggest gender, costume, or action.

A few scenes, however, depict human figures in poses or with attributes that suggest that a specific action or narrative element was intended. As noted above, several drawings depict warriors, either men standing and holding weapons, or men actively engaged in fighting. Drawing **2** depicts a man walking left holding a bow in his right hand and an arrow in his left. Similarly in **5** the figure holds what appears to be a bow on his left shoulder and wears a sword at his side.[38] Drawing **31** depicts a man walking left, with his left arm bent and the hand placed on the hip, and a sword along his right leg, similar to **5**. Drawing **98** shows a man walking right; his left arm, extended in front of him, is bent up at the elbow and he appears to hold a weapon like a mace with the head pointed back at him (this is analogous to, although not identical with, the weapon held by the figure in **44**, discussed below). Drawing **33** depicts a standing male holding a shield and a large spear to the right (alternatively, this could be a disproportionately large bow and arrow, analogous to the weapons in **2**). The figure is quite clumsily rendered, with an odd combination of full front and profile figure, but the depiction of the weapons is quite clear. Drawing **37** preserves only a partial section of weapons, a shield and spear (or bow and arrow), but it is likely that these were held by a human figure which is not preserved.

A few drawings depict warriors engaged in hostile action. Drawing **14** is the most detailed example. In this drawing two warriors stand and face each other with their arms extended towards each other; the figure at the left appears to hold a sword in his right hand, while the figure at the right has a pointed projectile extending from the right hand, presumably also a weapon. Both figures appear to be shown with helmets on their heads, and the right figure's helmet has a crest indicated on it. The scene strongly suggests a depiction of a confrontation between two armed warriors was intended. Similarly drawing **59** shows two scenes of men facing each other in hostile confrontation. None of the figures appears to be holding weapons, although the right figure of the pair at the far right of **59** wears a sword by his side.[39] Instead they raise their fists towards each other as if about to engage in a fist fight. Drawing **81** depicts a simpler version of two individuals fighting. The figures, rendered as virtual stick figures, stand and face each other, with arms extended out towards the opposite figure and the hands of the two figures interlocked, as if in struggle. The figure at the right is both poorly drawn and poorly preserved, so few internal details can be seen, but on the figure at the left we see a belt across the figure's waist and two fleshy buttocks.

The figures shown wearing the long costume, in **71**, **77**, **88**, and **94**, convey a different, more stately impression. Drawings **71**, **77**, and **94** depict standing males wearing a similar costume, a long gown with voluminous folds indicated by vertical lines (few internal lines are visible in **94**); the gown is fastened at the waist by a belt with an elaborate belt buckle (this is shown most clearly on **77**). The figure has a flat-topped cylindrical object on his head, probably a type of headdress. The rendering of the head and headdress is often so simplistic that it is difficult to read clearly, but this seems to be some official head covering, such as a crown. In all three of these figures the chin area flows directly into the gown with no indication of a neck, suggesting that the figure had a long flowing beard that hangs over the front of the gown. This feature appears most clearly shown in **77**, although in none of the figures is any detail of a beard, such as individual curls, shown. It is difficult to determine if any of these figures is engaged in some activity. The figure in **71** holds one arm, probably the right, back and outstretched; the figure may be holding a weapon such as a spear. The figure in **77**

---

38. The sword appears as a rectangular projection along the lower edge of the figure's tunic; this is not immediately apparent in this drawing but is clearer in other drawings, e.g., **44**.

39. This sword too appears as a rectangular projection along the lower edge of the figure's tunic; compare with **5**, **31**, **44**, **46**, and **101**.

may have the left arm outstretched. No arms are visible on **94**.

Drawing **88** also depicts a human figure in a long gown striding to the right. While this drawing lacks the detail of **77**, it is clear that the costume, headdress, and pose of this figure are somewhat different from the figures discussed above. There is no belt on the costume, and the only internal detail shown is a vertical fold in the garment's hem. The large rounded head suggests that a rounded head covering of some kind was intended. The figure's hair is gathered in a knot at the nape of the neck; it is uncertain whether a beard is indicated. The figure may have one arm extended before him, but no other details are shown.

A small number of scenes with human figures merit particular attention, since they depict subjects not paralleled elsewhere in the drawings. Two examples, **44** and **98**, show a male figure walking to the right. In each drawing the figure is holding one arm back and brandishing a weapon, as if about to strike someone or something. On both examples the handle of the weapon is turned so that the mace head is next to the human figure's head, a potentially awkward position for striking another object. In **98**, the figure appears alone and the potential object of the blow is not shown. Drawing **44**, however, depicts a more complex scene. Here the male figure wears a short kilt with a fringe and a decorative belt, and has a sword fastened by his side. His left arm, bent forward in front of him, holds the cord of a bag that dangles in front of him; in the bag we see a hare upside down. Traces of another set of hare's ears and head are visible next to the bag; this is probably part of a trial drawing that was abandoned. The figure holds a weapon, probably a mace or ax, with its right arm. The implication is that the figure is brandishing the weapon as if to strike the hare in the bag.

Drawing **46** also portrays a complex and unusual scene. In this piece the drawing style is considerably simpler, but the scene is nonetheless interesting. Along the left side of the incised surface is a standing male figure facing right. The figure wears a short kilt and has a sword or dagger at his side. Above his head is the flat-topped cylindrical headdress; this appears to be the same headdress as was noted on the figures wearing the long gown, although the crude style of the drawing makes certain identification difficult. The figure's arms, indicated as single lines, are shown outstretched in opposite directions, the right extended straight out while the left extends back with the elbow bent up. Two birds in flight appear on either side of the figure. The presence of the birds may be co-incidental, since many of the drawings show unrelated figures next to each other. The position of the figure's arms, however, suggests that he has extended his left arm to attract the bird at right, the direct object of the figure's gaze. The scene appears to be a depiction of falconry, showing an individual who holds out one arm for the bird to perch on, while with the other arm he swings a lure to attract the bird. Falconry may also be the subject of **19**, which shows two birds perched on an outstretched object. The bird at right is clearly a raptor, as indicated by its sharp curved beak, and the object on which it perches may be a human arm with protective covering.[40]

Drawing **101** also presents an interesting scene, in which a standing figure is shown with the body and face full front. There are no indications of clothing on the figure apart from five horizontal lines across the figure's waist that probably indicate a type of belt; an object attached to the figure's left side may be intended as a sword. The figure's hairstyle is unusual: it is parted in the center and fastened in two braids or ponytails. The arms are outstretched on either side of the body with the left arm bent up at the elbow, and the right arm down, while the legs are in right profile. The legs suggest that the figure is walking to the right, or perhaps running or dancing, since the left leg is kicked up in the air. Drawing **50**, shown in profile, also depicts a figure whose arm and leg position suggest that he is moving or dancing. This figure has no internal details to delineate a costume, headdress, or weapons of any kind.

The identity of these human figures is hard to determine. The details of costume, head covering, and weaponry are consistent and detailed enough to suggest that the individuals who drew these scenes had a specific visual model in mind. That model may lie outside Gordion, since the human figures in these drawings present many striking parallels in pose and costume with figures in Neo-Hittite relief sculpture, and parallels for these scenes will be discussed below in Section 3. Yet there also seems to be some interest in connecting these figures with elements of contemporary Phrygian society. This is most evident in depic-

---

40. This was suggested by Rodney Young (1969a:275); discussed further by Roller, forthcoming.

tions of elaborate belts and belt buckles (**77** furnishes a good example). The burial tumuli at Gordion have yielded several examples of intricately worked metal belts;[41] clearly this was a form of personal adornment that was important to the Phrygians, which may account for its presence in these drawings.

The status of the figures is also uncertain. One would assume that most were intended to represent human beings engaged in various activities. The addition of details of costume, such as the belt and the distinctive cylindrical headdress, was intended to identify the figure and designate individuals of high social position. Parallels with contemporary Syro-Hittite models, however, lay open the possibility that at least some may have been intended as divine or semi-divine figures. The intent of the human pictorial scenes is also problematic. The figures are for the most part isolated individuals, or, in four cases (**14**, **59** left and right, **81**), a pair of figures fighting. Were they intended to represent contemporary life? The formidable fortification walls of Gordion certainly suggest the potential for military activity in the contemporary community. Moreover, two intriguing scenes noted earlier, **19** and **46**, may show representations of falconry, an activity that could have been carried out by contemporary residents of Gordion. Yet other scenes, such as the striding warrior holding a hare in a bag (**44**), the warrior with a lion (**98**), the figure with a beak-shaped head, perhaps intended to depict a composite human-animal creature (**74**), the figure shown in full frontal pose (**101**) suggest allusions to a more complex narrative function, not necessarily connected with casual observations of daily life. These are all issues to which I will return in Section 3.

Let us look at another pictorial category, animals. Animals form the most frequent subject matter, with some type of animal occurring on approximately three-quarters of the incised stones.[42] The single most common animal is a bird, found on nearly half of the incised stones. Various poses appear, including birds at rest and in flight. Many consist of simple outline drawings, but in several cases great care was taken to depict internal details such as wing and tail feathers; noteworthy examples include **3**, **5**, **9a**, **11**, **16**, **19**, **20**, **62**, **66**, **69**, **72**, **77**, and **96**.

Several different types of birds can be recognized. One that recurs regularly is a raptor, or bird of prey, easily recognized by its curved beak and talons, emphasizing the bird's predatory nature. Depictions of the Gordion raptors fall into standard and repetitive patterns. The most common pose depicts the raptor in profile, sitting at rest with wings and tail folded and talons outstretched as if about to perch on something; good examples can be seen in **5**, **8**, **9**, **11** right, **16** left and center, **19**, **20** right, **26**, **54**, **69**. Less commonly, a sitting raptor is shown with outstretched wings, e.g., **3**, **11** left, **16** right, **20** left, **55**.

In addition to the depictions of raptors, there are many depictions of tamer fowl, some of which may be domesticated birds. Examples include **59** and **82** left and center, pheasant-like fowl; **14**, perhaps a sitting grouse; **41**, **50**, **71**, perhaps also **2**, birds that have the long neck, beak, and legs of a stork; **27** and **50**, which look like sitting hens; **94**, possibly also **92**, a goose. Drawings **67** and **104** depict a bird with a distinctive high crest, perhaps a type of crane, and **82**, **94** right, and **96** lower right show a bird with a long, elaborate folded tail; this too could be a crane, or perhaps a peacock. Other depictions of birds follow a set pattern that is not detailed enough to identify a distinct species. One is the undifferentiated bird in profile; this can be seen in **8**, **11** right, **14** left, **65**, **70**. Others show the outstretched wing span of a bird in flight; note examples on **8**, **46**, **62**, **72**, **74**, **77**, **82** right, and **92**. Here the emphasis is less on the individual species of bird and more on the appearance of the airborne bird as if seen from the vantage point of the human viewer below.

Virtually every bird is shown as an isolated entity, sketched independently and not interacting with other figures, human or animal, that appear in the same scene. In some instances several birds are shown in a row, e.g., **5**, **11**, **16**, **20**, **69**, as if someone was experimenting with drawing various bird profiles. In **5** a hu-

---

41. For bronze belts from early Gordion tumuli, see Young 1981:17–20, TumP 34–36, from Tumulus P; 147–54, MM 170–180, from Tumulus MM; 207–8, TumW 25–26, from Tumulus W.

42. This statistic should be considered approximate, since it is uncertain what percentage of the total number of stones with incised drawings was saved. It is clear from comments in the field notebooks that many stones with very simple marks, i.e., lines, crosses, arrows, etc., were not saved. In counting the number of depictions of animals in the extant corpus of incised stones, I consider every stone on which an animal form is found, even if the picture of the animal is clearly secondary to the main scene depicting a different subject.

man figure stands in the center with raptors on either side of him, but there is no interaction between them. Two interesting exceptions to this practice were noted above: **46** depicts a male standing with outstretched arms while birds fly around him, and **19**, although more poorly preserved, appears to depict two raptors perched on an object which may be an outstretched human arm. Both of these may illustrate scenes of falconry, the first depicting a man twirling a lure to recall the raptor, while the second showing the raptors on the trainer's arm.

The lion is the next most frequently represented animal, found on approximately 25% of the examples. The lions are presented in much more consistent fashion. All are shown in profile, as if striding forward.[43] They are normally shown with open mouth; in a few cases sharp teeth are clearly visible (**80**, **102**), and some have a long tongue hanging out (**1**, **7**, **10**, **38**, **48** left, **53**). Several lions are shown with prominent claws (**4**, **6**, **29**, **47**, **53**, **58**); often these are unusually long and curved, more reminiscent of a bird's talons than feline claws. The combination of teeth and claws serves to emphasize the animal's ferocity. Some of the lions are done in simple outline, but several were provided with distinctive internal details, such as prominent shoulder muscles (**6**, **29**, **48**, **53**, **98**, **102**), a wrinkled muzzle (**1**, **45**, **48**, **80**, **99**), a neck ruff that can appear almost like a collar (**1**, **4**, **6**, **48**, **53**, **95**, **99**, **102**), and a semicircular or angular mark indicating the cheek (**1**, **4**, **6**, **51**). A few examples (**10**, **29**, possibly also **98**) show the full mane of the adult male lion. On one stone, **80**, a particularly well preserved pair of lions have carefully detailed faces on which the face whiskers are clearly visible. Where the gender of the animal can be determined, all the lions are male, with one prominent exception, **85**, a nursing lioness whose teats are clearly shown.

The method of drawing the Gordion lions falls into a repetitive pattern, as if the drawing were following a standard model. The animal's nose and the curve of its head and back were drawn first, then legs were added, and finally internal details. This can be demonstrated from examples where the inciser made multiple attempts at drawing, abandoning an incomplete form and then starting another similar form nearby.

Note the double nose on **10**, a double tail on **83**, and the double lion's back on **47** and **84**.[44]

All of the lions on the Gordion incised stones appear as isolated figures, standing alone and not interacting with any other figure, human or animal. This is so even when more than one animal appears on the same stone. As noted above, there are several depictions of armed warriors, but no scene of a human figure hunting a lion appears among the incised drawings.

A variety of other animals also occurs, all appearing much less frequently than either a bird or a lion. Five stones depict horses (**10**, **12**, **72**, **82**, **104**), all shown in profile. In addition, there are two billygoats (**10**, **96**), one stag (**71**), an animal that may be either an ibex or a type of wild cattle (**72**, **73**, **100**), an animal that may be a gazelle (**75**), and a hare (**44**), as well as a few quadrupeds either so poorly preserved or so sketchily drawn that their identity is uncertain, and at least one example of a fish (**87**). Several of the depictions record lively details: the billygoats have prominent horns and beards, one horse (**72**) is shown galloping with a striking mane and tail, the stag stretches its neck to display a fine set of antlers, and the ibex (or cattle) have impressive sets of horns. One animal drawing—the hare carried in a bag by a hunter (**44**)—forms part of a complex picture that suggests a narrative function (parallels for this scene will be discussed in Section 3), but the other examples depict the animal as an isolated figure, not interacting with a human figure or forming part of a complex scene.

I will return to a fuller consideration of the meaning of the animal drawings in Section 3, but, given the breadth and complexity of the examples, a few summary remarks are in order here. Taken together, the depictions of animals reveal an intriguing mixture of animal forms that follow a prescribed pattern and animals with individual features that show close observation of nature. The drawings of the lions are the most formulaic: the animals are found in a limited range of poses, most frequently walking in right profile, and certain details, such as the open mouth, bared teeth, neck ruff, shoulder muscles, and curled claws, are depicted in very standard and repetitive patterns. Several of the depictions of birds also follow a repetitive pattern, a bird of prey in right profile with prominent

---

43. The great majority of the lions face right, although a few face left, e.g., **7**, **45**, **53**, **99**.

44. See infra, Section 4, for further examples and discussion of multiple attempted drawings.

beak and talons being the most common example. Others, however, suggest a keen eye for detail, and this is even more true of the less frequently depicted animals. This suggests that the lions and, to an extent, the birds of prey were depicted for their symbolic value, while other bird species and other animals reflect the artist's observation of the world around him. Taken together, the drawings of animals offer a shifting perspective between recurring symbolism and observation of daily life.

Depictions of architectural structures form another highly interesting subject. One architectural type that recurs in several drawings is an elevation of a tall building with a pitched roof. One block, **9a** and **9b**, now in two non-joining pieces, contains drawings of three such structures, and a smaller illustration of the same architectural type but with less detail appears in **46**.[45] In each case the drawing depicts the rectangular wall of a building; this is surmounted by a triangular pediment, indicating that we are looking at the short end of a building with the roof gable above. In one of the drawings (**9a**-right) a door is visible in the building's end wall. In two cases (**9a**-left, **9b**) the building is taller than it is wide, while in the other two drawings (**9a**-right, **46**) the building's façade is nearly square. These factors strongly suggest that the drawings depict the elevation of one end of a Phrygian megaron, such as those that comprise the most common building type in the Citadel complex, including Megaron 2 itself. These presumably had a pitched roof and a doorway in the short end of the building (for the plan of the standard Gordion megaron, see Fig. 3).[46]

Let us look at the three architectural elevations depicted on **9a** and **9b** in greater detail. These have usually been discussed together as a unit, but close examination of the drawings reveals that they differ from each other in several ways, indicating that the three drawings depict three separate structures. Reading from left to right, the building incised on the left side of **9a** depicts a tall narrow structure with a steeply pitched roof forming a high gable supported by a central vertical beam in the pediment. Above the central point of the gable are lines in the shape of a crescent; this is likely to be an intentional decoration on the roof, although it is difficult to be certain whether the drawing depicts a separate decorative element such as an akroterion placed on the building's roof or reproduces the visual effect of wooden rafters that continued above the ridgepole. Set into the center of the building's wall is a rectangle; this is likely to indicate a window, since it is too high above the ground level to be a door. In the pediment are lines forming small rectangles, one to the left of the central beam and two to the right; these appear to illustrate a set of windows in the pediment. The lower left portion of the building wall overlaps a drawing of a bird of prey, shown in right profile. The incised lines forming the building are heavier than those of the bird; thus it seems likely that the bird was drawn first and the building was incised later over the bird.

The center example also depicts the elevation of a building wall surmounted by the triangular end of a steeply pitched roof supported by a central vertical beam. Lines forming the side walls of the building continue beyond the top of the wall, although whether this reproduces an intentional construction feature or is just a product of sloppy drawing is uncertain.[47] The diagonal lines that outline the roof extend above the central ridgepole to form a V pattern; this is likely to be intentional, illustrating the extension of the sloping rafters above the ridgepole to create a decorative pattern on the roof. In the center of the building's façade is a double door composed of two leaves, each made from a row of vertical beams bound together with two horizontal cross timbers. To the right of the double door is a small rectangle, probably a window, while over the door is a circle with small lines inside it, presumably a form of decoration placed on the building wall. The building's wide double doors and its exterior decoration above the door suggest that it was an imposing structure of some importance.

The third architectural elevation, on **9b**, also shows the short end of a rectangular building with a gabled roof, but this drawing contains several unique

---

45. A drawing of **9a, b** made in 1956 by D. H. Cox has been reproduced several times in earlier publications; see Young 1957: pl. 90, fig. 12; Young 1965a:482, fig. 3; Young 1969a:272 top; Mellink 1983:357, fig. 1; Simpson 1998: pl. 180, fig. 16; Berndt-Ersöz 2006: fig. 119, but this drawing contains a number of inaccuracies (particularly in **9b**) and thus does not provide a good guide to the details of the representation.

46. Evidence for a pitched roof, Sams 1994b:212.

47. Similar lines can also be seen in the building elevation drawn at left; these seem more clearly to be the result of careless drawing.

features that set it apart from the other two. In this case the outline of the building's roof is drawn with parallel double lines, and the double outline extends well above the roof gable in a curved-V with inverted arms. The intent of the drawing seems to be to illustrate a decorative frame for the gable ends. This may well reproduce a decorative feature of stone, such as a stone akroterion with wings that curve inward on the point of the gable, of which actual examples have been found at Gordion.[48] There is no door in the front of a building, but an animal with a raised tail, drawn in right profile, is visible within the outlines of the building's front wall.[49] This is probably a lion, and here surely represents a type of decoration, either a relief sculpture or a painted drawing, placed on the building's façade. Next to the lion can be seen crossed diagonal lines forming a lozenge pattern; these are very faint, but seem intended to illustrate some form of geometric ornament that would also have decorated the building's front façade. The combination of lion and geometric pattern implies that this drawing represents the decorated front façade of an imposing public building. The lion on **9b** is too small to offer the level of detail visible in the drawings of lions discussed earlier, but the striding pose and raised tail of the animal are similar to the incised stone drawings of lions and suggest that this lion was intended as a symbol of power, further reinforcing the imposing nature of the building's appearance. Below the building is a series of horizontal parallel lines; these may represent stairs that led up to the building's entrance.

The building elevation illustrated in the far right of **46** is a simpler version of the previous three. In this drawing the short end of a building with a gabled roof is depicted; crossed lines extending above the point of the gable are likely to represent rafters extending above the ridgepole, on analogy with the building in **9a-right**. There is a doorway in the middle of the building façade, but no other internal details are visible. Below the building is a single horizontal line bisected by a vertical line; this may indicate a step or courtyard in front of the building.

In addition to the examples of the megaron elevation, another, completely different architectural form appears on **38**. On the left side of this stone is a drawing of a structure with a rectangular face, the top and bottom of which are indicated by two parallel horizontal lines; in its center is a tall vertical member, topped by a pointed triangular form, perhaps intended to suggest a tower. On either side of the central vertical structure, a pair of diagonal lines extends from its midsection to the upper left and right corners of the rectangular face. The effect is to suggest an elevation of a structure composed of a wooden frame braced by diagonal supports, with a large central tower. This could be part of a wooden fortification wall, such as a stockade, or it could be a gate with two leaves, although it would be surprising to see a tower placed in the middle of a gate, which is one reason for preferring the interpretation of a stockade wall. Alternatively, if the drawing represents a gate, the actual tower would have been placed at the side of the gate, and the drawing intentionally distorts the perspective to make the tower appear more conspicuous. Below this is a series of parallel horizontal lines; these may represent a set of steps leading up to the wall/gate or a stone base supporting it.

One further example provides further information about architecture at Gordion, a drawing on **8** that may replicate a section of a decorated standing wall. This stone is heavily incised with multiple scenes, but at the upper left corner is a form that appears to depict a wall made of two parallel faces of ashlar masonry, similar to the construction of Megaron 2 itself. One of these faces is decorated with a hooked meander pattern, perhaps alluding to decoration that was placed on the walls of buildings in the Early Phrygian Citadel.

Geometric patterns form another subject that recurs regularly among the Gordion incised drawings. These can range from fairly simple motifs such as straight and zigzag lines, squares and rectangles, the five-pointed star, and hand- and compass-drawn circles, to more complex and intricate patterns and forms. As in the drawings of anthropomorphic figures, the skill level of the drawings of patterns is quite uneven. Some of the incised stone drawings of geometric patterns were done by hand and can appear rather

---

48. Fragments of akroteria with inward curving wings were found in the level of the Early Phrygian Citadel preceding the Destruction Level; see Sams 1994b: pl. 20.3.2. One nearly intact akroterion with outward curving volutes was found in the fill above Megaron 2; Sams 1994b: pls. 20.2, 20.3.4, here Figure 16.

49. This feature was omitted from previously published drawings of this stone, but it can be seen in the photograph and is clearly visible on the actual stone.

clumsy. Others, such as the compass-drawn rosettes, were carefully done with a precision instrument.

Some of the patterns are basic elements of drawing that could be adapted to a variety of designs, including simple straight and zigzag lines (very common) and the compass-drawn circle or arc of a circle, found in **34**, **42**, **82**. There are also several examples of more complex patterns built on a circle, such as the vertical row of compass-drawn circles found on **82**. A more elaborate development of the compass-drawn circles was the rosette, a design comprising a circle with internal six petals formed by using the compass to draw arcs of the same circumference as the enclosing circle; note **10**, **70**, **72**, **75**, **82**, **85**.

Some of the simpler examples need not have any special significance, since forms such as lines, zigzags, and circles are all fairly basic drawing elements that were widely known and used. Other examples of complex patterns in the stone drawings, however, may have had special meaning for Early Phrygian Gordion, since they are similar to several of the designs used as decorative motifs in other media in Phrygian art, including painted pottery and wooden furniture. These can include concentric squares (**12**), meander patterns (**23**), diamonds and lozenge rows (**15**, **37**, **43**, **49**, **67**), and X-in-square or X-in lozenge designs (**10**, **20**, **30**, **57**, **82**, **103**). These same patterns suggest the types of designs that could have been used in perishable media, such as textiles.

In addition to the Megaron 2 drawings that depict geometric patterns, there are also drawings that appear to illustrate actual objects decorated with geometric designs. Drawing **37**, for example, depicts a square panel bounded by double lines above and below, with an internal row of vertical lozenges; a second, incomplete row of lozenges is found at the left. While the drawing is rather crude and was done freehand, it appears to represent the type of panel that might have displayed a row of lozenges, for example on wooden furniture. Drawings **49** and **67** seem even more likely to reproduce an actual object decorated with geometric inlay. Both include a drawing of a panel with patterns set in a frame. Drawing **49** illustrates a vertical strip with lozenges at left and a rectangular strip with a hooked meander at right, while **67** includes two horizontal strips with lozenges. These drawings may be an attempt to illustrate objects decorated with these patterns, such as strips of wooden inlay or textiles.

In addition to their decorative value, some of the geometric forms on the Early Phrygian drawings parallel symbols that occur in the corpus of pottery marks applied after firing on Destruction Level pottery, marks that were used for notations of ownership. Examples include the branch, the five-pointed star, the asterisk, latticing, and an X framed within a square or by parallel lines. This suggests that at least some of the patterns could have been incised onto the stones as marks of personal identity. Specific parallels for individual examples of owner's marks will be discussed in Section 3, but it is important to emphasize here that many of the geometric patterns on the stones are not random, but were regularly used in other media at Gordion, for the purpose of both aesthetics and personal identity.

Another interesting subject is furnished by three drawings of what appear to be cult objects. The drawings, found on three stones, **10** (left), **51** (center), and **94** (lower left), illustrate a form very similar to a Phrygian idol, a stone monument depicting a simplified humanoid form consisting of a head above a plain oblong that represents a schematic body. Such idols were a regular feature of Phrygian cult installations, and several are known from Gordion.[50] On one stone, **94**, the idol appears as an isolated figure with a simplified round head and oblong body. The drawing on **51** is somewhat more complex: it appears to represent a head, while the two upward curving lines extending out from the head probably indicate shoulders.[51] The figure on **10** also has shoulders, and in this drawing the disk-like face is enhanced by the presence of two eyes. The idols on **10** and **94** are isolated figures, unrelated to the other drawings on those two stones, while on **51** the head and shoulders of the idol are set on top of another rectangular form; this could indicate the body of the idol, or it may be intended to represent a step monument with an idol or semicircular disc on

---

50. For a discussion of stone idols in Phrygian cult, see Berndt-Ersöz 2006:56–58. Examples from Gordion include four under Tumulus B, Kohler 1995:20–21, TumB 17, pl. 11 A–B; 23–24, TumB 33, 34, 35, pl. 12 H–M; one from the Common Cemetery, Kohler 1995:21, n. 60; and several unpublished examples found in Tumulus E, Tumulus K, and the Middle Phrygian Level city; Roller 1999b:78, fig. 11, illustrates an example.

51. For the location of **51**, see Young 1958: pl. 21, fig. 3, and Young 1969a:271 top. The drawing published here has been reconstructed from excavation photographs.

top.⁵² Another form that may be a cult symbol appears in **60**, **94** (two examples), and **104**, with partially preserved examples on **17** and **37**. The design, a series of concentric circles drawn around a central line, could represent a maze pattern, but it may also represent a floral symbol with cult significance, such as a palmette or tree of life. The parallels for these Phrygian cult symbols will be discussed further in Section 3.

Finally, another class of material represented in the drawings comprises those marks that can best be called formless scribbles. A great many blocks with pictures of a human or animal form have a variety of random marks and lines in the background that have no connection to the main scene. In other instances (**18**, **24**, **32**, **34**, **39**, **61**, **63**, **68**, **76**, **78**, **84**, **89**, **93**, **97**) the major portion of the stone's incised surface is covered with formless marks. Since the stones with complex pictures or designs were the ones most likely to be saved, it is likely that many other stones with formless marks were found on the walls of Megaron 2 but not recorded; thus this type is probably more frequent than its presence in the catalogue suggests.

---

52. Prayon 1987:174 and Berndt-Ersöz 2006:120 suggest that the rectangular form below the idol head on **51** may be the oblong body form of an idol. Berndt-Ersöz 2006:120 offers an alternative interpretation, that this could represent a semicircular disc on the top of a step monument.

3

Subject Matter of the Incised Drawings: Sources and Possible Meanings

As the preceding discussion illustrates, the incised drawings are varied in technique, subject matter, and degree of artistic sophistication. These circumstances undoubtedly reflect both the variety of source material that influenced the drawings and a variety of motivations for incising them. Several drawings show distinct influences from artistic traditions outside Phrygia, while others portray themes that express local interests. Some of the drawings illustrate themes that also occur in other media, including stone sculpture, pottery decoration, and bronze and wooden objects. Some indicate familiarity with a complex iconographic tradition, but others probably represent the personal whim of the inciser. I will analyze potential sources for the various types of subjects found in the drawings here, then consider the reasons for their placement on the walls of Megaron 2 in Section 4.

Human Figures

The depictions of human figures offer a good starting point, since they form the most complex subject matter. The depictions of the human figure in the Gordion drawings reproduce the traditional rendition of the human form in ancient Near Eastern art: the face in profile but the eye full front, the shoulders and upper torso full front, and the lower torso, legs and feet in profile. This was a very old schema of representation, common in Anatolia and western Asia in the 3rd and 2nd millennia BCE and was still widely used in the early 1st millennium BCE. In addition, the hair style found on several of the figures, with the hair drawn back from the face and curling up into a pigtail at the nape of the neck, is also quite characteristic of the human form in Near Eastern art, as is the flowing beard over the long gown. The styles of costume, both the short kilt and the long gown, are also well known in western Asiatic art.[53]

Some of the drawings, however, are detailed enough to suggest a more immediate iconographic source, namely the visual programs of the Phrygians' neighbors in southeastern Anatolia and northern Syria, conventionally called Neo-Hittite.[54] This is true both in artistic style and in the choice of subject matter. Neo-Hittite relief sculpture furnishes a number of particularly close parallels. The costume of a belted kilt and shoes with upturned toes appears widely in

---

53. The schema for rendering the human form can be seen, inter alia, in the figure of a male divinity in the 14th century BCE relief from the King's Gate at Hattusas; Akurgal 1962: fig. 64–65. This figure wears the typical short kilt, but rendered with an eye in profile; for a round, full-front eye in a profile face, see a series of 14th century BCE gold figurines of deities from Carchemish; Akurgal 1962:53 top. The Carchemish deities also illustrate the short kilt and the long gown. For a figure with a flowing beard over a long gown, compare a late 2nd millennium BCE relief from Alaca Höyük; Akurgal 1962: fig. 93.

54. The term "Neo-Hittite" enjoys wide currency; cf. Akurgal 1962, Orthmann 1971, Genge 1979, Hawkins 1982, Hawkins 2000:3. The term refers to the early 1st millennium BCE use of a distinctive style and iconographic motifs that owe their origin to the 2nd millennium BCE art and iconography of the Hittite Empire. In practice, the cities where Neo-Hittite art has been found included a diverse spectrum of population groups, with Luwian and Aramaic-speaking peoples predominant. The style was consistently used by major cities throughout the region and seems not to be dependent on the ethnic origin of the population, so I will continue to use the term Neo-Hittite, even though the term is misleading, since Hittites themselves did not create the material. For a discussion of this problem, see Hawkins 2000, I:1–3; Aro 2003:281–85.

Neo-Hittite reliefs; compare reliefs from Arslan Taş, Babylon, Carchemish, Körkün, Malatya, Tell Halaf, and Zincirli, with Gordion drawings **5, 14, 44, 46,** and **59**.[55] Most of the Gordion figures appear to be bare-headed, although the right figure in **14** wears a helmet with a crest; this is less common in Neo-Hittite reliefs, although such a crest does appear in a relief from Karatepe, worn by two standing warriors facing each other.[56]

The parallels extend to the drawings of armed men and men engaged in combat. The practice of depicting a warrior with a sword at his side, projecting beyond the kilt, found in Gordion drawings **5, 31, 44,** and **59**, appears in Neo-Hittite reliefs from Arslan Taş, Babylon, Carchemish, Körkün, and Pancarlı.[57] A few Gordion warriors, **2, 33,** and **37**, stand and hold a bow and arrow, and one drawing, **5**, illustrates a warrior with a sword at his side and a bow on one shoulder; these are similar to a Neo-Hittite warrior found in a relief scene from Arslan Taş.[58] There is no Gordion drawing depicting a warrior actually shooting a bow and arrow in hunt or in battle, frequent themes in Neo-Hittite relief sculpture.

These characteristics of body pose, costume, and weaponry were both consistent and widespread in the Neo-Hittite repertory of sculpture, and so the presence of these features in the Gordion drawings need not suggest anything more than a general familiarity with this style. Some of the more complex Gordion drawings with human figures, however, furnish more precise parallels with specific centers in southeastern Anatolia and north Syria.

The Gordion drawings depicting pairs of combatants provide one set of parallels. One Gordion stone, **59**, illustrates two pairs of two men in combat; here the antagonists are unarmed, as if about to engage in a fist fight. This too appears in several scenes in Neo-Hittite relief sculpture: note a relief from Zincirli and a pair of winged genies on a relief found in Aleppo.[59] This latter pair has arm positions quite similar to those of the righthand pair of fighters on the Gordion drawing.

An even more detailed example, Gordion drawing **14**, depicts two antagonists squaring off against each other with drawn swords. Reliefs depicting foot soldiers appear in several sites in southeastern Anatolia and northwestern Mesopotamia, although the scene of actual combat between two evenly matched opponents is relatively rare in Neo-Hittite relief sculpture.[60] One good parallel for the Gordion drawing, however, comes from the Aramaean levels at Tell Halaf, on one of the small orthostate reliefs from the west palace.[61] The Halaf relief depicts two antagonists facing each other, both wearing a short kilt but otherwise nude. In both the Gordion drawing and the Halaf relief the left figure reaches out his left hand towards his opponent, while the figure at the right extends his left arm, which holds a sword that he thrusts towards his opponent. In both works the fingers of the figure at left are prominently shown. The two works differ in some details: the left figure in the Tell Halaf relief puts his hand on his opponent's head, while on the Gordion stone the left figure only grabs towards his opponent; also the Tell Halaf figures are bareheaded while the Gordion figures wear helmets. Yet the similarity between the two in both overall composition and in details such as the fingers strongly suggests that the correspondences are not accidental.

Parallels with Neo-Hittite relief sculpture are even clearer in Gordion drawings that depict more clearly articulated human figures with a higher level of detail. There are two Gordion drawings that depict a male figure advancing on foot while wielding a weapon, **44** and **98**. In both cases the figure strides from left to right, with the left leg forward and right leg back. The figure is bareheaded and the only costume is a short kilt. In both drawings the figure is shown with the chest area full front and the arms extended out to either side, although the position of the right arm

---

55. Reliefs from Arslan Taş, Orthmann 1971: pl. 4e; Babylon, Orthmann 1971: pl. 5b; Carchemish, Orthmann 1971: pls. 23e, 25d, 26a and d, 33d, 35e; Körkün, Orthmann 1971: pl. 38f; Malatya, Orthmann 1971: pls. 40e, 41f; Tell Halaf, Orthmann 1971: pls. 9e, 9h, 10f; Zincirli, Orthmann 1971: pls. 58 a, c, d, f, 59f, 60a, 61b.
56. Orthmann 1971: pls. 16c, 18a, b.
57. Arslan Taş, Orthmann 1971: pl. 4e; Babylon, Orthmann 1971: pl. 5b; Carchemish, Orthmann 1971: pl. 33d; Körkün, Orthmann 1971: pl. 38f; Pancarlı, Orthmann 1971: pl. 48h.
58. Orthmann 1971: pl. 4e.
59. Zincirli relief, Orthmann 1971: pl. 56a; Aleppo relief, Orthmann 1971: pl. 4c.
60. Orthmann 1971:403–4, gives examples from Tell Halaf and Carchemish.
61. Orthmann 1971: pl. 10c.

is not entirely clear in **98**, where the drawing of the human figure was drawn over a lion and is overlaid by other random lines and cross-hatching. Both figures hold a weapon, probably a mace, in the figure's right hand in **44**, and in the left in **98**. In stance, gesture, and weapon, both figures seem to be a variation on the theme of the "Smiting God," a well-established subject in Anatolian relief sculpture that was developed during the Hittite Empire period and was widely used during the early 1st millennium BCE to represent the Storm god.[62] It is unclear whether the male figures in the two Gordion drawings were intended to represent deities, since neither wears the conical cap that was a regular means of indicating divinity in Hittite and Neo-Hittite iconography. In **98** it seems surprising to see the figure holding the weapon in the left hand, and it is possible that this is a misunderstanding of the original scene in which the deity holds a lightning bolt or other object in the left hand.[63] The figure in **98** is drawn over a lion; this may be another instance of one drawing superimposed on another drawing of unrelated subject matter, several examples of which were noted in Section 1, but it is also possible that the maker of the Gordion drawing deliberately combined the two subjects. The combination of striding male figure and lion could indicate familiarity with the Neo-Hittite tradition of showing the Smiting God standing on the back of a lion, as can be seen in a relief from Malatya.[64]

The scene depicted in **44** is a more complex version of the subject. Since the scene is the only drawing on the stone, it is considerably easier to read. This drawing also shows a man in a short kilt with a sword at his side who strides to the right; the long fringe on his kilt swings forward, as if to indicate motion. The figure's hair is drawn back into a distinctive pigtail. In his left hand he holds a captured hare in a bag, while with his right he swings back a blunt weapon, an ax or mace, as if to strike the animal. While these are all characteristics of the Smiting God,[65] the bare-headed Gordion figure does not appear to be a deity. The figure is more likely to be a hunter and as such finds several parallels in Neo-Hittite relief scenes of a hunter who holds his prey in his left hand and a weapon to be used to dispatch the animal in his right. A good example can be found at Pancarlı, where the hunter, a human figure wearing a short kilt and a pointed cap, holds a lion cub upside down by the tail.[66] Two reliefs from Zincirli are also similar to the Gordion drawing, although here the hunter is a composite creature, a human body with a lion's head, which holds a deer upside down.[67] The method of holding the weapon, with the head of the ax turned inwards, seems an awkward way to hold a weapon for striking, and so its occurrence on both the Neo-Hittite monuments and the Gordion drawing reinforces the suggestion that the Gordion artist was following a Neo-Hittite model.

In addition to the general similarities with the Smiting God prototype, the detail of the prey, a hare, connects the Gordion composition with an Anatolian model. The scene of a god holding a hare in the right hand with the left hand drawn back and poised to strike is attested on a Hittite seal of the Empire period, found in Thebes, in Boiotia, demonstrating that the scene was widely dispersed.[68] A more immediate parallel is furnished by an Iron Age relief from Kültepe, site of a Luwian city in Tabal. Here the striding figure carries a spear across his body, while in his left hand he holds a hare upside down from a string, with a bird of prey above the hare.[69] The method of carrying the hare is comparable to that depicted in the Gordion drawing, although the Gordion work lacks the bird. Like the Pancarlı figure, the Kültepe figure wears a belted short kilt, and on both the Pancarlı and Kültepe reliefs the standing figures have a long beard and a high pointed cap, the traditional marks of a divinity. In contrast to these and to the Zincirli hunters, who are clearly not human, the Gordion hunter, bareheaded and clean shaven, appears to be an ordinary human figure. Thus the Gordion drawing appears almost as a composite of traits found in several Neo-Hittite scenes, but an exact replica of none of them.

---

62. Collon 1972 discusses the history of the type; Bunnens 2004, esp. pp. 58–60, gives several 1st millennium BCE examples.
63. The god with the lightning bolt can be seen in Bunnens 2004: pls. 1–6.
64. Orthmann, 1971: pl. 42f.
65. Bunnens 2004:59.
66. Orthmann 1971: pl. 48h.
67. Orthmann 1971: pls. 58c, 60a.
68. Porada 1981:47–49, no. 25.
69. Özgüç 1971:82, fig. 7; Orthmann 1971: pl. 38b; Aro 1998:173–74, B 133; Aro 2003:316, pl. XIV. Özgüç 1971:82, identifies the bird as an eagle, but it could also be a falcon.

The Neo-Hittite prototypes, in emphasizing the power of the divinity or demon, suggest that a more symbolic meaning was intended, but since the Gordion figure is an isolated example, we do not know if this scene too carried some symbolic significance.

A different Neo-Hittite model may lie behind another Gordion drawing, **101**, that depicts a figure with a full-front face and torso, and arms and legs in profile. While a full-front pose is less common than a profile view in Neo-Hittite sculpture, fairly close parallels can be noted at several sites. A relief on a large statue base from Sam'al (Zincirli) depicts a male figure between two lions, which he holds by their manes.[70] A comparable scene is known from Carchemish.[71] A relief from Tell Halaf depicts a figure in a similar pose, here flanked by two bull-men who support a winged sun disk.[72] In each of the Neo-Hittite works the kneeling figure is a hero or figure of myth that masters or is supported by strong animals or composite creatures.[73] Gordion drawing **101** is a very basic linear sketch and thus it might seem somewhat far-fetched to compare this with the more complex sculptural scenes noted above. Yet the Gordion drawing displays an attempt to capture several details of the Neo-Hittite models, including the elaborate belt on the costume, the shoes with upturned toes, and the distinctive hairstyle showing the hair parted in the center and drawn to either side of the face in two pony tails or braids. The Gordion figure appears alone, and so we cannot tell if this too was intended as the center figure of a heraldic "master-of-animal" pose, but its debt to a Neo-Hittite model seems clear.

In addition to the Gordion human figures who wear the short kilt, a few figures are shown with a long gown. One type, the long gown with an elaborate belt and a high cylindrical headdress, is best seen in Gordion drawing **77**, with more sketchy examples in **71** and **94**. The long, belted gown also finds numerous parallels in the Neo-Hittite repertory. This is the standard costume of an authority figure in Neo-Hittite art, indeed widespread in the art of western Asia, in both relief sculpture and sculpture in the round, where it can be used to depict both human figures, i.e., a ruler, and divinities.[74] Such a male authority figure is normally shown with a long flowing beard; this may be the intent in the Gordion drawings also, since in each of these drawings the chin of the figure is very indistinct and melds directly into the gown, as if the Gordion drawings were trying to reproduce the effect of the long beard that extends over the front of the gown. Neo-Hittite figures with this costume are usually shown with long hair that flows directly onto their shoulders, and this feature too seems to be present in the Gordion drawings, although in the Gordion drawings no internal details of hair and beard are shown.

Not every detail of costume in the Gordion figures can be connected with a Neo-Hittite prototype. The cylindrical hat worn by the figures in the Gordion drawings (also visible in **46**) is much less common in Neo-Hittite sculpture; normally a deity wears a pointed cap and a human ruler wears a rounded cap or is bareheaded. A rare example of the cylindrical headdress can be seen on a pair of reliefs from the palace at Sakçagözü, where it is worn by two antithetically placed genie figures, although these reliefs are later in date than the Gordion Destruction Level.[75] It is possible that the cylindrical hat found on the Gordion figures may be a local headdress denoting authority, just as the broad belt with elaborate belt buckle appears to be local to Phrygia (note especially **77**).

Another type of long gown can be seen in **88**, on a figure striding to the right with one arm extended forward. Both the garment and the pose can be paralleled in Neo-Hittite relief sculpture, specifically in a relief from Carchemish that shows two male figures, both divinities, standing on top of a lion; the rounded head covering of the Gordion example is found on the Carchemish figure at the left as well.[76] A similar garment, headdress, and pose appear on other Carchem-

---

70. Orthmann 1971: pl. 62e; Akurgal 1962: fig. 127.
71. Orthmann 1971: pl. 32d. Another relief from Carchemish (Orthmann 1971: pl. 32e) shows a kneeling figure in a similar pose, although here the figure is a composite creature with human body and a bird's head.
72. Orthmann 1971: pl. 12b.
73. For a discussion of the type, see Orthmann 1971:440–47.

74. Neo-Hittite parallels include a relief from Djekke, Orthmann 1971: pl. 5d (divinity); Carchemish, Orthmann 1971: pl. 23a (divinity), Orthmann 1971: pl. 35g (human ruler); Maraş, Orthmann 1971: pl. 45h (human ruler); Zincirli, Orthmann 1971: pl. 57e (human ruler), pl. 63a (human ruler).
75. Orthmann 1971: pls. 49a, 50c. Orthmann, p. 138, assigns this relief to the Late Neo-Hittite IIIb period, second half of the 7th century BCE.
76. Orthmann 1971: pl. 23a.

ish reliefs of human figures in procession, including musicians and warriors.[77] The sketchy nature of the Gordion drawing makes it uncertain what type of figure is intended, although a weapon seems to be indicated at the figure's right side, which would suggest a human male.

As this review of the Gordion drawings with human figures illustrates, the majority of the Gordion figures were derived from Neo-Hittite style and subject matter, but do not directly reproduce any extant work of Neo-Hittite sculpture. The individuals who made the Gordion scenes were clearly familiar with the conventions of Neo-Hittite relief sculpture, as the close parallels in body poses, hair styles, costume, attributes, and gestures of the figures indicate. Yet the subject matter of the Gordion drawings of human figures represents a highly eclectic selection of stock images and poses, without any suggestion of a systematic program.

We should also note some areas in which there are few correspondences between Neo-Hittite art and the Gordion drawings. The composite creature, a combination of human and animal or of two different animals, had long been a popular subject in the art of western Asia but is rare on the Gordion incised stones. This type may be represented by a single example on the right side of **74**, a figure with human legs, an indeterminate torso, and a head ending in a pronounced point like a beak. This could represent a simplified version of a human figure with the head of a raptor that has a pronounced beak, a figure known from several Neo-Hittite sites.[78] The Neo-Hittite bird-man, however, is usually a protective figure, often shown with his arms raised in a gesture of prayer, while the Gordion figure carries a long spear, implying that this is an aggressive figure.

We should also note two Gordion drawings that appear to depict scenes of falconry, a subject that may well reflect a scene of ordinary life in Gordion. One of the drawings, **19**, appears to show an outstretched human arm with two birds resting on it. While this is paralleled in a number of scenes in both 2nd and 1st millennium BCE Anatolian art, there is no reason to think that the Gordion scene copied a Neo-Hittite model; rather the scene probably reflects interest in falconry at Gordion.[79] The other drawing, **46**, which I have interpreted as a scene of a falconer swinging a lure to attract the bird to return to him, is a subject that does not appear in the extant corpus of Neo-Hittite material, and here too we should assume that the scene illustrates a contemporary event.

Animals

The choice of iconographic model for the Gordion drawings of animals seems more varied. Neo-Hittite prototypes exist for several of the animals on the Gordion drawings, especially the lion and the stag, while depictions of other animals, especially the bird and the horse, seem more strongly influenced by observation of the animals themselves.

The depictions of lions show the clearest evidence of influence from a Neo-Hittite prototype. Like their Neo-Hittite counterparts, the Gordion lions are shown in profile. They normally stride forward with open mouth and bared teeth. Specific details characteristic of Neo-Hittite representational style, such as the band on the neck, the treatment of shoulder musculature, and prominent curved claws, occur regularly in the Gordion drawings. Several Gordion drawings of lions exaggerate these features, suggesting that they were imitating an artistic representation rather than a living animal. Note the Gordion lions with prominent heads, tongue, or teeth: **6, 7, 10, 25, 29, 38, 45, 53, 80, 99, 102**. The claws of the lions in the Gordion drawings are particularly distinctive: they are unnaturally long and curved and in many cases look more like the claws of a raptor rather than a lion; good examples are furnished by **4, 6, 53, 58**. These are all features that appear regularly in Neo-Hittite depictions of lions, both reliefs and sculpture in the round; note examples from Ain Dara, Carchemish, Malatya, Zincirli, and Göllüdağ.[80]

Because these characteristic visual traits, especially the striding pose, open mouth, and prominent

---

77. Orthmann 1971: pl. 29d (musicians); pl. 31b–d (warriors).
78. See the examples listed by Orthmann 1971:320–23.
79. Canby 2002 discusses representations of falconry in Hittite and Neo-Hittite visual media and illustrates several examples. See also the discussion infra, n. 104.
80. Ain Dara, Orthmann 1971: pl. 1a; Carchemish, Orthmann 1971: pls. 20b, 23a, 27a and b, 32e, g; Malatya, Orthmann 1971: pls. 39b, 41a; Zincirli, Orthmann 1971: pls. 60 b, 61d and e, 62c; Göllüdağ, Aro 1998:411, B116–119.

claws, recur regularly in many Neo-Hittite centers, their presence in Gordion indicates a general familiarity with the stylistic canon of Neo-Hittite art. Some details in the Gordion drawings, however, suggest access to direct models from Neo-Hittite centers. One is the presence of a distinctive half-moon, like a cheek piece, found above the neck ring of the lion. Found in Megaron 2 drawings **4, 6, 51**, and possibly **1**, this feature is visible in lions or leonine-composite creatures from orthostate sculpture on the Herald's Wall at Carchemish, and also on one of the orthostates from Zincirli.[81] The use of cross-hatching to indicate the mane is another Neo-Hittite detail, found on Gordion drawing **98b** and on reliefs from Maraş and Zincirli.[82] Another specific feature of the Gordion drawings with close Neo-Hittite affinities is the tongue of several of the lions. This can be extended out and away from the open mouth, often with a pronounced curve or angular turn. Examples include **1, 10, 38, 48**, and **53**, and possibly **7** and **33**.[83] An almost identical example does occur in one of the Carchemish reliefs, a lion-sphinx from the Herald's Wall.[84] This work is particularly close to **38**, in which the animal's tongue does not extend from the interior of its mouth, as a natural tongue would, but appears almost as an addition to the end of the mouth. Another detail specific to Neo-Hittite sculpture is a small circle found on the rear haunch of the animal, seen in a relief from Maraş.[85] This feature, which does not appear to imitate any natural part of the animal's anatomy, finds an almost exact parallel in Gordion drawings **29** and **53**. Neo-Hittite parallels may also help explain the nature of two problematic drawings of lions, **1** and **4**, both of which were originally interpreted as dogs.[86] The animals in both drawings, however, have much in common with other Gordion depictions of lions, such as the open mouth, sharp bared teeth and extended tongue (**1**), curved claws on the feet (**4**), and the pronounced neck band (**1** and **4**). In both cases, the V-decoration on the neck band may be a simpler version of the half-moon cheek-piece discussed above. Note as a parallel a relief of a lion from Zincirli which also has an unusually long slender body, neck, and face, proportions more similar to a dog than a lion.[87]

The Gordion lions are not merely slavish copies of the Neo-Hittite lions, however, for we can detect two quite distinctive styles in the Gordion material. Some Gordion drawings depict a lion with a rather squarish face and angular mane, e.g., **4, 48 left, 80, 98b**. Others have a more rounded face and a wavy mane that more closely represents animal fur; for good examples, see **10, 38, 48 right, 102**.[88] Both types of lion are found in Neo-Hittite sculpture, although at different sites.[89] This suggests that the Gordion drawings drew on a variety of sources and artistic styles, absorbing them into the Phrygian drawings as well as into other media. We will see that both styles of sculpted lions were retained in Phrygian visual tradition, exemplified by those found on grave monuments in the Phrygian Highlands.[90]

One drawing of a Gordion lion, **25**, has a slightly different character. The drawing shows a rampant

---

81. Orthmann 1971: pl. 26b, the lion in a Master of Animals scene; pl. 27b, a lion-headed sphinx; and pl. 27d, a composite lion-human figure. From Zincirli, note a lion from the outer Citadel gate, Orthmann 1971: pl. 60b. The half-moon cheek piece was absorbed into Phrygian drawing style, since we find it on painted pottery from the Gordion Destruction and post-Destruction Levels; see Sams 1974:184–86, fig. 4-5 (a bull) and 10-11(a lion); Sams 1994a: no. 1074, pl. 131.

82. Maraş, Orthmann 1971: pl. 44b; Zincirli, Orthmann 1971: pl. 56d.

83. The animal in **33** appears more like a fish than a lion, but it has the same type of prominent curved tongue as the others, so I include it in this context.

84. Orthmann 1971, Carchemish, pl. 27b. The prominent tongue also appears on several of the painted animals on Gordion pottery, cf. TumP 55, Young 1981: pl. 17C.

85. Orthmann 1971, Maraş B/2, pl. 44b.

86. Young 1969a:273–74. See supra, n. 37.

87. Orthmann 1971: pl. 60b. We may also recall a later Greek example, the rather dog-like lions on the terrace of the Letoon at Delos; Boardman 1978: fig. 269.

88. A similar duality of style can be noted in the wooden lions from Tumulus P, where one example, TumP 107, Young 1981: pl. 22c–f, has an angular face, and two others, TumP 108, single lion, Young 1981: pl. 22g–i, and TumP 109, lion and bull fight, Young 1981: pl. 23a–c, have a more rounded face and curly mane.

89. For examples of the more angular-faced lion, see the sculpture from Ain Dara, Orthmann 1971: pl. 1a, and Carchemish, Orthmann 1971: pl. 26b, 27b; contrast these with the lions with more rounded faces from Malatya, Orthmann 1971: pl. 39a–c, and Zincirli, Orthmann 1971: pls. 58b, 60b.

90. Note the contrast between the square-faced lions from the Arslantaş monument, Haspels 1971: figs. 131–134, and the more rounded lion of the Yılantaş monument, Haspels 1971: figs. 143, 148. This will be discussed in greater detail in Section 5.

lion with a round head, round eye, button nose, and rounded mouth open at a 90° angle. These features are also present in two works of sculpture in the round from Gordion, two stone lions uncovered in the fill above Megaron 2 (Figs. 17, 18).[91] The sculptures are of the same white poros stone as that used in the building's walls, and were presumably made to decorate the megaron. Drawing **25** seems close enough to the sculpted lions that it almost appears to be a sketch for them.

A unique figure among the Megaron 2 drawings of lions is the nursing lioness with prominent teats, **85**, a representation that has no parallel in Neo-Hittite art. It may be a drawing taken from actual observation of the animal, but the nursing lioness may also be an image with special meaning to the Phrygians, since a pair of female lions with cubs (but without teats) is found on the sculpted façade of the Arslantaş tomb in the Phrygian Highlands.[92]

The depictions of lions offer the closest connection with a Neo-Hittite model, but other animals appearing in the Gordion drawings may also have a Neo-Hittite prototype. One is the stag with impressive antlers, depicted in drawing **71**. A similar animal appears in four reliefs from Zincirli, one of which, a relief from the outer Citadel gate, forms a particularly close model; note especially the correspondences in the treatment of the antlers, the hump on the back of the stag's neck, the eye, and the shoulder muscles.[93] A relief from Carchemish furnishes another parallel, although less close than the Zincirli relief.[94]

In contrast, other depictions of animals seem to be independent of an external model. The horses found in Gordion drawings **10**, **12**, **72**, **82**, and **104** offer a case in point. The first two examples are very simply drawn, with rather squared noses and diamond-shaped eyes, especially **12**. They are reminiscent of a wooden horse found in Tumulus P, the child's burial. The diamond-shaped eyes are also found in three ivory plaques from Megaron 3, one of the large megarons in the Early Phrygian Citadel.[95] The horses depicted in drawings **72** and **82** have a more impressive mane and tail and a long neck; these are features that do not appear in the horses depicted in Neo-Hittite reliefs, although such a mane appears on the horse in one of the ivory plaques from Megaron 3.[96]

Another Gordion animal, a goat, found in **10** and **96**, also has a distinctive character. Both of the Gordion examples are billygoats, as is clear from the beard and sharp horns depicted on the animal, and one, **10**, wears a collar, suggesting that it is domesticated. Goats do occur in Neo-Hittite relief sculpture (note an example from Tell Halaf),[97] but they lack the beard of the Gordion goats and are shown standing on their hind legs and looking back, while the Gordion goats stand on all four legs and face forward. Goats also appear on a small number of Phrygian stamped and painted vessels from the Destruction Level, although these too are not very similar to the goats from the Megaron 2 drawings. The goat silhouettes with slender bodies and long horns, imitating Alişar IV ware decoration, have little in common with the goat in **10**. The goats found on painted pottery from the tumuli and post-Destruction contexts have a more stately appearance with long upright necks and distinctly articulated legs and hooves, features that the Gordion drawings lack, and no collar is shown on the goats on painted pottery.[98] The lack of correspondence with other artistic treatments of goats suggests that the goats on the stone drawings were modeled on an actual animal.

---

91. Gordion inventory numbers S 35 and S 43, Young 1956a:261–62, pl. 92, figs. 42, 43; Simpson 1998: fig. 5-6.
92. Haspels 1971: fig. 131, 132. See also the discussion below, n. 165.
93. Orthmann 1971: pls. 56c, d, 57g, h. The closest parallel is with Orthmann 1971: pl. 57g.
94. Carchemish relief, Orthmann 1971: pl. 33e.

95. Tumulus P horse, see Young 1981:50–51, TumP 106, fig. 22 A, B, pl. 22 A, B; note also TumP 112, pl. 24 C–E, identified as a deer or bull, but very similar to **12** in the body type of the animal. The diamond-shaped eyes are found in three ivory plaques depicting a deer, a griffin, and a horse; Young 1960: pl. 25a–c.
96. Young 1960: pl. 60, fig. 25c; see also the logo on the title page of this volume.
97. Orthmann 1971: pl. 10b.
98. Goats on Alişar-style pottery made at Gordion, see Sams 1994a: no. 932, pl. 126, and on pottery imported from Alişar, Sams 1994a: pl. 161, nos. 170–171 (could also be a deer); a goat as a stamped motif on Destruction Level pottery, Sams 1994a: fig. 61, 1000. See also post-Destruction level examples, nos. 1082–1085, pl. 133. Polychrome painted goats on post-Destruction level pottery, Sams 1994a: nos. 1065, 1066, 1070–72 (composite drawing), fig. 45; no. 1069, fig. 46; on pottery from Tumulus P, Young 1981: TumP 55–57, pl. 17c–f. Another example from Tumulus K-III, no. 6, Körte and Körte 1904:56–57, pl. 2.

A few Gordion animals occur infrequently: an ibex on **72**; a quadruped with a long horn, presumably some type of cattle, **73** and **100**; a snake, **73**; a fish, **87**[99]; and an animal head that may be a gazelle, **75**. These drawings presumably record a sketch of the actual animal (although an alternative explanation for the gazelle, **75**, is offered below).

I have reserved a discussion of the depictions of birds to the end of this section, since birds form the most numerous and multifaceted class of animals found in the Gordion drawings. The great variety of birds shown, including raptors, ducks and/or geese, seated birds that could be hens, grouse, or pheasants, storks, crested birds (perhaps cranes), and others, and their frequency indicates the importance of representation of avian life to the Phrygian artists. Yet the sources of the bird pictures and their meanings are varied and complex, reflecting both external and internal influences.

Depictions of raptors deserve special mention, since the raptor was clearly of special importance to the Phrygian artists. Not only are raptors the most frequently depicted type of bird, but the greatest care was given to the representation of their appearance. Unlike the depictions of human figures, lions, and stags, the Gordion drawings of birds show little affinity with the art of western Asia. This is not for the lack of potential models, since birds of prey figure prominently among Neo-Hittite visual symbols. In the Neo-Hittite tradition, birds of prey could be a key symbol of cult: they appear in Neo-Hittite reliefs depicting the sun disc, where the wing span of a raptor supports the disc, and the bird of prey logogram appears in the Luwian name of the goddess Kubaba, an important divinity widely worshipped in southeastern Anatolia, especially in Carchemish.[100] In public court art, a bird of prey could be carried by an attendant of a ruler, presumably as a symbol of status, as can be seen on a relief from Sakçagözü.[101] The features of a raptor could be incorporated into a range of composite creatures, such as winged lions, winged genie figures, and human figures with bird heads, found in orthostate reliefs from several sites, including Gordion.[102] Many of these emphasize the physical traits of a bird of prey, such as large and elaborately feathered wings or a hooked beak.[103] Clearly the symbolism of the bird of prey—its power, its swiftness, its skill as a hunter—carried important ideological meaning. In private art, raptors appear on several funerary stelae from southeastern Anatolia, where they allude to the deceased's interest in hunting and falconry.[104] These raptors surely reflect real life examples, with the added connotation of elite status.

The raptors that appear in the Gordion drawings are normally shown alone, and only rarely are part of a larger narrative scene. The intent of the Gordion drawings seems to be to convey, not a symbolic vision of the bird's attributes or an allusion to status, but the actual appearance of the bird. Often the drawings emphasize the wings and tail and sharp talons of the raptor, although even in these cases the emphasis seems to be on the bird at rest, not the powerful and impressive wingspread found in the Neo-Hittite winged sun disk. The Gordion drawings do not depict the multiple layers and varying sizes of feathers, as are shown in the Neo-Hittite winged sun disk or composite creatures. This is not for a lack of detail, for many of the pictures of birds are among the most careful and detailed of all the Gordion drawings; note examples **3, 5, 11, 69**. Thus while the Gordion drawings of raptors

---

99. Pictures of individual fish are rare at Gordion, although depictions of fish were scratched onto pottery of the post-Destruction Level period; Roller 1987: fig. 43, 2C-5, 2C-7, 2C-13. There are several depictions of animals eating fish from both pre- and post-Destruction Level material: on pottery, Sams 1994a: no. 1051; on an ivory plaque found in Megaron 3, Young 1963:355, fig. 8; on a wooden figure from Tumulus P, Young 1981: TumP 111, pl. 24a, b; and on a red sandstone statuette of the goddess Matar from a Middle Phrygian context, Mellink 1983: pl. 73, 1, Roller 1999b:76, fig. 12.

100. For an example of a winged sun disc, see a relief from Tell Halaf, Orthmann 1971: pl. 12b. On the raptor logogram used for the name of the goddess Kubaba, Hawkins 1981, 2000.

101. An official carrying a falcon appears in a processional relief from the palace at Sakçagözü, Orthmann 1971: Sakçagözü A/7, pl. 50a.

102. For discussions of these composite creatures, see Orthmann 1971:320–50. A bird-man can be seen on an Early Phrygian relief from Gordion; Sams 1989: pl. 130, 1.

103. Examples of the hooked beak from Ain Dara, Orthmann 1971: pl. 3b; Carchemish, Orthmann 1971: pls. 26d, 32f; Zincirli, Orthmann 1971: pls. 55a, 59b. Examples of a prominent feathered wing, Carchemish, Orthmann 1971: pls. 27b, 28b, 33b, 33f.

104. Note the presence of falcons among the possessions of the deceased depicted on funerary reliefs from Maraş, Bonatz 2000b:99, nos. C54, C63, C64, C65; the last depicts a boy standing on his mother's lap holding a falcon with a restraining cord tied to its leg, surely a beloved possession; cf. Young 1969a:275.

followed a set pattern, it was a pattern based on actual observation.

This is also true of the other types of birds depicted in the Gordion drawings. The drawings present a virtual aviary of birds, some perhaps domesticated, such as hens, **27**, **50**; ducks or geese, **92**, **94**; birds with long elaborate tails like a peacock, **82**, **92**, **95**, **96**; and some wild birds such as storks, **2**, **41**, **50**, **71**; pheasants, **59** and **82**; birds with prominent crests that may be cranes, **67**, **104**; and others whose identity is uncertain but are clearly not raptors, e.g., **14**, **38**, **65**, **66**, **82** (multiple examples), and **89**. None of these appears in the art of the Neo-Hittites, and so it seems likely that these were all drawn from life examples.

The interest in depicting a variety of bird life is not limited to the stone drawings from Megaron 2, but occurs widely in contemporary or nearly contemporary objects found at Gordion in a variety of media. Depictions of birds of prey shown in profile occur on the painted pottery from the Destruction Level; note a Destruction Level vase with a row of metope panels containing a simple sketch of a bird with a long neck, similar to the drawings of a bird on **50**, **71**, and **96**.[105] A molded pottery bird with a curved head and long neck was attached to a sipping chalice from the Destruction Level; this is reminiscent of similar birds depicted in **50** and **67**.[106] A large painted krater of Brown-on-Buff related ware, found in the rebuilt Middle Phrygian Citadel, is decorated with a scene of two fighting hawks shown in the raptor-at-rest profile view found on the Megaron 2 drawings.[107] Two wooden figurines depicting birds of prey, both with a pronounced curved beak and herringbone feather pattern, were found in Tumulus P.[108] Two additional objects from Tumulus P depict a broad-billed bird, either a duck or a goose, that is reminiscent of the broad-billed bird in **94**; one of these, cast in bronze, formed an ornament on a bronze chalice handle and the other is a mold-made pottery vessel.[109]

Why were birds such a common subject in these drawings? Certainly the region around Gordion has a rich variety of bird life today, especially along the river, and one presumes that this was even more true in the early 1st millennium BCE. Scenes of the natural activities of wild birds, for example of birds fishing, with fish still hanging from their mouths, were depicted in other examples of Gordion art.[110] One would assume that the many examples among the Gordion drawings of birds in flight, with wingspans drawn as if seen from the ground, also represent a contemporary interest in observing and depicting avian wildlife.

Yet it is well known that depictions of birds, particularly birds of prey, had an important symbolic value to the Phrygians. The bird of prey was a well-established symbol of strength and power in the hunt and appears with several divinities in Hittite cult objects from the 2nd millennium BCE.[111] In the 1st millennium BCE, the bird of prey was a key symbol of the Phrygian Mother goddess, Matar, and appears regularly in depictions of her from Gordion and other sites in central Anatolia.[112] Figurines of birds of prey, in stone, bronze, and wood, have been found throughout the Early and Middle Phrygian levels at Gordion,[113] and it is widely assumed that many of these were votive offerings to the goddess Matar. Because of this it has often been assumed that the frequency and level of detail in the depictions of birds in the Megaron 2 stone drawings result from interest in the Matar cult and reflect the prominence of this cult in Gordion.[114]

This interpretation, however, has a number of drawbacks. One key problem is that all of the images of the goddess Matar with a bird are later, often considerably later than the 9th century BCE date of the incised stones. The status of Matar in the Phrygian pantheon in the late 9th century BCE is far from

---

105. Sams 1994a: no. 933, fig. 43.
106. Sams 1994a: no. 859, pl. 104.
107. Sams 1994a: no. 1067, fig. 46.
108. Young 1981: TumP 148 and 149, figs. 31 and 32, Pl. 28a, b.
109. Young 1981, the bronze ladle, TumP 9, Pl. 8i; the vase, TumP 50, pl. 16a, b.

110. See above, n. 99.
111. Mellink 1983:351–52.
112. Mellink 1962; Mellink 1983:351–54; Roller 1999b:109.
113. In addition to examples cited by Mellink 1962 and 1983, note an inscribed alabaster hawk from Gordion, Young 1969b, no. 63; Brixhe and Lejeune 1984:124–25, no. G-136. There are also many unpublished examples.
114. Young 1969a:275; Mellink 1983:357–59; Simpson 1998:638–39. The prominence of the cult of Matar in Gordion, and in Phrygia in general, is well established from the large number of monuments dedicated to the goddess and from the fact that she is the only deity depicted in anthropomorphic form. See Roller 1999b:71–115.

certain. There are no representations of Matar from the Destruction Level or earlier levels, nor is there unequivocal evidence of sacred spaces or objects dedicated to her, so we cannot be certain what attributes were associated with the goddess during the Early Phrygian period. As noted above, the incised stones contain a number of complex scenes depicting human beings, and at least some of these appear to be patterned after a Neo-Hittite model depicting a deity. But in every case the figure in the Gordion drawing, whether deity or human, is male; no female figures are present.[115] This is all the more noteworthy when we consider that many representations of Matar in Phrygian cult reliefs show a close stylistic affinity with the Neo-Hittite images of the goddess Kubaba, who was especially prominent at Carchemish.[116] Since other Megaron 2 depictions of human figures were patterned after Neo-Hittite models, one might expect a comparable interest in depicting Matar, if her cult were a prominent feature of Phrygian religious practice in the 9th century BCE.[117] Overall, the lack of evidence for Matar's prominent status in the Phrygian pantheon during the Early Phrygian period seriously undercuts the assumption that all representations of birds of prey found in the incised stone drawings must be symbolic of her cult.

We should note that there is very little evidence for cult practices of any type in the Early Phrygian Citadel; thus the absence of evidence for the Matar cult need not be a conclusive argument. It is possible that at this date the Phrygian goddess was part of the Gordion pantheon, yet was not represented in anthropomorphic form, a circumstance that has been postulated for other Phrygian deities.[118] Thus the raptor could symbolize the deity without an image of the deity being present. In support of this hypothesis, we should note that a few of the raptors in the Megaron 2 drawings, **20** and possibly also **5**, are shown with a collar, implying some form of special status. This could refer to a symbolic connection with a deity, something that was almost surely the case for several small figurines of collared raptors from the Middle Phrygian period, including one with a dedicatory inscription.[119] However, in the majority of the raptor drawings the bird lacks a collar or other special markings that might suggest connection with a deity. Moreover, if we assume that all the raptors depicted on the stone drawings were sacred symbols, then we would have to consider a potentially symbolic implication for the frequent appearance of other types of birds, e.g., storks, ducks, geese, cranes, and others, and this seems very unlikely.

If most of the birds of prey found on the incised stones are not cult symbols, then why are they so common? One possible answer may lie in two examples in which the bird of prey appears not as an isolated figure but as part of a more complex scene. One is **46**, which depicts a male figure with outstretched arms and two birds in flight; as discussed in Section 2, this may represent a scene of falconry, in which the man holds a lure to attract a bird to land on his outstretched arm. Falconry may also be the subject of **19**, a drawing that illustrates a pair of sitting hawks on an object, perhaps an outstretched arm, and **21**, a drawing illustrating a bird of prey in a cloak or what may be a falcon's hood.[120] Falconry is attested as a notable interest among the elite in Syro-Hittite cities,[121] and

---

115. Note especially **44**, **88**, and **101**. One possible exception to this may be a sculpted relief of a figure in a long gown seated on an elaborate throne, found in the pre-Destruction Level; Sams 1989: pl. 130, 3. The relief clearly depicts an imposing figure of authority, although not enough of the piece survives to determine whether the figure is male or female, human or divine.
116. Mellink 1983:354–55; Roller 1999b:47–48.
117. It is true that the logogram for Kubaba in Neo-Hittite inscriptions was a bird of prey, shown in profile view with prominent curved beak and talons, similar to several of the Gordion drawings of raptors, but it is by no means clear how closely the Neo-Hittite Kubaba was related to Phrygian Matar, since the cults of the two goddesses show significant differences; see Roller 1994; Roller 1999b:48–53.
118. Berndt-Ersöz 2004 postulates a similar set of circumstances concerning a male deity, namely that a dominant Phrygian male deity, which Berndt-Ersöz calls the Phrygian Male Superior god, was represented as a schematic idol or as a bull, but not in anthropomorphic form; see also Berndt-Ersöz 2006:158–72. Mellink 1983:358–59, proposes that anthropomorphic images of Matar first appeared at the end of the 8th century BCE; see also Roller 1999b:83, and Berndt-Ersöz 2006:209–10.
119. Note an inscribed alabaster figurine of a bird with a collar, Young 1969b:287–88, pl. 72, no. 63; Brixhe and Lejeune 1984:124–25, no. G-136. On Phrygian images of raptors with collars, see Mellink 1962.
120. Roller, forthcoming. Young 1969a:275 also suggested that 19 represents a scene of falconry.
121. Note the presence of falcons on funerary reliefs from Maraş cited above, n. 104, Bonatz 2000b, especially C65.

it seems quite reasonable to assume that falconry was popular with the Phrygian elite also. This may help account for the frequency of birds of prey among the Megaron 2 stone drawings.

This suggestion does not preclude the possibility that the drawings reflect contemporary interest in the raptor for its symbolic value. Birds of prey have long been associated with swiftness, keen eyesight, and excellent hunting abilities, and depictions of them often express the wish to transfer these qualities to the elite of a society and to a divinity. Apart from the rare presence of a collared raptor and the potential scenes of falconry, however, the Megaron 2 drawings do not contain any direct allusion to such symbolic meaning. They only permit us to conclude that the bird of prey was a popular subject for representation, a circumstance that may result from several factors: the frequency of raptors in the environment around Gordion, the actual use of the bird in falconry, and the symbolic value of a raptor as a divine attribute and/or an elite status symbol.

In sum, the scenes of animals among the Megaron 2 drawings present an intriguing mixture of highly stylized representations taken from the artistic tradition of southeastern Anatolia and northern Syria and more naturalistic figures that appear to have been drawn from the observation of actual animals, both wild and domestic. The lion and to a lesser extent the stag seem to have been chosen for their symbolic value, particularly the lion for its strength and ferocity. The Megaron 2 lions appear to have been sketches, some highly detailed and complete, others more schematic and tentative, that were patterned after the standard representation of a lion in Neo-Hittite art. We may even wonder if these lions were imitating a program of sculptural lions that adorned a gateway or an important building in Gordion, or, alternatively, served as practice pieces for sculptural relief. This seems particularly plausible in the case of **98**, where the lion is shown in low relief (this issue is discussed more fully in Section 4). Several fragments from a program of sculpted orthostates, including a lion, survive from the pre-Destruction Level Citadel at Gordion[122]; moreover, the two stone lions in the fill above Megaron 2 (here Figs. 17, 18) further demonstrate that such sculptural depictions were indeed used in the Early Phrygian Citadel. The many representations of birds, in contrast, present more complex interpretive possibilities, with some examples, particularly those of raptors, having symbolic value, while others reflecting observation of contemporary avian life and the activities connected with this. The depictions of other animals, the goats, horses, and others, all seem to represent attempts to depict these animals based on actual observation of the animal. The composite animal, a fabulous creature comprised of a combination of two or more animals, such as a sphinx, a griffin, or a winged bull, does not occur among the incised Gordion drawings. This may suggest that the drawings of animals, like those of human figures, were not intended to suggest a wider narrative function.[123]

Architecture

While only a few of the stones contain depictions of architectural structures, these depictions offer valuable information on the architecture of the Early Phrygian levels at Gordion. The illustrations of the short end of a rectangular gabled building traditionally called a Phrygian megaron (three examples on **9** and one on **46**) were surely taken from observation of actual structures at Gordion, since these architectural features are verified by the plans of the megara found in the Destruction Level Citadel. Therefore we should assume that **38**, a drawing that is likely to represent a city wall or gateway, also illustrates a structure in Early Phrygian Gordion.

---

122. The pre-Destruction Level orthostates are discussed by Sams 1989; the lion is no. 1, pl. 129, 1–2. For the chronology and the relationship of this material to pre-Destruction architectural levels, see also Voigt 2005:29. As Sams 1989:449–50 notes, these Early Phrygian orthostates show clear signs of Neo-Hittite influence.

123. Fabulous creatures, both human-animal figures and composite animals, while frequent in the art of western Asia, are not common in Early Phrygian Gordion, although a few examples are known. These include a griffin on one of the orthostate reliefs from the pre-Destruction Level city, Sams 1989: fig. 130, 1; a griffin on an ivory plaque from Destruction Level finds in Megaron 3, Young 1960: pl. 25b; sphinxes on a series of ivory horse trappings from the Terrace Buildings, Young 1962:166–67, figs. 24–25; and examples from Early Phrygian tumuli, a sphinx in a panel on a painted jug from Tumulus P, TumP 56, Young 1981: pl. 17d–e, see also Sams 1974:176; a wooden figurine of a griffin from Tumulus P, TumP 111, Young 1981:52, pls. 23h, 24a–b; and four siren attachments on each of two bronze cauldrons from Tumulus MM, MM 2, and MM 3, Young 1981: pls. 51–57.

Let us look first at the megaron elevations. Their identity and function have been much discussed, often without careful attention paid to the actual appearance of the drawings. I will focus on the three megaron drawings on **9**, since the drawing on **46** is so simple that it adds little detail. As discussed in Section 2, the three buildings illustrated on **9** are different enough that we should assume that they represent three separate structures. Clearly all three illustrate a megaron elevation, but this offers little help in determining the buildings' functions, since in the Gordion Destruction Level the megaron type was used for various purposes, ranging from the Terrace Buildings, sites for food preparation and textile production, to Megaron 3, probably a residence for the elite. It seems likely, though, that at least two of the buildings illustrated, **9a-right** and **9b**, depict important buildings of high status. These both have a decoration conspicuously placed on the building's front surface, a rosette or similar ornament on **9a-right**, and a lion and geometric pattern on **9b**; **9b** also has an akroterion on the roof. Drawing **9b** may well illustrate a residence or audience hall of a ruler, since the combination of roof ornament and lion, a common symbol of power, on the front wall, communicates an imposing sense of substance and authority. Drawing **9a-right** could also be an audience hall or reception room; this suggestion is based on the presence of the roof ornament, the wall ornament above the door, and the wide double doors that could swing open to provide a clear view of the interior.

The identity of **9a-left** is less certain. It too has a curved ornament on the roof but no door in the wall. The lack of any distinctive decoration suggests that this is not a special or unusual building, and the presence of a window in the wall further suggests that we are looking at the back of the structure; if this were a view of the front wall of a building, we would expect a front door, since a building with no door in the front entrance makes little sense. Assuming this is the back view, the curved pattern above the roof ridgepole would represent timber rafters that extended above the gable. The windows in the pediment are likely to represent actual windows present in the original building that were needed to provide light, air ventilation, and smoke escape. Such windows are essential features in a building that has an interior hearth but no chimney, exactly the interior arrangement of almost all of the megara in the Gordion Destruction Level. The representation of such practical details reinforces the assumption that the drawings are depicting features found in Early Phrygian architecture in Gordion, although they do not enable us to determine the function of **9a-left**.

The three megaron elevations on **9** have excited much attention because of their resemblance to the architectural structures that appear in several cult reliefs in the Phrygian Highlands. From this it has been deduced that the Gordion drawings must depict a cult structure such as a temple.[124] Several arguments have been advanced to support this interpretation. Chief among them are the similarities between the structures depicted in these drawings and those represented in several of the Highland reliefs. Both sets of depictions reproduce the short end of a building with a gabled roof and a door in the center of the wall. The central doorway in **9a-right** recalls the door depicted in reliefs such as the principal Midas City relief and the Arslankaya monument,[125] while the rectangle in the center of the wall in the building on **9a-left** resembles a cult niche, found in several carved façades of the Phrygian Highlands. The windows in the pediment of **9a-left** are also found in several Highland cult façades, as is the akroterion on **9b**. Finally, the juxtaposition of the building in **9a-left** with the bird of prey invites the suggestion that this depicts a temple of the Phrygian goddess Matar, since a bird of prey was a frequent attribute of the goddess.

None of these arguments is fully compelling. The general similarity between the building type in the Megaron 2 drawings and that found in Phrygian cult reliefs stems from the fact that both illustrate the short end of a megaron. The megaron type, however, was used for so many buildings with different functions in the Gordion Destruction Level that we cannot simply assume that a megaron elevation signifies cult function. Another problematic issue is the window in **9a-left**, which some have considered a niche, on analogy with the cult niches in the rock

---

124. Mellink 1983:357; Sams 1997:241; also implied by Berndt-Ersöz 2006:201.

125. The Highland reliefs that reproduce architectural forms are discussed in detail by Haspels 1971:73–93; Roller 1999b:84–96; Berndt-Ersöz 2006:21–40. Midas City, Haspels 1971:73–76, figs. 8–13, Berndt-Ersöz 2006:232–34. The Arslankaya relief, Haspels 1971:87–88, figs. 186–91, Berndt-Ersöz 2006:222–24.

monuments of Phrygia.[126] This too is unconvincing: the drawing presumably was intended to represent an actual building, and as discussed above, a real three-dimensional building would be unlikely to have a niche but no door in its front wall.[127] The connection of the windows depicted in the pediment of **9a**-left with Phrygian cult function is also tenuous.[128] The purpose of the window is to be sought in its practical use to facilitate air ventilation and smoke escape, not in cult function.

The curved ornament on the roof of the Megaron 2 architectural drawings is another point of contact with the akroteria depicted on many of the Highland cult façades.[129] On the Megaron 2 drawings, the curved ornament could represent sloping rafters extending beyond the roof gable, or it could represent a separate stone akroterion, a decorative feature of which several examples are known from Early Phrygian Gordion.[130] Yet the akroterion by itself need not be a symbol of cult practice. Whether made of timber or stone, the curved akroterion was a decorative feature intended to make a building appear more conspicuous, and therefore more noteworthy. Its presence in these drawings indicates that the buildings illustrated fulfilled some special function in the community, but it does not tell us what that function was.

A major factor that has been thought to connect the drawings on **9** to Phrygian cult practice is the presence of the bird of prey overlapping the building in **9a**-left. As noted above, a bird of prey was a common attribute of the Phrygian Mother goddess, Matar, and appears in conjunction with images of the goddess from several Phrygian sites, including Gordion.[131] It remains very uncertain, however, whether the raptor in this drawing was intended as a direct reference to Matar, or indeed to any deity. Many of the interpretive problems discussed above in connection with the drawings of raptors are relevant here too: the lack of evidence for the Matar cult in the Early Phrygian settlement, the uncertain meaning of the raptor in the corpus of Gordion drawings, and the lack of any clear connection between the raptor drawings and cult practice. Moreover, as discussed in Section 2, a great many of the Megaron 2 drawings show one figure incised on top of another, often superimposing two drawings with unrelated subject matter. Because of this, the conjunction of the bird with the building elevation need not imply a relationship between the two. If the presence of the bird over the building is intentional, it could be intended as a sign of status, recalling the prestige associated with a bird of prey and with falconry; in this case the bird tells us that the building depicted on **9a**-left, like the other two megaron elevations, was a building associated with the elite of the community.

In sum, we can say that the drawings of the megaron architectural type illustrate examples of actual Gordion architecture, and that they depict three different structures in the Early Phrygian Citadel. The presence of the roof ornaments, the imposing double door in **9a**-right, and the decoration on the walls of **9a**-right and **9b** strongly suggest that at least two of the buildings were structures of high status in the community. However, the drawings do not supply enough information to determine with certainty what the function (or functions) of the buildings depicted on them was.

Drawing **38** is also likely to represent an actual structure, although one of a completely different character. The parallel horizontal lines at the top and bottom of the structure and the diagonal lines that run at an angle from the upper corners suggest bracing for a wooden construction. This could be a fortification wall topped by a tower, or it could represent the double leaves of a gate, although in that case the tower would seem awkwardly placed in the middle. It is possible that the drawing compresses two angles of view into one drawing, and thus could depict a gate with a tower

---

126. Mellink 1983:357, interpreted the square in the middle of the "building" wall in drawing **9a** as a niche. Berndt-Ersöz 2006:28, states that it could be either a window or a niche. On cult niches in architectural façades from the Phrygian Highlands, see Berndt-Ersöz 2006:21–29. As Berndt-Ersöz notes, only four of the Highland façades have a niche that is not at ground level, and in one of these, the Areyastin Monument, the niche is clearly a substitute for a larger, unfinished panel, Berndt-Ersöz 2006:29.

127. This point is discussed in greater detail in Roller, forthcoming.

128. A relief imitating a window with closed shutters is found on three of the carved façades in the Phrygian Highlands, the Areyastis Monument and the Unfinished and Hyacinth Monuments at Midas City; Berndt-Ersöz 2006:33.

129. Berndt-Ersöz 2006:29–30.

130. Sams 1994b:212–13.

131. Examples include four cult reliefs from Gordion: Mellink 1983: pl. 72, figs. 1–3, pl. 73, fig. 2, Roller 1999b: figs. 7 and 12; a cult relief from Ankara, Roller 1999b: fig. 8; and a statue found near Ayaş, Naumann 1983:67, no. 21.

in the walls next to it. The horizontal lines below could represent a set of steps leading up to a gate, or alternatively, a series of stone courses on which a wooden gate or wall was built. No such structure has been found in the Early Phrygian Destruction Level, but a gate or wall made of wood could easily have perished in the fire that destroyed this level of the settlement.

Geometric Designs

The Early Phrygian drawings furnish numerous examples of geometric shapes and symbols. The frequency and ubiquity of geometric patterns found in the drawings offer a further example of a feature well attested in the Phrygian visual repertory. The Phrygians' affinity for this type of artistic vocabulary is readily apparent in the complex decorative language found on a variety of other media from the Early Phrygian Destruction Level or from tumuli close in time to the Destruction Level; these include wooden furniture, painted decoration on pottery, and the pebble mosaic on the floor of Megaron 2 itself.[132] Such patterns, built around basic shapes as circles, squares, diamonds, Xs, and the like, are often combined in intriguing and aesthetically satisfying ways. One presumes that these same patterns were also used in, perhaps even developed for, the textiles that formed a significant part of the economy at Gordion.[133]

Patterns built on a circle appear regularly. The vertical row of compass-drawn circles found on **82**, for example, was a device also used as a decorative element on painted pottery.[134] The compass-drawn rosette with six internal petals (note **10, 70, 72, 75, 82, 85**) appears to be a simplified version of the rosette that was used as a decoration on several examples of wooden objects, including the small rosettes on the inlaid serving stands from Tumulus MM and on wooden objects from Tumulus P.[135] A similar six-petal rosette forms the central element in the pebble mosaic from Megaron 2 (Fig. 8), and also appears on several examples of painted pottery from the Destruction Level.[136] Some of the rosettes on the Megaron 2 stones, e.g., **10, 75, 82**, are incomplete; these could be the result of careless drawing, or alternatively, practice designs for an artist testing his tools.

Several other geometric designs that occur in the drawings find parallels in other media. Concentric squares, found in **12**, appear on painted pottery and on furniture from Tumulus P, as wooden inlay on a table top and on the upper part of the serving stand.[137] A variety of designs built on the concentric square pattern, in differing color combinations and degrees of complexity, can also be seen on the Megaron 2 pebble mosaic.[138] Another pattern, the hook meander on **23**, appears on both pottery and on wooden furniture from Tumulus P and Tumulus MM.[139] Drawings **10, 20, 30, 57**, and **82** furnish examples of a row of Xs framed by two vertical lines or an X set in a square. An X framed within a panel occurs at Gordion on both stamped and painted pottery, on wooden objects, and among the patterns used in the Megaron 2 pebble

---

132. For geometric patterns in Phrygian furniture, see Simpson 1988, Simpson and Spirydowicz 1999; for geometric designs on painted pottery, Sams 1994a:134–73. On the pebble mosaic floor of Megaron 2, see Young 1965b:10–11; Salzmann 1982: no. 48, pls. 2–3.

133. On Phrygian textiles in personal dress, see Boehmer 1973. Some actual examples of textiles were found in Tumulus MM, Young 1981:294–310, and in Megaron 3 and Terrace Building 4. The Terrace Building complex at Gordion has yielded abundant evidence, including loom weights, footprints for looms, and spindle whorls, well analyzed by Burke 2005, to demonstrate that textile production was an important part of the Gordion economy. The pebble mosaic floor of Megaron 2 suggests what these textiles might have looked like, since the mosaic creates an effect very much like that of patterned rugs scattered on a floor.

134. Sams 1994a, vertical rows of concentric circles, fig. 19 no. 500, fig. 36 no. 882, fig. 42 no. 931; concentric half-circles framed vertically in a panel, fig. 36 no. 882, cf. fig. 65, semicircle panels 1.

135. Young 1981: fig. MM 378, 379, fig. 104. Two small rosettes with six petals are found below the main central rosette. Note also the rosette on a wooden box and a wooden disk from Tumulus P, Young 1981: TumP 139, fig. 29 (box), TumP 138, fig. 28 (disk).

136. Rosette on the pebble mosaic, Salzmann 1982: pl. 2, fig. 2. For examples on painted pottery, see Sams 1994a: fig. 45, fig. 46, nos. 1067, 1069.

137. Concentric squares on painted pottery, see Sams 1994a, examples on the chart on fig. 64, latticed panels 2 and 3. Concentric squares from Tumulus P, note the inlaid table: Young 1981: TumP 154, fig. 39E, Simpson and Spyrodowicz 1999: fig. 74; and the inlaid serving stand: Young 1981: TumP 151, fig. 33, Simpson and Spyrodowicz 1999: fig. 63; and an inlaid strip from an unknown piece of furniture, Young 1981: TumP 163, fig. 47.

138. Salzmann 1982: pl. 2, fig. 2; pl. 5, fig. 4 (detail).

139. The hook meander on pottery, cf. Sams 1994a: fig. 63, 3A and B. The hook meander on furniture, note the serving stand and footstool from Tumulus P, TumP 151, 157 Young 1981: figs. 33, 42; and both serving stands and the inlaid table from Tumulus MM, Young 1981: MM 378, 379, 388.

mosaic.¹⁴⁰ Diamond patterns and lozenges, i.e., a vertical or horizontal row of diamonds, occur on incised stones **37**, **43**, **49**, and **67**, and the same patterns are found frequently on stamped and painted pottery and in designs on wooden objects.¹⁴¹ The pebble mosaic in Megaron 2 furnishes further examples of lozenges, with both plain and concentric diamond patterns.¹⁴² A single lozenge with internal cross-hatching can be found in **15**, and **103** reproduces a lozenge with an internal X; further examples include a pattern of diamonds formed by cross-hatching on **10**, **22**, and **82**. This motif too appears in painted pottery.¹⁴³ The motif of a row of triangles, found in **43**, can also be paralleled in pottery decoration.¹⁴⁴

Another potential meaning present in the geometric patterns is that of personal identification, a form of non-verbal signature. Some of the geometric patterns in the drawings are virtually identical to the nonverbal marks incised onto Gordion pottery after firing, where they appear to have been intended as a form of owner's mark. Examples of patterns found in the drawings that were used as owner's marks on pottery from the Early Phrygian period are as follows: the branch on **28**, **39**; a five-pointed star on **1**, **11**, **31**, **60**; an asterisk on **32**; latticing on **22**, **40**, **42**, **59**, **61**; a row of Xs between two parallel lines on **10**, **20**, **82**; and the compass-drawn circle on **34**, **42**, **82**.¹⁴⁵ The pottery of the Middle Phrygian period, the 8th through 6th centuries BCE, furnishes even more parallels. The branch, five-pointed star, asterisk, latticing, an X framed within a square or by parallel lines, and a row of lozenges, all designs found in the Early Phrygian stone drawings, continue to occur regularly among pottery marks, and another pattern, a wheel pattern found on **94**, also appears.¹⁴⁶

It might be argued that it is merely coincidental that the patterns and symbols found in the Megaron 2 stone drawings also occur in pottery marks. Certainly some of them, such as the asterisk, latticing, and five-pointed star, are very basic symbols that can occur independently in a variety of contexts and cultures; their presence in the stone drawings could be merely coincidence, without any intent to reproduce a specific pattern. As noted in Section 2, there are many irregular lines and scratches on the stones that are likely to be random marks without any deeper significance. Some of the geometric symbols could also be the result of random drawings without meaning.

The frequent occurrence of these symbols in a variety of contexts suggests strongly, however, that some of them did carry a meaning to the person who placed it on the stone, either of personal identity or some more abstract value. The branch, for example, was a symbol regularly used as both a graffito and a stamp on pottery vessels from the Hittite Empire period in Boğazköy.¹⁴⁷ It also occurs in a variety of contexts in the first half of the 1st millennium BCE in Anatolia, on stamp seals and as a mason's mark, and it was used as a letter in a Phrygian alphabetic graffito from

---

140. X in panel on stamped pottery, Sams 1994a:1003–4; on painted pottery, Sams 1994a: no. 882, fig. 36, pl. 110, and no. 930, pl. 108. The pattern is found on a wooden saucer with bar handles from Tumulus P, Young 1981: TumP 121, fig. 25, and forms the motif used on the border and in some of the internal inlay of the wooden serving stand, TumP 151, fig. 33. For the pebble mosaic, cf. Salzmann 1982: pl. 2, figs. 2 and 4.

141. For lozenges on stamped pottery, see Sams 1994a: fig. 60, 992 and 1000; on painted pottery, Sams 1994a: fig. 63 bottom. Lozenges are a frequently used design on wooden furniture; they are found on both serving stands from Tumulus MM as a background design for the main panels and in the circles around the central rosettes, Young 1981: MM 378, 379, figs. 104, 107, and in several of the decorative panels that formed part of the inlaid table, MM 388, figs. 110, 111. Lozenge panels are also found on the Tumulus P furniture, Young 1981: TumP 151, fig. 33, serving stand; TumP 157, fig. 42, on the border of the footstool; and TumP 164, fig. 48, inlaid strip from an unknown piece of furniture.

142. Salzmann 1982: pl. 2, 2; pl. 4, 2; pl. 5, 2; this volume, Figure 8.

143. Sams 1994a: fig. 63 bottom.

144. Sams 1994a: fig. 62.

145. The non-verbal owner's marks have been treated extensively by Roller 1987; for specific parallels, see the following: the branch, 2A-7, a black polished vessel from Tumulus MM; five-pointed star, 2A-1, 2A-9, 2A-27; asterisk, 2A-4, 2A-5, 2A-6; latticing, 2A-9, 2A-12, 2A-13, 2A-17 through 25; XX between parallel lines, 2A-10; compass-drawn circle, 2A-15, all from the Destruction Level City. These last two designs were also treated above under the discussion of patterns potentially taken from furniture or textiles. The branch also occurs as a stamped pottery design, Sams 1994a: fig. 61, 1003.

146. Roller 1987: nos. 2A-38, 2A-45, 2A-53, 2A-55, 2A-65, 2A-91, 2A-121, the branch; nos. 2A-28, 2A-31, 2A-51, 2A-56, 2A-64, 2A-70, 2A-97, the five-pointed star; nos. 2A-29, 2A-30, 2A-80, asterisk; nos. 2A-36, 2-66, 2A-74, 2A-79, 2A-148, 2A-150, latticing; nos. 2A-58, 2A-68, X in square; nos. 2A-86, 2A-93, X's between parallel lines; 2A-96, 2A-106, row of lozenges; no. 2A-54, the wheel.

147. Seidl 1972: nos. A 121-217, B 24-27. See the discussion in Roller 1987:10–11.

Boğazköy and more regularly as an alphabetic letter in the script systems of Lycia and Lydia.[148] The repeated use of the same sign in different contexts and over a long period of time suggests that the branch was not just a decorative element, but conveyed some meaning to the people of central Anatolia. Similarly the X within a square and the wheel pattern, both attested on the Megaron 2 stones, also occur in other contexts in 1st millennium BCE Anatolia; the X in a square is found both as a countermark on coins and as a mason's mark, and the wheel was also a coin countermark.[149]

Taken together, the presence of such recognizable Anatolian symbols on the Megaron 2 drawings suggests that some of the geometric symbols were intentionally incised, perhaps as a form of personal identification mark. Clearly there is no systematic method of marking the stones, such as would be used for masons' marks; rather, the use of known patterns and symbols suggests that the individuals who incised the surface of the Megaron 2 stones felt free to leave some personal record of their presence.

The use of patterns that served as marks of personal identification raises a further question, namely the relationship of these patterns to a system of writing. One pattern with relevance to this question, found at the far right of drawing **54**, is a form that resembles a pitchfork, here with seven prongs. The form appears to be a more elaborate version of a similar symbol with three prongs that was later used both as a non-alphabetic pottery mark and as a letter in an alphabetic pottery graffito.[150] This symbol straddles the boundary between alphabetic and non-alphabetic marks, since it is also found in coin countermarks and as a mason's mark from other regions of 1st millennium BCE Anatolia.[151]

Another potential source of influence on the symbols in the Megaron 2 drawings could be symbols used by the Luwian hieroglyphic script system. While no sustained text in the Luwian language is known from this region, there are a handful of characters in the Megaron 2 drawings that are similar to logograms in the Luwian script system, suggesting that the individuals who incised them were familiar with the Luwian writing system. As potential Luwian logograms[152] that appear on the Megaron 2 drawings, we can note GAZELLA, similar to the head of a horned gazelle on **75**; the Gordion drawing clearly illustrates a head only, not the whole animal. Other potential logograms include FLUMEN, two sets of parallel wavy lines that occur on drawings **32** and **64**. On these stones the lines seem carefully and intentionally drawn and are unlikely to be random scratches, yet do not resemble an animal or other object. Another candidate is found on **93**, where two sets of parallel zigzag lines resemble the logogram FULGUR.

The Luwian hieroglyphic logogram AVIS,[153] the raptor, should be mentioned in this context, given the large number of birds of prey depicted on the Megaron 2 stones. The Luwian logogram depicts a bird of prey in profile, with the sharp beak and curved talons clearly visible; in two alternative logograms the bird's wings are outstretched. All three of the Luwian AVIS forms occur regularly among raptors depicted on the Gordion stones. The Luwian symbol was used as a determinative for the name of the goddess Kubaba, an important female deity in the Luwian pantheon. The raptor was a cult symbol of the Phrygians also, not as a part of a name but as the regular attribute of the Phrygian goddess Matar at Gordion. As I discussed above, it is unlikely that every occurrence of a raptor on the Gordion stones signifies a religious image. However, it is noteworthy that there are multiple representations of the raptor in the Early Phrygian drawings, and that several of these have outstretched wings similar to the Luwian logograms $AVIS_2$ and $AVIS_3$. As we have seen, the raptors depicted in the Megaron 2 drawings could be associated with hunting and falconry, and therefore could have served as a symbol in which the associations of both kingship and cult practice were interwoven. The use of the same symbol in the Luwi-

---

148. For the occurrence of the branch on stamp seals and as a mason's mark, see Roller 1987:102–3, Chart B. For its occurrence in an alphabetic text from Boğazköy, Neumann 1975:76–84, no. 3; in alphabetic script systems of other Anatolian languages, see Roller 1987:101, Chart A, Lycia and Lydia.

149. Roller 1987:12–14 and 102–3, Chart B.

150. The sign as a pottery mark, Roller 1987: nos. 2A-33, 2A-39, 2A-99; the sign as a letter of the Phrygian alphabet, Brixhe and Lejeune 1984: G-112; Roller 1987:34–35, note especially no. 2B-2, a 6th century sherd.

151. Roller 1987:12–14 and 102–3, Chart B.

---

152. The logograms cited follow the system of Hawkins 2000, I:26–27, tables 2 and 3.

153. Hawkins 2000, I:26–27, tables 2 and 3, Avis (128); Avis2 (132); Avis3 (130).

an hieroglyphic script to denote a powerful deity who was a protector of cities and a supporter of the rulers of Carchemish could well have reinforced these associations among the Phrygians.

The presence of these Luwian logograms (if this interpretation is correct) should not be construed to mean that the Phrygian inhabitants of Gordion in the 9th century BCE were literate. Indeed, the absence of written texts in any script system from this level of the settlement strongly suggests the opposite.[154] It does suggest, however, that the inhabitants of the site were aware of the existence of the writing system in neighboring states to the southeast and of its potential to communicate information. As is well known, when the Phrygians did adopt a script, they used a modified form of the Greek alphabet, first attested in the graffiti on objects from Tumulus MM, from the second half of the 8th century.[155] The allusions among the Megaron 2 stone drawings to the Luwian hieroglyphic script system, however, suggest that the Phrygians knew of the Luwian system of writing and chose not to adopt it, despite the presence of extensive influence from Neo-Hittite visual iconography on the Early Phrygian settlement.

Phrygian Cultural Symbols

A few symbols that appear in the Early Phrygian drawings may be forms that had special meaning to the Phrygian residents of Gordion. Here I am not considering personal marks of private individuals, but rather symbols that recorded aspects of Phrygian cultural identity. One such area of cultural identity is cult practice. Two types of illustrations are relevant here. Some objects depicted in the drawings appear to be illustrations of actual cult artifacts, while others are symbols that can have multiple meanings, of which cult imagery can be one. Among the former are objects found in three drawings, **10**, **51**, and **94**, that almost surely represent aniconic Phrygian idols. The aniconic idol was a stone sculpture in simple humanoid form that is a regular feature of Phrygian cult shrines, found throughout the extent of Phrygian influence in Anatolia.[156] Some were carved in relief onto rock surfaces, while others are free-standing figures, often positioned on top of step monuments. In some cases the idol consists of little more than a round disk set on top of an oblong block, while on others some anthropomorphic characteristics such as facial features and distinct shoulders are present.[157] Gordion drawing **94** illustrates the simplest type of idol, merely a round disk above an oblong block; this is also the type most frequently found in Phrygian cult monuments. Drawing **10** depicts a similar idol but with the addition of two eyes, while the idol on Gordion drawing **51** illustrates an idol with pronounced upturned shoulders; this drawing also depicts an oblong block that could represent either the body of the idol or the monument into which it was set.

The precise identity of these idols has been much debated, although it is generally agreed that they represent a deity. Some see them as an earlier or simpler form of Matar, the Phrygian Mother goddess, while others interpret the form as a representation of another deity (or deities) in the Phrygian pantheon.[158] The presence of idols in the Early Phrygian drawings at Gordion does not help resolve this debate, but does demonstrate that such idols were a feature of Phrygian cult practice during the Early Phrygian period. This is an important point, because to date no examples of

---

154. I will omit any discussion of an alphabetic text on a Phrygian bowl from Megaron 10, Brixhe and Lejeune 1984:98, G-104, since this vessel was found in a disturbed context and it is uncertain whether or not the vessel and graffito belong to the Destruction Level; see Brixhe 2002:26.

155. On alphabetic writing from Tumulus MM, see Brixhe in Young 1981:273–77. Several additional alphabetic graffiti, probably all proper names, are present on one of the large logs above the tomb chamber in Tumulus MM; these were first noted in 2007 and further studied in 2008. I owe this information to Richard Liebhart.

156. Naumann 1983:92–100, pls. 9–11; Berndt-Ersöz 2006:56–58, 159–61. See also Summers 2006 for a recently discovered example in Kerkenes Dağ, east of the Halys River at the eastern limit of Phrygian cultural expansion.

157. For examples with facial features, four idols from Boğazköy, Naumann 1983: pl. 9a–d. For examples with shoulders, see Berndt-Ersöz 2006: figs. 65–67, 70–71, 81 (a single and a double idol), 82 (two idols), 87–90, all from the Phrygian Highlands. An example with clearly articulated head and shoulders was found in an 8th century BCE shrine at Boğazköy; here the idol was set on a stele, flanked by two upright and horizontal stelae decorated with reliefs of lions, bulls, and a human figure hunting on horseback; see Beran 1963; Naumann 1983: pl. 9e; Prayon 1987: fig. 26, pl. 35; Prayon 2004:620, fig. 4; Berndt-Ersöz 2006: fig. 113.

158. Naumann 1983:92–100, Roller 1999b:77–78, fig. 15, and Prayon 2004:613 connect the idol type with the Matar cult, while Berndt-Ersöz 2006:160–161 suggests that the idol could represent either a male or female deity.

these aniconic cult idols has been recovered from an Early Phrygian context. Several examples of similar idols are known from Gordion, but all were found in contexts from the Middle or Late Phrygian settlement.[159] Typical Phrygian cult features such as step monuments, niches, and platforms carved into live rock are, however, attested at Dümrek, a Phrygian sanctuary located on a high point overlooking the Sangarios River about 40 km northwest of Gordion.[160] Ceramic finds demonstrate that the Dümrek sanctuary was in use throughout the Early and Middle Phrygian periods, providing evidence for continuity of cult practice at the site from an early period. Given these circumstances, it would not be surprising if humanoid idols were also in use during the Early Phrygian period at Gordion.

Other subjects in the drawings may also convey symbolic value, although their meaning is less clearcut. One is the rosette. The six-petal rosette is easy to draw with a compass and forms an attractive visual ornament, so it is not surprising to find it recurring on the stone drawings as well as in other media. To the Phrygians, however, the rosette may well have communicated more than simply an esthetically pleasing pattern. As noted above, the rosette appears on wooden objects, the serving stands and a wooden box, found in the tumuli P and MM, tumuli that were surely the burials of the ruling elite. It also appears on large kraters decorated with painted designs, probably also used by the elite members of the community, and forms a central element in the mosaic of Megaron 2, which, as discussed in Section 1, is likely to have been an audience or reception hall for the Phrygian ruling elite. This suggests that the rosette could have been a floral symbol denoting royalty, much like the royalist French fleur-de-lis.

Another potential meaning for the rosette is suggested by its presence in the wooden serving stands from tumuli P and MM, where it forms the centerpiece of a complex iconography of curved legs with lion paws and maze patterns built around an interlocking cross design.[161] This placement of a central ornament surrounded by maze patterns parallels a similar arrangement of decorative patterns found on several cult façades of the Phrygian Highlands, including the main façade at Midas City and the Büyük Kapıkaya, Maltaş, and Arslankaya monuments, among others.[162] On the Highland façades, the position occupied by the rosette in the serving stands is taken by a cult niche, one that in two instances, the Büyük Kapıkaya and Arslankaya façades, contains an image of the goddess Matar. The presence of a similar decorative schema on both the Gordion serving stands and the Highland cult façades could mean that the rosette on the serving stands was a symbol of a deity, perhaps Matar.[163] Alternatively, the rosette on the serving stands could also be a symbol of royalty, intended to signify the close relationship between the Phrygian ruler and a deity.[164]

It seems overly deterministic, however, to assume that every rosette found in the Early Phrygian drawings conveyed a symbolic value. The rosettes on the stone drawings do not appear consistently with a set arrangement of patterns, but are found with a variety of different animals and other objects. Under these circumstances we cannot be certain whether the rosettes on the Megaron 2 drawings symbolized a deity, and it is even less certain that the deity was Matar, particularly since, as noted above, there is no definitive evidence for the status of the Matar cult in Early Phrygian Gordion. On the other hand, the rosette may well have been a popular symbol because it was an emblem of cult and/or elite identity for the Early Phrygians. One drawing that encourages this interpretation is **85**, where a rosette was incised over a drawing of a nursing lioness. As we have seen, the lion in Neo-Hittite art was a frequent means of alluding to strength and power; this animal, however, is always male. The presence here of a rosette together with the female lion, with emphasis on the maternal act of nursing, suggests that the drawing alluded to the combined images of

---

159. See the examples discussed above in Section 2, n. 50. Note also the 8th century BCE example from Boğazköy, supra n. 157.

160. Grave, Kealhofer, and Marsh 2005.

161. Young 1981: TumP 131, fig. 33; MM 378, MM 379, figs. 104, 107.

162. On these Phrygian cult monuments, see Berndt-Ersöz 2006:232, no. 30 (Midas City), 224, no. 27 (Büyük Kapıkaya), 227, no. 24 (Maltaş), and 222, no. 16 (Arslankaya). On the similarity of the geometric ornament found in the Highland façades to that of the Gordion wooden serving stands, see Haspels 1971:103; Simpson 1998:633–39.

163. Simpson 1998:633–39.

164. Note the suggestion of Roller 1988:49 that the cult façades in the Phrygian Highlands depicted a royal residence and symbolize the close relationship between ruler and deity.

power of a female deity united with that of a ruler, as symbolized by the rosette.[165]

Another intriguing allusion to cult practice is a pattern formed by a series of concentric circular lines extending out from a central vertical line. This is found on **60**, **94** (two examples), and **104**; **17** and **37** may depict partially preserved examples. Despite minor variations, the drawings on all five stones are similar enough to suggest that the persons who drew them had a common model in mind. The subject is enigmatic. It may represent a maze of some sort, since it is known that Phrygian artists incorporated maze patterns into the designs of the elaborate wooden furniture found in Phrygian burial tumuli.[166] The design may also depict a floral pattern, such as a palmette. For a parallel one can note a Phrygian stele of the 5th century BCE from Vezirhan, with inscriptions in the Greek and Phrygian languages; at the top of the stele is a head, almost certainly that of a deity, wearing a tall floral headdress.[167] The headdress is particularly similar to the drawing on **60**. It is possible that in these drawings we see another aniconic cult symbol, a floral ornament such as a palm tree or a tree of life design, one that could have symbolized a deity.

Summary

When we consider the range of source material found in the stone drawings, we see a diverse mix of themes taken from the Neo-Hittite visual repertory of southeastern Anatolia and Syria and subjects that seem to be specific to Gordion and Phrygia. The latter group is very broad: it includes marks that evidently represented little more than the whim of the inciser, such as random lines and circles, and more complex themes that were to play a larger role in later Phrygian art. Looking at the material as a whole, however, several general patterns can be noted. With only a few exceptions, the scenes that depict human figures imitate an iconographic tradition that was created outside Phrygia. The cultures of southeastern Anatolia and northwestern Syria had a long tradition of portraying the human figure in complex narrative scenes, and several of these can be recognized on the Gordion stones. On the other hand, the borrowings of the human figure scenes seem to have been rather selective. The depictions of human figures represent an eclectic assortment of themes that stress action, such as fighting or hunting, or a statement of authority and status, e.g., the imposing figure in a long robe. Some of the more complex scenes are drawn from Neo-Hittite models that contain a deeper programmatic meaning, such as a desire to advertise the power of divinities or the authority of a king. Within the Gordion drawings, however, the scenes with human figures appear randomly and in isolation, not as part of an extended iconographic program. It is possible that the scenes of human figures were imitating a formal program of relief in early Gordion that is lost to us. The orthostate reliefs with figured scenes from the pre-Destruction level indicate that relief sculptures depicting complex scenes were made for public display in the Early Phrygian Citadel,[168] and the Gordion drawings of human figures could have been sketches that reflect a similar type of relief program. Many of the drawings of human figures, however, lack specific details, such as divine attributes or indications of identity. This makes it uncertain whether the incised drawings imitate specific examples of relief sculpture or merely reflect general Phrygian familiarity with the Neo-Hittite style and corpus of subject matter.

The scenes of animals present a much more mixed picture. Animals form by far the largest category of subject matter, in both number and variety. Most scenes of animals cannot be construed as part of a narrative sequence, but are simply isolated representations of the animal in a few fixed poses. The most common animal subject, a bird, may be connected in part to the art of southeastern Anatolia; a bird of prey shown in profile and at rest formed a regular subject in Neo-Hittite tradition, both in the visual arts and as an ideogram in the Luwian hieroglyphic script. However, the variety of birds found on the Gordion drawings and the poses in which they are shown go well beyond what can be found in the Neo-Hittite visual tradition.

---

165. Simpson 1998:638–39, fig. 19. Simpson proposes that the rosette was an aniconic symbol of Matar, the Phrygian Mother goddess. I am less certain about a one-to-one correspondence between the rosette and a specific deity, but I agree with Simpson's suggestion that the drawing conveys symbolic meaning.
166. Simpson 1988, esp. pp. 28–29.
167. Anadolu Medeniyetleri II, 1983:60, no. B 146. The stele and inscriptions are discussed by Neumann 1997.

168. Sams 1989.

Moreover, there are some Gordion scenes that depict or allude to falconry and are likely to reflect the interests of contemporary residents at Gordion. These points suggest that many drawings of birds reflected actual observation of avian life.

Lions, the second most common class of animal, are shown in a more limited range of poses. The standard drawing of a lion is repeated so regularly and consistently that in this case the artists were surely drawing from an established template of how a lion should be depicted. That template was furnished by the representation of lions in Neo-Hittite art rather than by real life observation. Since lions appear quite frequently among the Early Phrygian drawings, this theme must have been important to the Phrygian artists. The close dependency on the Neo-Hittite prototype suggests that, like several scenes of human figures, at least some of the lion drawings were test sketches for a program of sculptural lions. The treatment of the lion in **98**, where the stone around part of the lion is cut away to create the beginning of relief sculpture, strongly supports this. Two more lion drawings, **8** and **25**, further reinforce this suggestion, since in these drawings the lions are shown with a prominently drilled pupil in the eye, a feature found on two stone lions from the fill above Megaron 2 that were probably originally placed on the megaron roof.[169] The artist(s) who made these two lion drawings on the Megaron 2 blocks could have been experimenting with the techniques of sculptural preparation for inlay that would have been used for sculpture in the round. Alternatively, the drawings could be imitations of lions that were depicted in relief sculpture or in other media at Gordion.

While we cannot be certain why there was such strong interest in the representation of birds and lions, some explanatory hypotheses are worth considering. In the Neo-Hittite visual tradition the popularity of the lion, or composite leonine figures, stems directly from the symbolic qualities associated with the lion, namely strength, ferocity, power—all qualities that the ruling elite wished to claim for itself. Did the lion have the same meaning to the Phrygians? The two stone lions found above Megaron 2 (Figs. 17, 18) would have certainly embellished the building and made it more conspicuous, potentially conveying the authority of a human ruler or the power of a divinity, or both. Similarly the strong interest in representing birds of prey conveys a complex message: contemporary interest in falconry and the prestige of hunting, the desire to transfer the positive qualities of the raptor, e.g., its speed, keen eyesight, and predatory nature, to the human elite, and a well-established association in Anatolia between the raptor and divinity.[170] In the case of both animals, there may have been multiple associations at work, drawing on both practical and ideological sources of inspiration.

Other animal types appear substantially less frequently and thus their meanings are harder to discern. One, the stag, was also a long-established symbol in Anatolian iconography, and the similarity of the Gordion examples to stags in Neo-Hittite reliefs suggest that this animal also was probably taken from a Neo-Hittite model, although here too its meaning to the Phrygians is uncertain. The others are most likely to record the observation of the actual animal.

Other subjects found in the drawings also record visual images from contemporary life at Gordion. The drawings of architecture were surely taken from actual models. They offer a sense of what the important buildings in the Citadel complex looked like and help convey the impact these buildings made on the contemporary observer. The frequency of complex, aniconic geometric patterns reflects the Phrygians' interests in such patterns to decorate other visual media, particularly those in use in their daily lives, such as pottery, furniture, and textiles. It may also result from the use of such patterns as a means of personal identification, widely attested on contemporary and later Phrygian pottery from Gordion. The limited number of script signs from the Luwian hieroglyphic script, while showing awareness of this writing system, also serves to reconfirm how much more common the use of non-verbal patterns and symbols were. This mix of external and internal source material in the drawings will have interesting implications when we come to assess their authorship.

---

169. Young 1956a:262, pl. 92, figs. 42, 43. See n. 91 and the discussion supra on the similarity between the lion in **25** and the sculpted lions.

170. Note the discussion of Collins 2004.

4

Origin of the Drawings and Their Placement on Megaron 2

We now come to the question of when and why were the drawings incised onto the walls of Megaron 2 and the Citadel Gateway, and by whom.[171] One thing seems certain: the drawings were not part of an intentional program of decoration, but were incised without regard for the final appearance of the walls. Indeed, the presence of stones with multiple drawings done one on top of another, stones with random lines over figured scenes, and stones with gouges probably intended to delete the figured drawings (**44** and **58** provide good examples) suggest the opposite, that the drawings are the product of informal impulses that represent the personal interests of the individual or individuals incising the stones. Such random drawings, or graffiti, are very common on architectural structures, public and private, found in many chronological periods and locations. Motivations to make such drawings are extremely varied; they can include statements of political or religious affiliation, desire for personal or political protest, intent to cause damage to a surface representing an alien political or religious tradition, individual destructiveness, i.e., vandalism, and simply the desire to leave a personal record of one's presence. Few of these reasons seem a probable explanation for the Gordion drawings. Neither the drawings on Megaron 2 nor those on the Gate Building would have been easily visible and so they would have been ineffective as political or ideological statements. Nor do they seem to be intentional vandalism; the drawings on the sides and back of Megaron 2 would have barely been visible from the building's front courtyard, and the marks are generally too light to cause any significant damage. Thus the most likely motives seem to have been the desire to record observations of the contemporary Early Phrygian environment and leave a personal record of one's presence.

This leaves unanswered the questions of who would have made the drawings, and under what circumstances. As noted in the Introduction, Rodney Young, the original excavator of Megaron 2, interpreted the drawings as the marks of casual passers-by who incised directly onto the megaron's standing walls while hanging around the building.[172] (Young was unaware of **104** and **105**, the drawings on the Early Phrygian Citadel Gateway.) There are, however, several practical reasons why this interpretation should be modified. Megaron 2 was located within the elite quarter of the Early Phrygian city to which entry was limited by an outer and an inner gate; moreover, the megaron was an imposing building that surely had an important public function. These factors make it improbable that casual visitors would have had access to the building, much less the opportunity to incise graffiti onto its walls. The position of the drawings on the walls' surfaces also makes Young's explanation unlikely. In areas where the location of the incised drawings on the walls could be determined, primarily on the southeast corner and the

---

171. My discussion focuses primarily on the drawings on Megaron 2, although these remarks are also applicable to **104**, the one complex drawing in the courtyard of the Gate Building. I will omit **103**, since the drawing appears to have been incised onto the blackened surface of the stone, suggesting that the incised mark was done after the fire that destroyed Megaron 2, and also **105**, the drawing of the zigzag line on the inner face of the gate, since this is a lightly incised, fairly simple design that could have been done either during or after the gate's construction.

172. Young 1957:323; Young 1958:142–43; Young 1963:353–54; Young 1969a. Young reconstructed the situation as follows: "its [i.e., Megaron 2's] three sides exposed to and temptations for idlers who took full advantage of the free space for their scribbling," Young 1958:143.

south/back wall of the building, it is clear that a number of the blocks with incised drawings were too high on the wall to be within easy reach of someone standing on the ground or, alternatively, were so close to the base of the building that the potential graffiti artist would have to be lying almost flat on the ground.[173] Young argued that a raised stone projection along the east side of Megaron 2 was a bench that could have been used by individuals while scratching their drawings on the wall,[174] but Sams' close study of the architectural remains of the area demonstrates that the east wall projection was built at a later stage, when there was no longer full access around the side and back of the building.[175] Moreover, several of the drawings were very deeply incised and in a few cases seem to be attempts at relief sculpture (**98** is a good example of this). Such complex stone work would have taken extra time and special tools, not likely to be available to the casual visitor. Further, if the drawings were incised onto blocks on the standing wall, it is difficult to account for the fact that some blocks were covered with drawings, while others were left blank. On the south/back wall of the building, for instance, the lower part of the exterior face of the wall was formed from large rectangular poros blocks with smoothed exterior surfaces, but no incised drawings were found on these blocks. Only the upper portion of the wall, built from a series of smaller blocks placed in vertical piers that alternated with upright wooden beams, bore incised marks (see Fig. 12).[176] The lower part of the wall would have furnished an equally or even more convenient surface for graffiti, yet these surfaces were left untouched. For all these reasons it is seems unlikely that the drawings were incised onto the standing walls of Megaron 2 or the Citadel Gateway by members of the general public.

So when would the drawings have been incised onto the walls of a major public building and gate? One possible scenario is that the drawings were incised onto the individual blocks before the megaron or gateway complex was constructed. This could have been done during the construction process, after the blocks had been cut to size and the outer surface finished but before the blocks were built into walls. It might seem odd that only the outer, finished surface, the surface that was intended to be exposed as the outer wall surface, was incised and that there are no incised marks on the top or bottom surfaces which were destined to be concealed by the wall's construction. In most cases, however, apart from the outer block face, very few of the other surfaces, the surfaces to be concealed within the walls, were finished with a smooth face; thus the blocks' other faces did not offer a potential field for drawing.

A significant point in support of this explanation is the presence of several blocks with incised drawings that are upside down or sideways to the upright direction of the block in a standing wall. At the right end of **46**, a bird of prey was drawn at a 90° counterclockwise angle to the main scene. Along the left end of **52**, a bird was drawn at a 90° counterclockwise angle to the drawing of a human figure in the center of the block. A similar situation can be observed on **100**, where a bird is drawn at one orientation, and a horned animal was drawn at a 90° angle to the bird. On **41** a bird and the head of another bird are drawn at an oblique angle of approximately 135° counterclockwise to the lower edge of the block. On **87**, a bird is drawn at a 90° counterclockwise angle to the figure above it. On **89**, a bird is drawn at a 135° counterclockwise angle to the base of the stone. It is hard to imagine how these drawings could have been done unless they were incised onto a block lying flat on the ground, where someone could draw on the block from different angles.

If we accept the argument that at least some of the drawings were placed on the stones before the building was built, then the individuals who incised them would be surely be those who had access to the stones during the construction process. Why would they have done this? The subject matter of the drawings suggests that several factors could have been at work. One possibility is that some of the drawings were sketches for a program of visual ornament in another medium or, alternatively, were copies of the figures used in such a visual program. As was extensively discussed in Section 3, almost all scenes of human figures and several of the animal figures, especially the lions, imitate the style and iconography used in the sculptural programs of the

---

173. Drawing **48**, an incised stone uncovered in 2004, is a good example of this, since it is a carefully incised drawing situated in the second masonry course, about 20 cm above ground level.
174. Based on this hypothesis, Young 1957:323 called the space between the east side and Megaron 2 and Megaron 1 the "waiting room."
175. Sams 1994a:2–3.
176. Young 1962:160. See the discussion above, Section 1.

Luwian and Aramaean states of southeastern Anatolia. Many of the drawings could have reflected the themes found on a program of sculpted orthostates, based on a Neo-Hittite model. Such Neo-Hittite influence is clearly seen in the series of sculpted orthostates from Gordion (mentioned in Section 3) that was probably used to decorate a building (or buildings) from a level preceding the Destruction Level. The subject matter of the Gordion orthostates includes the profile body and forward-turned head of a lion; a hoofed animal, perhaps a bull; a male figure who swings a lion cub upside down; a hoofed animal being attacked by a clawed creature; a griffin with upraised arms; and an elaborate throne with a human figure seated on it.[177] While there is little overlap between the subjects on the sculpted orthostates and those found in the incised drawings, the orthostates offer concrete evidence for what was probably an ambitious program of sculptural ornamentation for an important official building or series of buildings. Further evidence comes from the drawing on **9b**, the elevation of the Phrygian megaron that illustrates a lion on the center front wall. This drawing records an image of a lion that surely functioned as a decorative feature on an actual building wall. Some of the drawings on the Megaron 2 blocks could be the product of the same artistic and political impulse that produced such decorative programs for Early Phrygian architecture, illustrating the familiarity of local artists with the Neo-Hittite style and the desire to imitate that style, encouraged by its use in official sculptural programs on public monuments.

If the drawings were done by those involved in the process of construction or monumentalization of the Early Phrygian Citadel, this would explain a number of idiosyncratic features found in the drawings. The random lines, zigzags, and circles could be the result of individuals who were testing tools or making practice drawings of basic symbols such as compass-drawn circles and rosettes. It would also explain why many drawings were placed one on top of another, as individuals re-used the same surface to hone their skills. This hypothesis also explains the approach used for the drawings of animals. As noted in Section 2, almost all of the Gordion lion drawings follow a very standard pattern of execution; this can be demonstrated by the repetition of the lines creating the head, mouth, ears, feet, and other features of the lions in several of the drawings. Several drawings show what appear to be test patterns, i.e., the outline of the lion was started and then abandoned (note **8**, **10**, **12**, **46**, **47**, **50**, **79**, **82**, **83**, **93**), or were redone with details such as the head (**1**) or tail (**53**) changed. Some even appear to be sketches in which the lines were corrected by a more experienced hand, e.g., **72**, **84**. These characteristics can be found in a drawing of human figures, too; note **71**, where there are several attempts at drawing the figure's headdress. The drawings that were heavily scored over as if to erase the original scene (**44**, **58**, **81**) could also be a product of the process of correction for redrawing. All of these factors suggest that these were sketches that reflect local workmen's knowledge of the Neo-Hittite court style, perhaps even the work of those involved in the creation of the Gordion orthostates.

The examples of stones with the beginnings of relief sculpture, e.g., **31**, **33**, **59**, **95**, **98**, also reflect knowledge of a program of public relief sculpture. The technique used on the incipient relief sketches on the Megaron 2 stones noted above is consistent with that found on the Early Phrygian orthostates. In both cases the drawing was incised in outline form onto the stone and then the stone around the figure was chiseled away. A similar technique was used to create a sculpted relief depicting a lion found in a pre-Destruction Level context and can also be clearly seen in the carved orthostate of the hoofed animal (a bull?), one of the sculpted orthostates from the pre-Destruction Level series noted above.[178]

A further point in favor of this interpretation is found in the connections between the drawings and the few extant works of Phrygian sculpture from the Early Phrygian Citadel. The lion in drawing **25**, with its mouth open at a 90° angle, is extremely similar to the form of the sculpted stone lions found in the fill above Megaron 2 (Figs. 17, 18). The drilled pupil of the lion's eye in drawings **8** and **25** is another feature found in the sculpted lions, and also appears in the lion and griffin orthostates noted above, whose pupils

---

177. Sams 1989: pl. 129, 1, 2 (lion); pl. 130, 4 (hoofed animal); pl. 129, 4 (male figure with lion); pl. 129, 5 (hoofed animal with clawed creature); pl. 130, 1 (griffin); pl. 130, 3 (seated figure). On the date and extent of Neo-Hittite influence, see Sams 1989:449–53.

178. The stone lion is Gordion inventory number S 99, unpublished. For the hoofed animal, see Sams 1989: pl. 130, 4.

were drilled to receive inlay.[179] One of the lions from the orthostate series was carved with its tongue hanging out at a right angle to the mouth, a feature found in drawings **1**, **10**, **38**, and **53**.[180]

At this point, several potential objections to this explanatory hypothesis need to be addressed. Perhaps the most compelling objection lies in the drawings' potential to deface the blocks that were destined for a major public building. Why would workmen have done this? While we cannot answer this definitively, we can look at the question in the context of the architectural development of Early Phrygian Gordion. The Destruction Level was built above an earlier level of the urban settlement which comprised a number of substantial stone buildings, presumably formal public buildings.[181] These seem to have been deliberately dismantled, and some of the stones from them may have been reused for the succeeding Destruction Level buildings. It is possible that some of the stones used to build Megaron 2 (and perhaps also the Citadel Gateway) were salvaged from buildings in the earlier level of the settlement. The difficulties of acquiring stone suitable for building were such that no one wanted to waste it, even if the outer surface of the stone had already been marked by incised drawings. This would help explain why the Megaron 2 stones were of unequal dimensions. It might also suggest why the stones were available to be used as surfaces for drawings, since if the drawings were done on the stones after they were dismantled from one building but not yet designated for use in another building, they would have been considered surplus construction material and thus were available for drawings and sketches. Even if the stones used to construct Megaron 2 were newly cut specifically for this one building, there may well have been a lag between the removal of the stone blocks to the city and their incorporation into the building's walls, which would have allowed time for individuals to incise these drawings onto the stones.

A further and more serious objection to this hypothetical scenario concerns the question of why the drawings were not removed from the stone blocks after it was decided to use (or reuse) these stones for the construction of a major public building. This may be impossible to answer with certainty, but we can suggest that the presence of the drawings may not have seemed as intrusive to the people living in the Citadel as they seem to us. Drawings on the rear wall of Megaron 2 would not have been visible from the front of the building. Drawings placed on the east wall, the side wall facing Megaron 1, and those on the west wall, parallel to the substantial interior wall that separates the outer courtyard from the inner courtyard in front of Megaron 3, would also have been hard to see, since the passageways along the side of the megaron were only accessible through a narrow space that would have precluded direct sunlight on them. Moreover, the spaces around Megaron 2 did not give access to any other buildings or courtyards and in any case were too narrow to accommodate a significant amount of foot traffic, making it unlikely that there was any regular movement around the sides and back of the building, apart from support personnel connected with the building. Therefore only the front of the megaron would have received regular attention. Since the drawings were barely visible from the building's front face, presumably it was not thought necessary to remove them.[182] We should note that many of the drawings are very light and are hard to see even now. The Young excavations in 1956 completely missed **48**, still in situ in the east wall of Megaron 2 in 2004, and also missed **104**, the drawing in the north court of the Citadel Gateway. Drawing **104** was not noted until the early 1990s, even though the gate and court buildings had been cleared in the 1950s and the wall with the incised stone stood open and visible. It is possible that **104**, the incised stone in the Gate Building, was covered with plaster when it was first excavated in the 1950s, and

---

179. Note also the series of drill holes of varying sizes found in **50**; these too could have been practice drill exercises.

180. Lions above Megaron 2: Young 1956a:262, pl. 92, figs. 42–43; Prayon 1987: nos. 13, 14, pls. 4e, 5a–b. See also Mellink 1983:357. Orthostates with drilled pupils, Sams 1989:449, pl. 129, 1–4 (lions) and pl. 130, 1 (griffin). Orthostate lion with tongue hanging from mouth, Sams 1989: pl. 129, 2.

181. Voigt 2005:28–30, a discussion of the PAP (Post and Poros) building of the pre-Destruction Level city. See also Voigt and Hendrickson 2000:48, fig. 6.

182. There is at least one other instance of a reused stone with an incised drawing, a gaming board incised onto a surface of a block from the Early Phrygian city gate, reused as a paving block in the Middle Phrygian gate, see Young 1955:12, pl. 6, fig. 25. This block was placed face down in the later gate so that the drawing would not be visible, presumably because the gate area received regular traffic.

only after the plaster fell off was the incised surface exposed.[183] If this is so, however, it further supports the idea that the stones were incised by individuals involved in the construction process, before the building (the Gateway complex, in this case) was completed.

We should remember that Megaron 2 itself is somewhat irregular, and the blocks are not of consistent size. Moreover, the alternation between stone piers and wooden upright posts and horizontal beams would have created a marked contrast in colors and textures that might well have detracted from the incised pictures on the exterior walls, particularly if the walls were not viewed close up. The front of the building, which probably was either open or consisted of a decorated wooden screen, would have formed the focal point of the viewer's attention, thereby drawing attention away from the side walls. One might also wonder whether the haphazard nature of the drawings and their presence on the walls of a public building would have troubled the Early Iron Age Phrygians. The whole plan of the central area of the Destruction Level Citadel has a somewhat informal arrangement that lacks symmetry and regularity.[184] Apart from the sculpted orthostates noted above, there is little evidence that the Phrygians used the formal visual iconography of court ritual to impress and intimidate the viewer, such as the public architectural sculpture found in Neo-Hittite states.[185] The mosaic floor of Megaron 2 (Fig. 8) is a case in point: the geometric patterns in the mosaic are loosely grouped around a rosette pattern in the middle of the floor adjacent to the central hearth, but the patterns themselves are completely random and their placement is irregular. There was no effort to create an overall design that focused the eye on a central point. This low key and informal approach to urban design and public visual monuments may reflect an attitude that would not have minded the low key and informal drawings on the side and back walls of the building.

A more serious objection to my explanatory hypothesis for the Gordion drawings lies in the fact that the majority of the incised stones whose position could be determined were placed in the walls of Megaron 2 with the drawings upright. Why would anyone go to the trouble of setting the incised stones with the scenes on them upright if they were casual sketches that most people would never see? While there is no certain answer for this, the question suggests additional reasons why the incised drawings were made. It is possible that some of the drawings meant something to the individuals who incised them and those individuals wanted some visible record of their presence, even if it would only be seen by a limited number of people. As noted above, several of the drawings include symbols that were later used as personal marks of identification, and it is entirely possible that these symbols fulfilled the same function during the Early Phrygian Period. Some may simply record the maker's view of his surroundings, e.g., drawings of local animals or of architectural structures located in Gordion. A few convey a distinctive personality through a sense of humor; **81**, for example, a drawing of two stick figures engaged in combat, seems almost a caricature of **14**, a scene of two helmeted warriors in combat, which is itself an adaptation of a Neo-Hittite scene.[186] Other drawings, particularly the aniconic idols, the lion, and the bird of prey, may have had religious symbolism to their makers. Still others could have symbolized cultural constructs reminiscent of southeastern Anatolia that may have been important to an individual who had ties to that region.

An alternate hypothesis for the placement of the drawings on the stone blocks is also possible, namely that the drawings, especially those on Megaron 2, were incised onto the walls of the completed building. As I argued earlier, it seems unlikely that the general public in Early Phrygian Gordion would have had access to Megaron 2, and so if we wish to determine who might have incised drawings onto the standing building, we need to consider when and to whom the walls would have been accessible. It seems unlikely that drawings would have been incised as graffiti onto the walls of Megaron 2 during its initial phase, when it was a free-standing building, because that leaves unexplained the broad stretch of surface on the

---

183. G. K. Sams, personal communication.

184. This is in part a result of the fact that the Destruction Level city plan incorporated structures from earlier levels of the city, e.g., Megaron 10 (see Sams 1994a:2–3, and Fig. 2 here), that stood on a different orientation from later buildings.

185. Contrast the irregular architectural plan at Gordion with the very different situation at Carchemish, discussed by Denel 2007.

186. For a discussion of **14**, see above, n. 56. For other observations on a sense of humor in Phrygian art, see Simpson 1988:38.

back wall that was not incised. The construction of the two storage sheds, Houses X and Y, would have covered the entire back wall of the building, making the blocks with graffiti there unreachable, and the construction of the Terrace Building complex would have made both the south and west walls of the building inaccessible. The only time when all the incised surfaces of Megaron 2 were available to potential graffiti artists would have been during the period of the construction of the Terrace Buildings, when the two side walls of the megaron were still unimpeded and the storage sheds had been partially demolished, still covering the lower part of the back of Megaron 2 (the part that has no graffiti on it) but leaving the upper part exposed. (This was the state of the building when it was excavated, cf. Fig. 11.) At this point the walls would have been exposed to view and the workmen, soldiers, and others involved in the construction project would have been able to incise drawings directly onto the standing walls.

These two scenarios need not be mutually exclusive. The opportunity to incise onto the blocks before construction would explain the figured drawings that are not upright, the blocks with relief work, and the careful and precise drawings of human and animal scenes, e.g., **44**, **53**, **69**, **80**. The workmen who drew onto the standing walls could have added random lines and scratches, patterns that served as personal identification marks, and more casual drawings, feeling free to add their own marks to stone blocks that already had incised drawings on them.

Another example of incised drawings on a public Phrygian monument, a series of graffiti found on two sandstone blocks in the main city gate at Kerkenes Dağ, offers support for this point. In this Phrygian settlement of the later 7th through mid-6th centuries BCE, located east of the Kızılırmak River in central Anatolia, graffiti were scratched onto blocks near the front of the gate chamber in one of the major city gates, termed the Cappadocia Gate by the excavator.[187] The graffiti includes several representations of an aniconic stele of the type discussed above in connection with Gordion drawings **10**, **51**, and **94**, and also random marks and two occurrences of the letter M. In the back of the same gate chamber was a cult monument, a step monument topped by an aniconic Phrygian idol.

This combination of pictures, letter forms, and formless marks, in a public gateway and near a cult shrine, provides an interesting corollary to the mixed subject matter of the Gordion drawings. While some two and a half centuries later than the Gordion drawings, the Kerkenes material offers an example of Phrygian incised drawings that, like those at Gordion, would have been visible in a public setting.

The extensive Neo-Hittite influence on the Gordion drawings is important enough to deserve further comment. As discussed in Section 3, a significant proportion of the drawings reveal the influence of Neo-Hittite style and subject matter. How would such Neo-Hittite visual models have reached Gordion? Two possibilities can be suggested. Those involved in incising the drawings could have included stone workers from regions where Neo-Hittite visual culture was the dominant mode of public art, who came (or were brought) to Gordion in order to carry out a program of sculptural relief intended to decorate the walls and buildings of the city and outfit it with the type of visual program thought suitable to advertise the growing power of the fledgling Phrygian state. Such outsiders could have worked with local Phrygian workmen who were imitating the style of their masters while developing their own subject matter and style in other drawings.

One circumstance that makes this suggestion plausible is the frequency of imitation and repetition in the drawings. Overall, the drawings show an unusual combination of the hand of someone familiar with the iconographic traditions of Neo-Hittite art and the sloppy work of a careless amateur. This suggests that some of the stone drawings reflect the output of individuals who were in the process of learning how to draw and, more generally, how to produce visual symbols important to their culture and to themselves. The homeland(s) of the artists who were training the Gordion apprentice craftsmen could have been fairly close to Gordion. One potential source lies in the cities of Tabal, the Luwian district immediately to the southeast of Phrygian territory around Gordion.[188] While monumental sculpture from Tabal has not been as systematically investigated as the sculptural programs of major southeastern Anatolian centers such as Carchemish, potential correspondences be-

---

187. Summers 2006:652–53, pl. 2.

188. On Tabal in the Iron Age, see Aro 1998; Hawkins 2000:425–33.

tween the two regions can be noted. An excellent example is **44**, a striding figure carrying a hare in a bag, a drawing that closely parallels a relief from Kültepe, a Luwian center in Tabal. The territory of Tabal has also furnished several sculptural treatments of lions, both in relief and in the round, that exhibit many of the characteristics of the lions in the Gordion drawings; note examples from Göllüdağ, Havuz, and Kululu.[189]

In support of the hypothesis of foreign craftsmen leaving their mark in casual drawings at Gordion, we may recall similar circumstances at Persepolis, where Greek craftsmen left their mark in an Achaemenian environment. I will not discuss the question of the impact of Ionian artists on the formal public sculptural program at the Achaemenian palatial center,[190] but the presence of graffiti in typically Greek manner on artifacts from Persepolis. Two such graffiti drawings provide vivid testimony both to the presence of Greek workmen in Persia and to their interest in drawing in their native visual idiom. One is a late 6th century graffito incised onto the foot of a statue of the Persian king Darius. The graffito, depicting two bearded male heads and two lions, bears such strong formal similarities to contemporary Attic red figure vase painting that it was clearly done by a Greek artist, or an artist trained in the Greek tradition. Yet it appears on the foot of an image of the king, an image carved in Achaemenian style.[191] Another example is a stone plaque dated to the late 6th century BCE found in the Treasury at Persepolis. On the plaque, a piece of local stone, is incised a scene of Herakles struggling with Apollo for the Delphic tripod, a quintessentially Greek subject that would have had little meaning to a Persian. This drawing too is clearly the work of a Greek artist at Persepolis, drafting a Hellenic subject (out of nostalgia for his homeland, perhaps?) on a piece of polished stone that would never have been seen in public.[192] Both of these examples show how workmen from another culture can work both in their native tradition and in the style and iconography of the dominant culture that employs them.

Alternatively, the drawings could have been done by local Phrygian craftsmen imitating the conventions of Neo-Hittite art found on small portable objects such as ivories, gemstones, and seals. Such objects, manufactured in Neo-Hittite centers and brought to Gordion as objects of trade or gift exchange, could have furnished models of Neo-Hittite subject matter and style to the Phrygian artists. As an example, we may note a set of ivory horse ornaments found in one of the Terrace Buildings from the Destruction Level Citadel that were imported from a Neo-Hittite center.[193] These include a set of side pieces decorated with a leonine sphinx; the lion head of the animal has a wrinkled muzzle, wavy mane, and tongue-like cheek piece, all features that appear on several of the lion drawings from Megaron 2. Ivory objects have been shown to form the source of subjects found on sculpted orthostates in other western Asiatic sites such as Tell Halaf, and imported ivory objects could easily have supplied models for the visual arts in Gordion also.[194] Another potential source could be scenes depicted on seals and sealings. At least one of the Gordion scenes, **44**, the hunter with the hare, was depicted on a seal from the Hittite Empire period,[195] suggesting this as a possible source for some of the incised drawings. A few examples of seals and sealings from the Hittite Empire period have been uncovered from Gordion, most from much later contexts, that display the iconography of deities and composite creatures that was also used in the Neo-Hittite repertory.[196] None of the extant seals offers a direct parallel to the scenes in

---

189. The Kültepe parallel is discussed supra n. 69; see Özgüç 1971: 82, fig. 7; Orthmann 1971: pl. 38b; Aro 1998:173–74, B 133; Aro 2003:316, pl. XIV. For lions, see Aro 1998: pls. 75–79 (Göllüdağ), pl. 83 (Havuz), pl. 105 (Kululu).

190. On this question, see Nylander 1970.

191. Richter 1946:28–29, fig. 26. The graffito would have been covered with paint and would not have been visible in the finished work; thus the Greek artist could express his own interest in drawing in his native style, knowing that it would not be seen.

192. Roaf and Boardman 1980.

193. Ivory horse ornaments, Young 1962:166–67, figs. 24–25; see also Voigt and Henrickson 2000:50.

194. Winter 1983, 1989, and in general, Winter 1987:355–56. Winter's arguments are addressed to the question of transfer of subjects and motifs among north Syrian centers and between north Syria and the Assyrians, but the theoretical model of transfer that she proposes would work equally well for transfer of motifs between north Syria and Phrygia.

195. Porada 1981:46–49, no. 25.

196. On early seals and sealings found at Gordion, see Guterbock 1980; Dusinberre 2005:20–22, nos. 1–18.

the incised drawings, but it is possible that seals with similar motifs were used at Gordion but have not survived.

This hypothesis would explain why many of the Gordion drawings, particularly those of human figures, show a general similarity to a Neo-Hittite prototype, yet omit many details. Several of the Gordion drawings replicate scenes depicting Neo-Hittite deities, e.g., **44** and **88**, yet omit such critical details as a headdress or other attributes that identify the deity. Drawing **101** furnishes another example; this drawing replicates the general form of the tamer-of-animals figure, yet is extremely sketchy, as if the person who made the drawing had only an outline to follow with few internal details. I have suggested above that part of the reason for this may have been a question of receptivity: the Gordion artists may have been uninterested in reproducing precise details of a Neo-Hittite prototype of a deity or narrative scene if the deity or narrative had little meaning to a Phrygian audience. The possibility that the Gordion drawing was copied from a much smaller prototype in which internal detail was omitted because of the object's small size offers a further explanation.[197]

Here too these alternative hypotheses need not be mutually exclusive. Both potential explanations, postulating imported craftsmen and imported objects, explain different features of the drawings. Some of the animal scenes, the lions, for example, are so close to a Neo-Hittite model in small details that it seems highly probable that they were made by someone trained in the Neo-Hittite visual tradition. In other scenes the connection with a Neo-Hittite prototype is much more imprecise, indicating an indirect model may have been the inspiration for a given scene.

As a whole, the drawings appear to represent the output of several distinct groups. The Neo-Hittite tradition of visual themes such as the lion, the stag, and complex scenes of human figures engaged in fighting, hunting, and regal poses could result from the efforts of individuals familiar with this tradition, whether stoneworkers native to the cities of neighboring Luwian centers or Phrygians imitating Neo-Hittite subject matter. Blocks with relief or drill work could be the product of artisans who were testing their tools or honing their skills in sculptural technique. Contemporary subjects such as Phrygian architectural structures, Phrygian non-verbal symbols, and local animals could be the product of local craftsmen and workmen who wished to leave a personal mark. Random lines, scratch marks, and cartoonish drawings could have been casual marks made for amusement by workmen who knew their efforts were not going to be seen by others.

---

197. Note the discussion of Miller 1988:85–88 on a similar process through which scenes from the repertory of Achaemenian art reached 5th century BCE Athens by way of seals and other small portable objects.

5

Conclusion: Contribution of the Drawings to an Assessment of Early Phrygian Cultural Development

Despite their rather haphazard character, the Megaron 2 drawings, together with the one complex drawing from the Early Phrygian Citadel Gateway, give us valuable insights into a range of visual themes of interest to the Phrygians at Gordion during a pivotal stage in the development of the city. This insight is accidental: the fire that destroyed the Early Phrygian Citadel and preserved the stones with drawings appears to be the result of random chance, not a conscious event.[198] It is therefore all the more interesting to consider what the drawings reveal about the status of Phrygian artistic development in the late 9th century BCE.

One notable factor that comes through clearly is the extensive impact made by the visual models of the city-states in central and southeastern Anatolia. Both the more complex Megaron 2 drawings and the sculpted orthostates from the pre-Destruction Level Citadel demonstrate that the developing political powers at Gordion turned to the Neo-Hittite cities to emulate their visual repertoire. The evidence for a complex program of visual imagery at Early Phrygian Gordion correlates with the architectural evidence from the pre-Destruction Level settlement to signal a major advance in the degree of political organization and cultural sophistication at the site.[199] The archaeological record indicates that before the 9th century BCE, the Phrygians had little experience in the representation of figured scenes, particularly scenes with human figures. The rich and well established cities of Luwian Tabal, for example, offered an influential and geographically available model of complex figured scenes through which the ruling elite could represent itself and its rituals in order to maintain its position of authority. The developing complexity of Phrygian society undoubtedly encouraged the Phrygians to turn to Neo-Hittite models to create such a program of figured ornament for themselves, one that would have been displayed in the context of an urban plan that was surely intended to be visually impressive.[200]

The Megaron 2 drawings also suggest, however, that many facets of the Neo-Hittite visual repertory were not adopted by the Phrygians. The more complex drawings of human scenes are few in number, are limited to a single example, and deliberately omit many distinguishing features, such as the attributes of a deity and the court panoply of a ruler. The rather casual and sketchy nature of the drawings certainly may be one reason for this, but it is also possible that another reason may lie in the area of cult practice. Many of the Gordion scenes with human figures follow a Neo-Hittite model in which a divinity or divine attendant plays a prominent role. As noted above, several of the Gordion drawings draw on Neo-Hittite images of divinities, such as the figure of the hunter carrying a hare, **44**, and the striding figure in a long gown, **88**, yet

---

198. Voigt and Henrickson 2000:52; Voigt 2005:32–35.
199. Voigt and Henrickson 2000:50 and Voigt 2005:29 discuss the discovery of a fragment of a sculpted orthostate in the level of Gordion 6B, the pre-Destruction Level city, that matches the sculpted orthostates published by Sams 1989, clearly demonstrating that the program of sculpted orthostates at Gordion was intended to be displayed in this level of the city.

200. The comments of Nylander 1970:11 and n. 3, on the need of a new power to "create a monumental art expressive of their new dignity and their special ethos," are relevant here.

present these figures without the attributes that advertises their divine status. We may suggest that one reason for the lack of detail in such scenes in Gordion lay in the desire of the local Phrygians not to imitate the tradition of cult and saga used by a different people, but to develop their own Phrygian traditions.

For that reason it is both interesting and instructive to look at the subjects found on the drawings that continued in use to become a regular feature of the Phrygian visual repertory. Of these by far the most common are the scenes of animals, especially lions and birds of prey. As discussed above, a large number of the lions in the Megaron 2 drawings exhibit strong formal similarities with the lions on Neo-Hittite sculpted reliefs, in details such as the neck ridge, the tongue, the tongue-like cheek piece on the face, and the prominent curved claws. Yet there are several lions in the Gordion drawings that do not follow the Neo-Hittite pattern so closely, but reveal characteristics that would be prevalent in later Phrygian representations of lions. Drawings **38** and **48**, right, offer good examples. Here the lions have very rounded heads, prominent ears, and open mouths, features which are strikingly similar to one of the monumental lions carved onto the rock façade of the Köhnüs Valley in the Phrygian Highlands, known as Yılantaş.[201] (Fig. 19) Another example is drawing **80**, with two lions, both with more angular bodies and squared faces with a prominent nose and whiskers; the mouth of the lion at right, open in what is surely intended to be a menacing roar, has traces of teeth in the lower jaw. The lions in this drawing seem to be close precursors to another prominent pair of stone lions carved over a tomb in the Köhnüs Valley in the Phrygian Highlands, known as Arslantaş.[202] (Fig. 20) While I am not proposing a direct transmission from the Early Phrygian drawings to the reliefs of the Phrygian Highlands, it seems highly likely that the lion entered the Phrygian artistic repertory under the circumstances we see here, namely through imitation of southeastern Anatolian models, and then was adapted to Phrygian taste and transferred into monumental sculptural form.

Even more striking are the examples of birds of prey. As I have argued above, the bird of prey, one of the most frequent subjects in the Megaron 2 drawings, may have been a popular theme for several reasons, including potential interest in falconry and observation of nature around Gordion. As is well known, however, the bird of prey was an important symbol of religious imagery to the Phrygians, particularly during the Middle Phrygian period, when it was one of the principal attributes of the Phrygian Mother goddess. Since no image of the Mother goddess is definitely known from the Early Phrygian period, we cannot be sure to what extent the birds of prey on the Megaron 2 drawings allude to religious practice. It is noteworthy, though, that when images of the deity holding her raptor appear, such as that found in the Ankara/Bahçelievler relief,[203] the form of the divine attribute follows the image of several of the raptors as shown in the Early Phrygian drawings (note **5, 9a, 11, 69**). Like the raptors in the drawings, the bird held by the goddess is shown in profile view with extended talons, a prominent curved beak, and striations to indicate the tail and feathers. As in the case of the lions, the form of the bird of prey in later Phrygian art derives directly from its appearance in Early Phrygian art, as attested in drawings such as these.

Overall, the great interest in the representation of lions and birds, especially raptors, may represent a stage of the development of a distinctive style of visual identity among the Phrygians. Both the lion and the bird of prey were symbols of long standing in Anatolia, in regular use from the early 2nd millennium through the 1st millennium BCE.[204] During the Bronze and early Iron Ages both animals had been associated with several different divinities, male and female. Their basic function seems to have been, not to identify one specific deity, but to communicate implications of status and power. As such, they would be attractive symbols of high status among elite in newly emerging Phrygian polity. Both the lion and raptor were to become attributes of the Phrygian Mother goddess, but I do not think that their frequent appearance in these drawings indicates a direct reference to this one deity alone. Rather, these two animals symbolize the royal house and the power of the divinities that served

---

201. Haspels 1971: figs. 141, 143, 146.
202. Haspels 1971: figs. 130–34.
203. Mellink 1983: pl. 71, 1; Naumann 1983: pl. 5, fig. 2; Roller 1999b: fig. 8. Note also a similar bird of prey in a red sandstone relief of the Mother from Gordion, Mellink 1983: pl. 73, 1; Roller 1999b:12.
204. Collins 2002; Collins 2004.

CONCLUSION

as patrons of the ruling authority in Phrygia.[205] Their regular appearance in the Gordion drawings results from the developing Phrygian interest in the animal symbols that encompass a broad range of references, human and divine.

Not only do the subject matter and style of several drawings look forward to the continuing development of Phrygian visual forms, but several technical details do also. I have already noted the drill hole for the eye of the lion in drawings **8** and **25**, a feature that also appears in a lion in the early sculpted orthostates and also in the stone lions found above Megaron 2.[206] The diamond-shaped eye that is found in some of the drawings of birds, e.g., **50** and **69**, and in the horse in **12** also appears in the three carved ivory inlay plaques from Megaron 3.[207] The predatory bird in a "marching" pose, with hooked beak, outstretched wings, and one foot stepping forward, occurs in drawings **3**, **11**, **20** and also on painted pottery from the early phase of the Middle Phrygian level.[208] Taken together, these details indicate that the artisans who made the drawings were very familiar with the forms of Phrygian visual expression that were used on several media, and that these features were to continue in use after the rebuilding of the Citadel in the Middle Phrygian period. This mix of subjects that are found nowhere else in Phrygian art and subjects that were to become regular features of the Phrygian visual repertory contributes to the sense of vividness offered by the drawings. It also confirms their position as a valuable snapshot of a society that had only recently moved beyond the shadow cast by the well established visual programs of the cities of southeastern Anatolia to assert itself as a distinctive culture on the central Anatolian plateau. The accident of the fire preserved the drawings at a pivotal stage of Phrygian art, as the Phrygians were moving beyond direct imitation of Neo-Hittite visual models to develop their own form of visual expression. Machteld Mellink's assessment of the visual culture of the finds from the early Gordion tumuli is valid for this material too: "In these works (the human and animal motifs found in the Destruction Level) the differences between Phrygian and Neo-Hittite (or other Near Eastern) art cannot simply be attributed to the inexperience of a beginning artist."[209] The same can be said of these early Phrygian drawings. As a valuable record of the interests and activities of the people in 9th century BCE Gordion, they have much to teach us about the character of the Early Phrygian state.

---

205. This point is well discussed by Collins 2004, esp. pp. 93–94; see also Collins 2002:331.
206. Early Phrygian orthostate, Sams 1989: pl. 129, 2; stone lion above Megaron 2, Young 1956a:262, pl. 92, figs. 42–43.
207. Young 1960: fig. 25a–c.
208. Sams 1974: no. 1038, pl. 55.

209. Mellink, in Young 1981:268.

II

Catalogue of Stones with Incised Drawings from Early Phrygian Gordion

The catalogue entries are organized according to the find spot of the stones. The first group, much the largest, comprises those incised stones found on or fallen from the walls of Megaron 2. These are arranged according to their position on the walls: first are those from the east wall, the left side as one faces the building; next are those from the south or back wall of the building.[210] No stones from the west or right wall of the building were preserved or inventoried, so none is included in the catalogue. Following the catalogue entries of the Megaron 2 stones are two examples of incised stones from House Y, one of a pair of small storage sheds behind Megaron 2. Next are the catalogue entries for three stones found in the fill above Megaron 2, and finally there are two entries for the two incised stones on the Early Phrygian Gate. Within this organization, the stones are numbered continuously. The numbered catalogue entries refer to the stones, not to the subject matter of the drawings, since often more than one subject appears on the same stone. Each catalogue entry contains the following information: the catalogue number and subject(s) drawn on each stone, then the Gordion Excavation inventory number, the location of the stone, the dimensions of the block, the state of preservation of each block, a description of the incised drawing(s) on the block, and references to previous publications of the stone or drawing, if any.

An explanatory note about the Gordion inventory numbers may be helpful. The original inventory numbers consist of two parts. The first was a number given to every object from the excavation, assigned in the order in which the object was inventoried. The second part contains a prefix of one or two letters indicating the medium from which the object was made and a second number, assigned in the order in which an object of that particular medium was inventoried. The first Gordion stone with an incised drawing to be discovered, **102**, was assigned a prefix of S for Sculpture; however, all subsequent stones with incised drawings were given a prefix of ST, for Stone. This change of nomenclature undoubtedly reflects the uncertainty of how to regard the incised stones, as potential works of art or as utilitarian objects.

Dimensions are all given in the metric system. The following abbreviations are used:

Dim. – Dimension
L. – Length
W. – Width
Th. – Thickness
PL. – Preserved Length
PW. – Preserved Width
PTh. – Preserved Thickness

In some cases the preserved area of the incised face was considerably smaller than the actual length and width of the block; in these examples, the dimensions of the preserved area of the incised face are given as well as the dimensions of the entire block.

---

210. As the plan of the Destruction Level at Gordion shows (see Fig. 3), Megaron 2 is oriented with the entrance towards the northeast and the main axis of the building running from northeast to southwest. However, the preliminary excavation reports consistently refer to the front of the building as the north and take the description of the cardinal directions from this orientation; see Young 1957:322–23. My discussion here follows Young's practice.

Stones from Megaron 2

1   **Star; lion; two men**
    4015 ST 255
    Megaron 2, east wall
    Dim. of block: PL. 0.32, H. 0.24, Th. 0.47
    State of preservation: single block preserving front, back, upper, and lower faces. Part of left side preserved, right side broken.

Description: drawing covers whole of incised face of stone. At left, five-pointed star; above this, two superimposed triangles forming flag-like designs. In center, head and neck of a large animal with its mouth open, teeth visible, tongue hanging out. Along the neck is a pronounced neck band with double-outlined curve along animal's cheek. Above the head, two rough outlines of animal's muzzle and nose, perhaps preliminary sketches that were abandoned. Animal is probably a lion, although the long slender muzzle is more suggestive of a dog. Above animal's head, a small human figure striding to left, hair in a small pigtail at nape of neck; figure wears short kilt, has outstretched right arm, left arm extended behind body with elbow bent. To the right of the animal, another small human figure, facing right, appears to wear helmet on head, no other details of body or costume visible.

Previous bibliography: Young 1969a:273; Prayon 1987: fig. 27c.

2   **Warrior; bird; formless marks**
    4016 ST 256
    Megaron 2, east wall
    Dim. of block: PL. 0.40, H. 0.23, PTh. 0.32
    Dim. of incised face: 0.22 x 0.29
    State of preservation: single block, preserves top and bottom surfaces, part of front and right side, left side broken. Incised surface has small pits overall.

Description: in center, standing male figure facing left; figure has large eye, nude except for short kilt with internal cross-hatching. Figure holds bow in outstretched right arm; left arm bent back, holds arrow or spear. Behind human figure is elongated object, perhaps a simple bird. At right, a simple geometric pattern of overlapping rectangles, integrated into end of arrow/spear. Other random lines in the field, probably unrelated to drawing of human figure.

Previous bibliography: Young 1969a:273; Prayon 1987: fig. 27b.

3   **Two birds; animal; bird; marks**
    4017 ST 257
    Megaron 2, east wall
    Dim. of block: L. 0.50, H. 0.15, Th. 0.32
    State of preservation: two joining pieces, mended, preserving whole block except for several large chips in incised front face; upper left and lower right corners gone, several large chips in center around mend of joining pieces. Sides of block at back modified to make a wedge shape.

Description: at far left, bird of prey facing right, wings outstretched, leg and talons extended. At right of bird, crudely drawn quadruped, identity uncertain. Four schematic legs visible, tail extends up and over head, other deeply incised lines parallel curve of tail, unclear how they relate to the animal. Above animal tail, head and beak of another bird; to right of bird, a crude face looking left. To right of quadruped, random lines, two triangular flags. At far right, bird in right profile, partially preserved.

4   **Lion; bird head**
    4018 ST 258
    Megaron 2, east wall
    Dim. of block: PL. 0.45, H. 0.18, Th. 0.20
    State of preservation: block mended from two joining pieces, preserves most of front face, top and bottom surfaces, and right side. Left side missing; large gouge in center front, much of lower half of front face missing. Drawing found only on right side of front face, appears complete.

Description: lion walking right; lion has crescent-shaped eye, pronounced ridge along neck, half-moon object along animal's cheek, long curved claws on feet, almost like talons. At far right, animal head, perhaps beginning of bird's head. Random lines in field.

Previous bibliography: Young 1969a:274; Prayon 1987: fig. 28b.

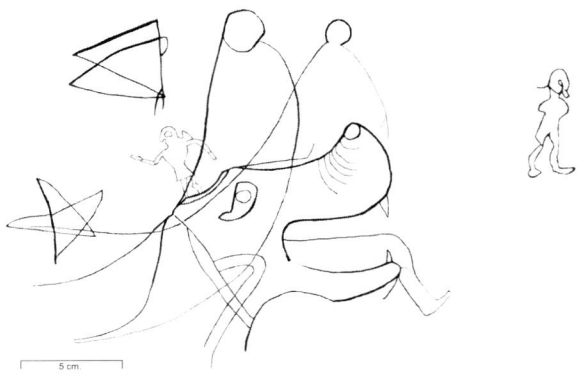

1: ST 255

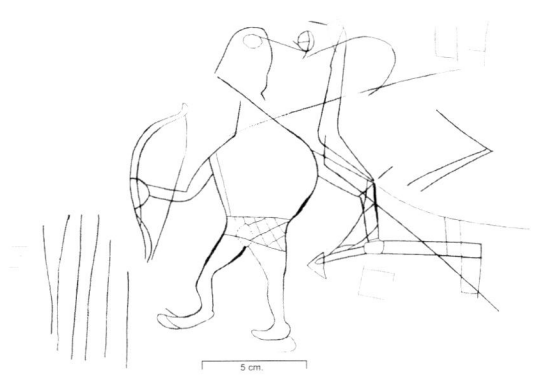

2: ST 256

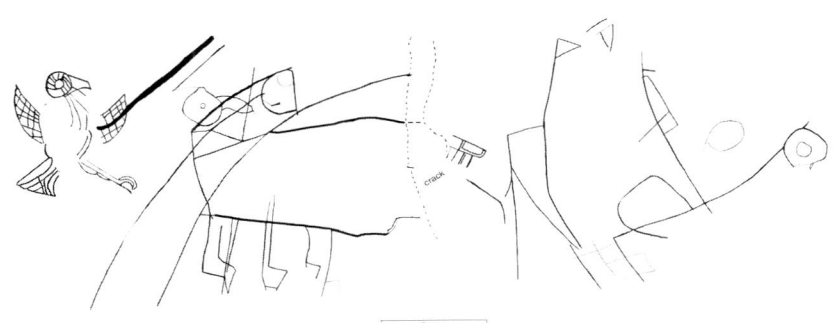

3: ST 257

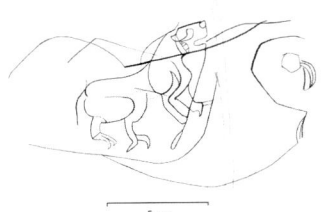

4: ST 258

5   Three birds; man; three birds
4019 ST 259
Megaron 2, east wall
Dim. of block: L. 0.44, H. 0.16, PTh. 0.34
State of preservation: block originally complete, now mended from two large and several joining fragments; right two-thirds of stone now missing, so description of all figures except for three birds at left is not from autopsy.

Description: at left, three birds of prey in a row facing right, each has pointed beak and talons; above second and third birds, crude latticing with irregular circle over it. In center, figure of a man walking left, wears short belted tunic, carries shield (or bow) in left hand, right arm outstretched. At right, bodies of two more birds facing right, head of another bird below and between them. Lightly sketched lines over bird at far right may be trace of another bird, abandoned.

6   Lion; random lines
4020 ST 260
Megaron 2, fallen from east wall
Dim. of block: PL. 0.40, H. 0.175, PTh. 0.20
State of preservation: block mended from several joining fragments; preserves surfaces of incised front face and top, bottom, and left faces; right side and back missing. Large chip on upper right corner of front face, several chips in center front at joins.

Description: lion walking right, lion has open mouth, small body, and disproportionately large head, and long curved claws on feet, almost like talons. Double line along neck, small tongue-like projection on animal's cheek. At right, several curved lines; one set may be beginning of bird's beak facing left.
Previous bibliography: Roller 2005:126, fig. 2; Roller 2008: fig. 1; Tsetskhladze 2007:297, fig. 2.

7   Lion
4021 ST 261
Megaron 2, east wall
Dim. of block: PL. 0.23, H. 0.15, PTh. 0.20
State of preservation: mended from several fragments, preserves upper and lower surface, left face and left edge; incised face has large crack in center, several chips in incised surface; only left side preserved, so extent of drawing unknown. Incised surface covered with many pits and cracks. Left side of block smoothed 0.17 m from front edge, then roughly finished.

Description: lion walking left, downward projection from mouth may be attempt to draw tongue hanging out (cf. **1, 38, 53**); only three legs now visible. Two sets of two parallel curving lines, one to left of lion, one above lion.

8   Lion; birds; pattern; man
4022 ST 262
Megaron 2, east wall
Dim. of block: PL. 0.42, H. 0.20, Th. 0.31
Dim. of incised surface: 0.40 x 0.20
State of preservation: block mended from several joining fragments, preserves front, top, and bottom surfaces; several cracks and abrasions on incised front face. Side edges missing.

Description: complex set of images, one superimposed on another, making the drawing hard to read. At upper left corner of preserved surface, two vertical lines enclosing squares, one with a meander pattern, perhaps illustration of a building wall with stone outer surface (like Megaron 2). Below this, two sitting birds facing right, one with head, one without. Below these, a large animal facing right, probably a lion, has prominent eye with drilled pupil; two front legs visible. Two legs to the left may belong to second lion at right. Over face of lion, large crescent-shaped object with lines in center, probably outstretched wings of bird in flight. Underneath this, beginning of another lion, one leg, outline of front of body, one ear, and nose visible. At right, small bird with long neck and beak facing right, incomplete. At far right, small male figure walking right, torso obscured by crack in stone. Random horizontal and vertical lines at right and below lion.
Previous bibliography: Roller 1999a:146, fig. 3.

9a-left   Two buildings; bird; animal
9b-right   Building; lion; latticing
4023 ST 263a, b
Megaron 2, east wall
State of preservation: two non-joining fragments from the same block of stone; catalogued

5: ST 259

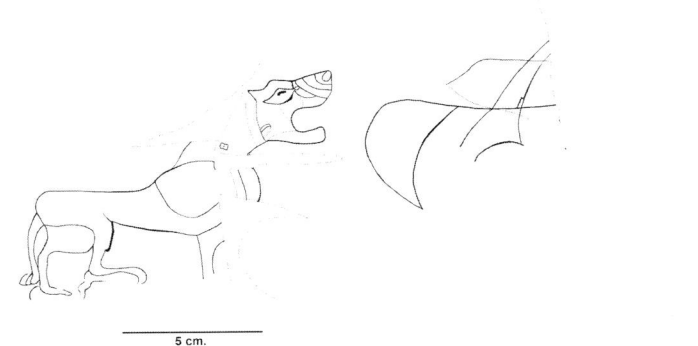

6: ST 260

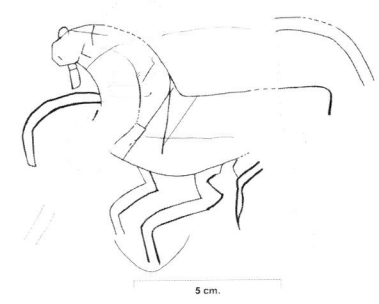

7: ST 261

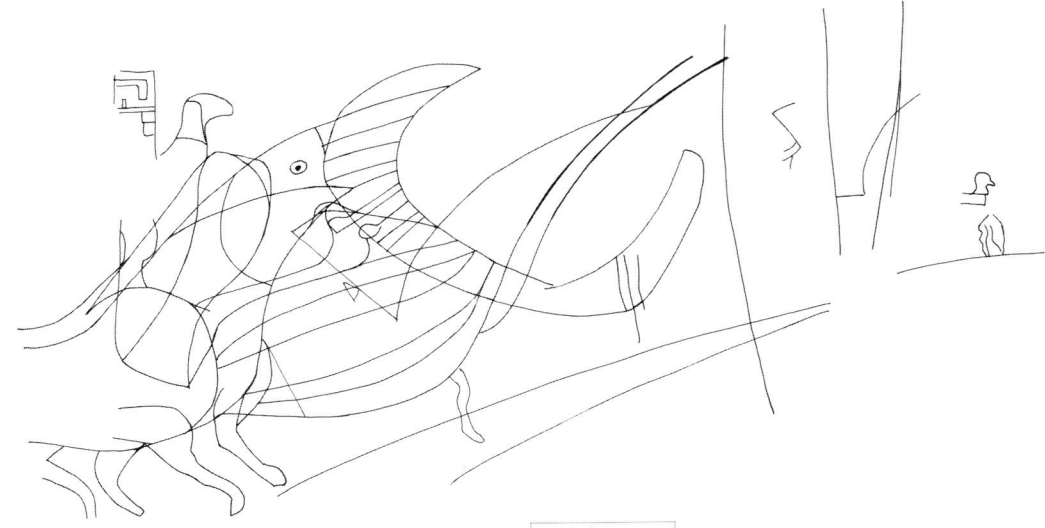

8: ST 262

separately as ST 263a and ST 263b. Top and bottom surfaces roughly finished with flat chisel; left edge of ST 263a also finished. Incised surfaces of both pieces pitted with small holes.

Dim. of block **9a**: PL. 0.19, H. 0.22, PTh. 0.18
Dim. of incised surface: 0.19 x 0.18

Description of **9a**, left fragment: at left, large bird of prey in right profile, diamond eye, pronounced sharp beak, outstretched talons. Over bird is a building, seen as if from narrow end of structure, with gabled roof, horn akroterion above center gable, central support for gable, and two windows in pediment visible. In center of the building wall, a large window cuts through bird's eye and beak. To the right, another building, also shown as from the narrow end, with gabled roof, central horn akroterion, and central roof support under gable; lines extending up on either side of the building are likely to be the result of careless drawing, not intentional architectural features. Below center of pediment is a rosette with eight petals, perhaps a decorative element on the building. In center front of building is a double door with two leaves; each leaf appears to be made of vertical beams bound by two horizontal beams. Small window to the right of the door. Below this, part of double-outlined rectangle and other formless lines in field. At lower left, rear part of a quadruped.

Dim. of block **9b**: PL. 0.16, H. 0.22, PTh. 0.16
Dim. of incised surface: 0.19 x 0.16

Description of **9b**, right fragment: at right, elevation of building, seen as if from narrow end of structure; building has gabled roof and horn akroterion indicated with double lines. On front of building, a lion facing to right, tail in air, legs bent as if animal is running. Very light diamond scoring over building. Below the building, a series of deeply incised horizontal lines; the topmost line forms the base of the building; other random lines between horizontal lines. Light checkerboard scoring to left of building.

Previous bibliography: Young 1956b:264, lower right; Young 1957: pl. 90, fig. 12; Young 1965a:482, fig. 3; Young 1969a:272; Mellink 1983:357, fig. 1; Prayon 1987: fig. 28a; Simpson 1998: pl. 180, fig. 16; Berndt-Ersöz 2003: fig. 103; Roller 2005:127, fig. 3 (9b only); Berndt-Ersöz 2006: fig. 119; Tsetskhladze 2007:296, fig. 2; Roller, forthcoming, fig. 1-3.

10 Lion; horse; bird; goat; symbols
4024 ST 264
Megaron 2, east wall, found in situ above stone bench
Dim. of block: L. 0.66, H. 0.24, Th. 0.30
Dim. of incised surface: 0.41 x 0.24
State of preservation: single block, some edges damaged, but all finished faces present. Clear traces of flat chisel marks. Left side very roughly finished, but surface was worked with flat chisel. Approximately two-thirds of incised surface present.

Description: Complex series of overlapping patterns: at left, a lion facing right, rounded head, nose, eyes, curly mane, wrinkled muzzle, and open mouth with tongue extended and curled up, all visible; beautifully drawn. Small circle and line above lion's head appears to be trial sketch for lion nose and face, abandoned. To the right and slightly below the lion, a horse, more crudely drawn; head lifted up slightly, ear pointed forward, four legs and tail clear. Above hind quarters of horse, a round object which becomes narrow, then flares out again and has flat lower surface. Two small circles in upper part look like eyes, whole figure reminiscent of schematic Phrygian idol. From flat bottom of this figure extend two long stilt-like projections, perhaps legs? To right of this, a sitting bird in right profile, incomplete. To right, a billygoat facing left, nose, line across muzzle with beard, curved horn, collar on neck; all four legs and tail visible and carefully drawn. Above goat, body of upright bird at rest, in right profile. Drawn over goat and both birds are three compass-drawn arcs, all very light, one forming a partial rosette with three petals present. All arcs are the same diameter, ca. 0.86 m. To right of upright bird and circles, an open, angular boomerang-shaped object with internal cross-hatching. To far right, two hand-drawn concentric circles. Behind hind quarters of goat extending to right edge of stone, large geometric pattern consisting of rectangle in double outline (three lines form right side), divided in half vertically by three vertical lines, each half has vertical row of X patterns drawn with three parallel lines (cf. 30). At left

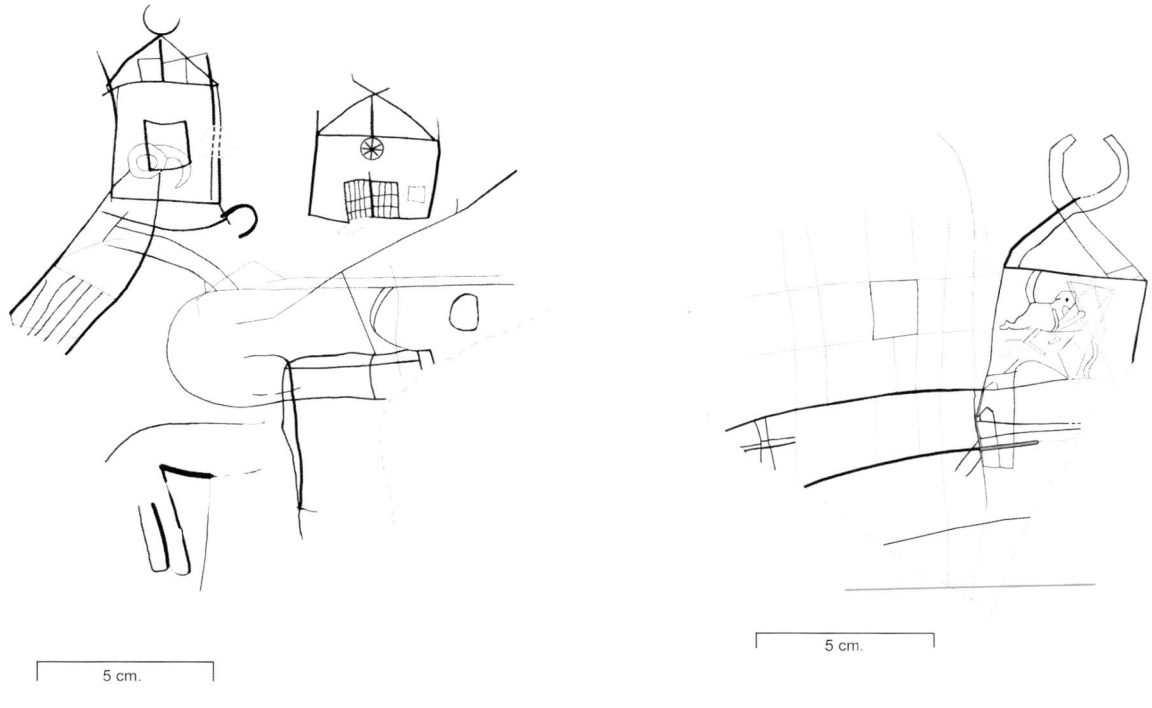

9a: ST 263a

9b: ST 263b

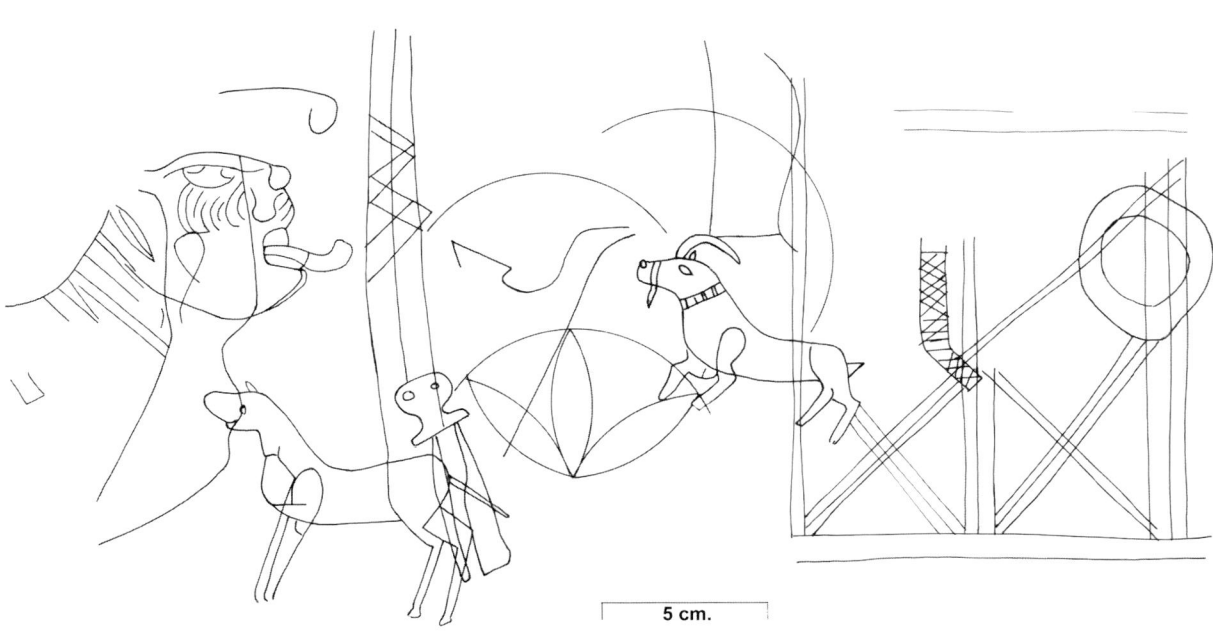

10: ST 264

center, to right of lion and behind round idol-like figure, three vertical lines, irregularly drawn, zigzag pattern lightly incised on this.

Drawing contains many overlapping patterns, but apparently geometric designs at right were drawn on first, then animal figures, horse on top of lion, Phrygian idol over horse, then lightly scored arcs.
Previous bibliography: Young 1969a:274 bottom; Prayon 1987: fig. 28d (uncorrected); Roller 1999a:147, fig. 6 (corrected).

11 Bird; star; bird
4025 ST 265
Megaron 2, east wall
Dim. of block: PL. 0.24, H. 0.23, Th. 0.08
State of preservation: single block preserves part of front, top, bottom, and left surfaces; back and right section of block missing.

Description: at top left, two parallel vertical lines, top of right line curved, joins left line. At right, a five-pointed star; below this, a large bird of prey facing right; eye, outstretched talons, wings, and tail carefully and intricately drawn, detailed lines on body, wings, and tail of bird indicate feathers. In lower right section of block, upright bird facing right, eye, beak, and talons visible, no other internal details. Above, faint outline of large bird in profile covers part of star and head of lower right bird. Other random lines in the field.
Previous bibliography: Young 1969a:274; Prayon 1987: fig. 28e.

12 Symbols; bird; horse; lion
4026 ST 266
Megaron 2, east wall face
Dim. of block: L. 0.56, H. 0.15, Th. 0.34
Dim. of incised surface: 0.52 x 0.15
State of preservation: single block of stone, some edges chipped, but otherwise fully preserved. No traces of burning. Powdery white stone, rough surface.

Description: At left, set of two concentric rectangles, each with double outline; next, a vertical band with diagonal latticing on interior. To the right, head and beak of a bird facing left; then an animal, perhaps a horse, three front legs, two rear legs, and tail visible; on horse's head, a diamond-shaped eye and two ears, one rounded, one pointed; random lines superimposed on animal. At far right, part of another animal, perhaps a lion walking right, only outline of torso, upper edge of neck, and beginning of hind leg present on stone; a few pairs of double lines, straight and curved, may indicate lion's fur.

13 Two animals, formless marks
4027 ST 267
Megaron 2, east wall face
Dim. of block: PL. 0.48, PH. 0.17–0.19, PTh. 0.29
Dim. of inscribed surface: 0.48 x 0.19
State of preservation: single block, several cracks and gaps on finished front surface. Block covered with salts. Right edge broken, other surfaces appear to be original, although all but front face very roughly finished. Marks of flat chisel clearly visible on all finished surfaces but front.

Description: at left, two curved lines which may have been outline of sitting bird body, overlaid by irregular L-outline drawn with multiple lines. To right, very light diamond scoring, above this, uncertain shape, may be an animal. On right side, quadruped, perhaps a horse walking right. Animal and bird drawings overlaid with series of deeply gouged parallel vertical lines which run over whole face of stone, applied after animal figures were drawn.

14 Two warriors; man; ball/sun; bird; lion
4028 ST 268
Megaron 2, east wall face
Dim. of block: PL. 0.28, H. 0.23, PTh. 0.45
State of preservation: single block, broken at left, preserves top, bottom, and part of right face, also part of incised front face. Right front corner missing.

Description: in upper left corner, lightly incised standing male figure who faces left, hair drawn back in pigtail at the nape of the neck. Light rectangular latticing above this figure. Central scene has several overlapping figures; main scene depicts two standing male figures who face each other. Both wear helmets (note the crest on the helmet of the figure at

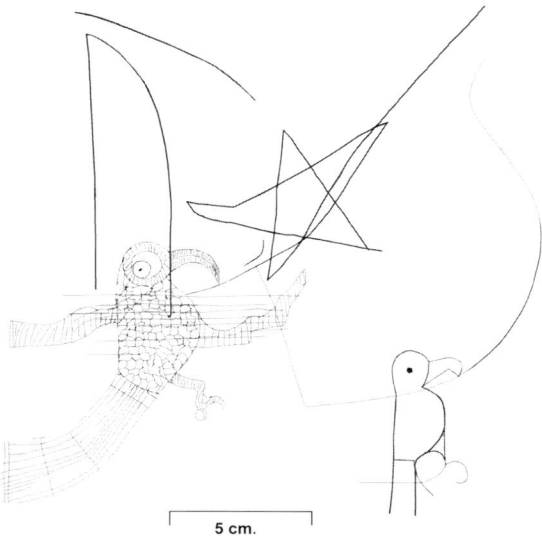

11: ST 265

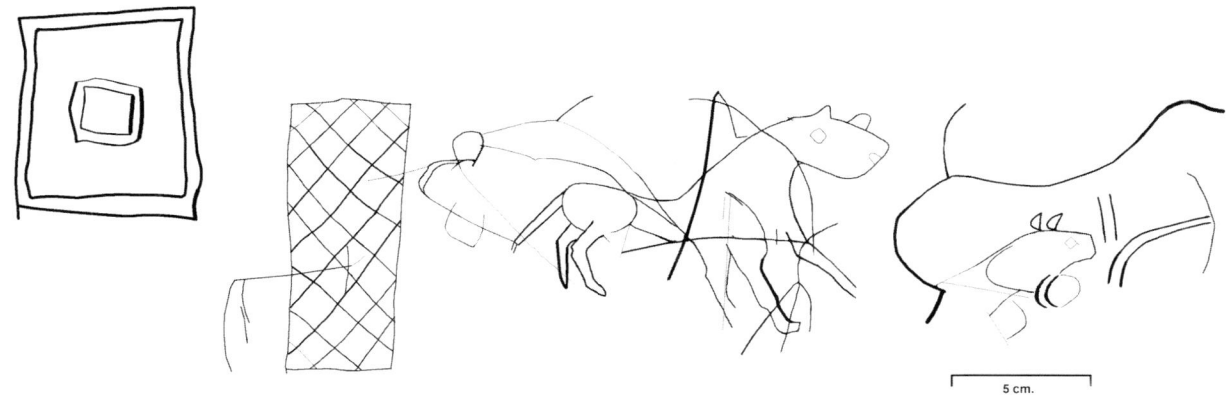

12: ST 266

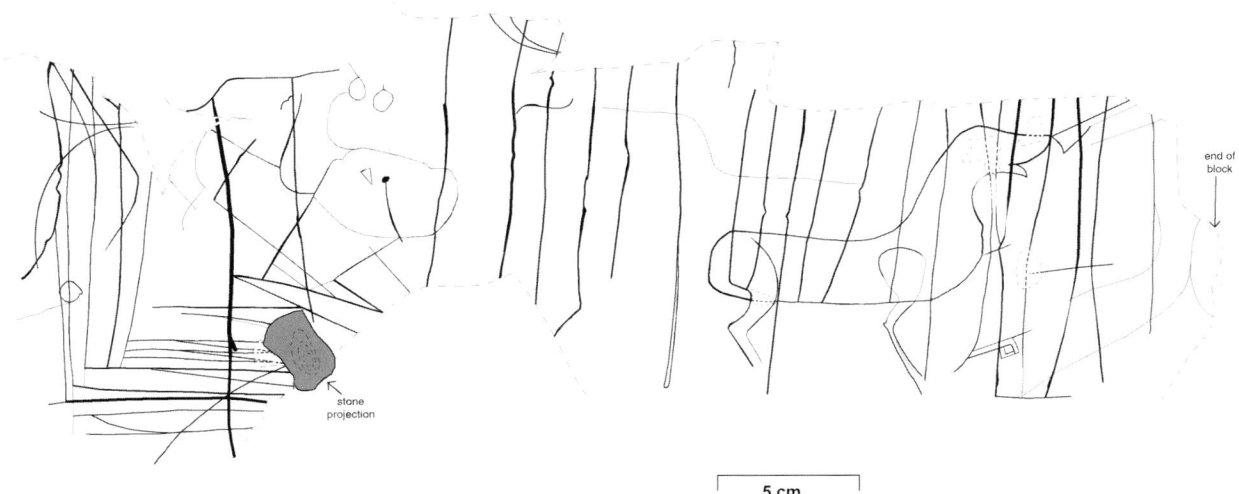

13: ST 267

right) and a short kilt or loin cloth. One prominent eye visible in each figure, also prominent nose, which may be nose piece of helmet. Man at left stands as if with chest to viewer, left arm extended towards opponent, three outstretched fingers clearly visible, right arm drawn back behind him, holds elongated object, probably intended to depict a sword held in right hand. Figure has rounded chest area, perhaps intended to depict a breastplate, wears short kilt over lower torso; one curved foot visible, perhaps to indicate shoes with pointed toes. Figure at right has similar costume, with helmet, kilt, and breastplate; stands with chest towards viewer, extends right arm towards opponent, has elongated hand that may be intended to show weapon; left arm back by his side.

Under right figure of armed pair, a lion walking right, body, tail, and three legs visible, head not preserved. Above left figure of armed pair, a bird in right profile, sitting, has small head and large body, perhaps a dove or goose. Near bird's head is a large round object, perhaps a sun or a ball in mid-air. To the left of this bird and overlapping sitting bird and left armed figure, outline of a much larger bird, upright and facing left; its prominent beak suggests a raptor.

Previous bibliography: Young 1957: pl. 90, fig. 11 (actual stone); Young 1969a:270; Prayon 1987: fig. 28c (drawing); Roller 2007: fig. 1 (corrected drawing).

15 Symbol: diamond
4045 ST 269
Megaron 2, east wall face
Dim. of block: PL. 0.21, H. 0.20, PTh. 0.16
State of preservation: single block, preserves small part of upper and lower surfaces and incised face, broken at right, left, and back. Trace of burning at left.

Description: large diamond with internal cross-hatching in center of incised area; one corner extended to make more regular diamond shape, extension area has no internal lines. Random lines in the field around diamond.

16 Three birds; formless marks
4046 ST 270
Megaron 2, east wall face
Dim. of block: PL. 0.20, H. 0.15, PTh. 0.22
State of preservation: fragment of single block, preserves top, bottom, and right surface, left edge missing. Several new chips in incised surface.

Description: three upright birds in a row facing right, all with the hooked beak of a bird of prey. Two birds at left crudely drawn; bird at right more carefully drawn, outstretched wings and tail have internal lines to show feathers. Irregularly drawn concentric circles over left two birds. Vertical scoring over all.

17 Hand-drawn arcs
4047 ST 271
Megaron 2, east wall face
Dim. of block: PL. 0.09, PH. 0.09, PTh. 0.12
State of preservation: two joining pieces (mended) preserve small section of one end of block, small part of drawing face and one side preserved.

Description: series of lines that appear to form part of a set of arcs from hand-drawn concentric circles. Similar designs on **37**, **60**, **94**, and **104**.

18 Symbols
4048 ST 272
Megaron 2, east wall face
Dim. of block: PL. 0.14, H. 0.17, PTh. 0.29
State of preservation: single piece, preserves parts of top, bottom, and incised front surfaces; both sides missing.

Description: series of irregular geometric patterns. In center, X in square, one side of square touches arc of hand-drawn circle; above and to the right, a row of in-and-out crenellated lines; at right, smaller circle with internal rectangles; above this, irregular arcs and latticing.

19 Two birds; possibly a human arm
4049 ST 273
Megaron 2, east wall
Dim. of block: PL. 0.24, PH. 0.16, PTh. 0.12
Dim. of incised face: 0.18 x 0.16
State of preservation: single block, top, both sides, and back surfaces broken, lower part of front face present, upper part abraded.

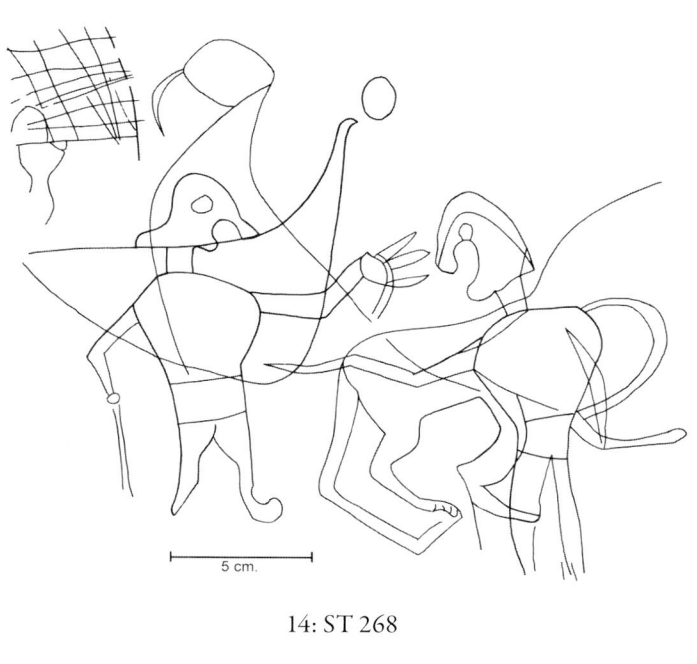

14: ST 268

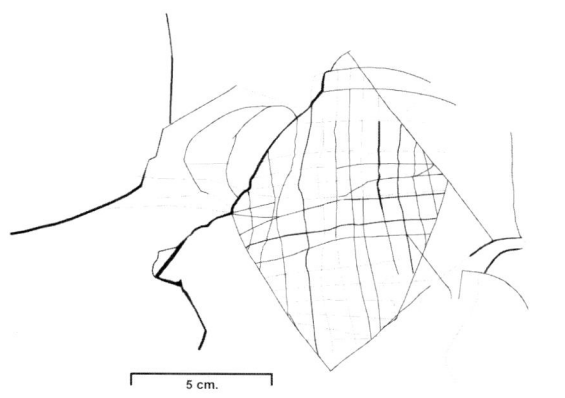

15: ST 269

16: ST 270

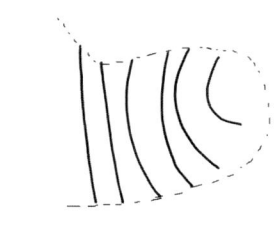

17: ST 271

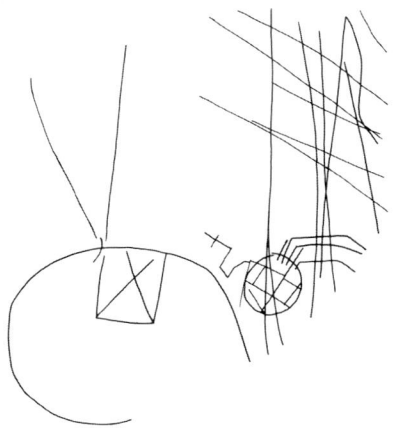

18: ST 272

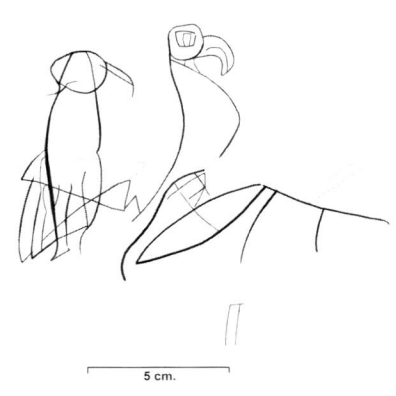

19: ST 273

Description: two birds of prey in right profile; both with prominent curved beaks. Bird at right appears to rest on an object represented by curved lines, perhaps a perch or outstretched human arm.
Previous bibliography: Young 1969a:275; Mellink 1983:358, fig. 2; Prayon 1987: fig. 28f; Roller, forthcoming: fig. 4.

20 Three birds; symbols
4050 ST 274
Megaron 2, east wall
Dim. of block: PL. 0.28, H. 0.21, PTh. 0.27
State of preservation: single block, broken at left; top, bottom, and right front surfaces present; large abraded area on upper right of incised front face; several large chips in incised surface.

Description: at upper left, vertical rectangle with irregular diagonal cross-hatching inside; curved lines to the left of this, perhaps beginning of a bird. Across lower half, three birds in a row, all in right profile, all have prominent beaks suggesting birds of prey; right bird has extra lines over it, now much damaged by surface chips. Left bird has outstretched wings.

21 Bird
4171 ST 281
Megaron 2, east wall face, found in situ above outside ledge
Dim. of block: PL. 0.24, H. 0.19, Th. 0.31
State of preservation: left section of block present, preserves left side; mended from two pieces joining front to back.

Description: bird facing right, head, beak, and eye visible, long narrow body, beginning of tail, no wings, legs, or other internal details present; drawing gives the impression of a bird of prey wrapped in a long cloak. Hand-drawn circles at right.
Previous bibliography: Roller, forthcoming, fig. 7.

22 Latticing
4172 ST 282
Megaron 2, east wall, found in situ above outside ledge
Dim. of block: PL. 0.26, H. 0.13, PTh. 0.22
Dim. of inscribed surface: 0.16 x 0.11
State of preservation: single block, part of incised face and lower face preserved, all other faces missing. Underside carefully smoothed, a few chisel marks observable, traces of mud plaster (fine light brown plaster) preserved.

Description: diagonal cross-hatching with horizontal lines to form triangle pattern.

23 Maze
4173 ST 283
Megaron 2, east wall
Dim. of block: PL. 0.25, PH. 0.125, PTh. 0.21
Dim. of inscribed surface: 0.25 x 0.12
State of preservation: single block, preserves part of incised front surface, and top and side surfaces. Right edge very rough, top roughly finished with flat chisel.

Description: maze pattern consisting of a double-outlined rectangle with internal design of swastika and interlocking hooks.

24 Symbol
4174 ST 284
Megaron 2, east wall
Dim. of block: PL. 0.28, H. 0.12, PTh. 0.24
Dim. of incised face: 0.23 x 0.12
State of preservation: block mended from two joining fragments of coarse limestone. Preserves part of incised front face and lower surface, large part of upper surface, and left surface. Several large chips in stone, right side and lower left edge missing.

Description: in center of preserved face, loop suspended from vertical line, inverted D at right joined to loop by two diagonal lines forming left-facing V. Other random lines in the field.

25 Asterisk; lion
4175 ST 285
Megaron 2, east wall
Dim. of block: L. 0.23, H. 0.16, Th. 0.24
State of preservation: single block, top, bottom, both sides, and front surfaces present. Front (incised) face cracked and has several gaps, covered with small pits and holes.

20: ST 274

21: ST 281

22: ST 282

23: ST 283

24: ST 284

25: ST 285

Description: at left, simple asterisk; at right, crudely drawn lion walking right. Lion has drilled hole for eye, mouth open at a 90° angle. Other random lines in the field.

26 Bird; two bird heads
 4176 ST 286
 Megaron 2, east wall
 Dim. of block: PL. 0.13, H. 0.19, PTh. 0.29
 Dim. of incised face: 0.13 x 0.10
 State of preservation: single block, preserves top, right, and bottom surfaces, small part of incised face.

Description: seated bird of prey facing right; lightly drawn head of another bird above. Upper part of bird's head and eye facing right visible along lower edge of surviving front face. Other random lines in the field.

27 Bird; symbol
 4177 ST 287
 Megaron 2, east wall
 Dim. of block: L. 0.53, H. 0.19, Th. 0.34
 State of preservation: block mended from two joining fragments, original dimensions preserved. Large abraded area in center of front surface; large chip at bottom of front surface near join.

Description: at top left, bird facing left, body looks like sitting hen, has large rounded beak; below this are two lines, perhaps legs of bird. At right, series of rectangles that look like superimposed blocks, curved line extending to right. All lines below bird are very faint.

28 Two branches
 4178 ST 288
 Megaron 2, east wall
 Dim. of block: PL. 0.28, Max. PH. 0.24, Th. 0.21
 Dim. of incised face: 0.24 x 0.19
 State of preservation: fragment of single block, broken all around, no original surfaces preserved. Incised surface rough and uneven, not finished like other incised stones.

Description: two almost parallel upright branches, nearly complete, apparently carved onto unfinished surface of stone.

29 Lion
 4179 ST 289
 Megaron 2, east wall
 Dim. of block: L. 0.24, H. 0.16, Th. 0.24
 Dim. of inscribed surface: 0.24 x 0.16
 State of preservation: block split in two joining halves, all original worked surfaces present; many chips and abrasions on all finished surfaces including incised front surface.

Description: lion walking right. Lion has curved claws, upward curling tail, small circles on front and back legs indicating musculature. Irregular incised lines indicate lion's mane. Lion's mouth open, but surface of mouth now abraded, cannot determine whether tongue was present.

30 Symbol
 4180 ST 290
 Megaron 2, east wall
 Dim. of block: PL. 0.33, H. 0.18, PTh. 0.31
 Dim. of inscribed surface: 0.30 x 0.18
 State of preservation: Single block, upper and lower surface and part of left side preserved. Back surface gone, broken at right.

Description: rectangle, approximately 0.11 x 0.12, with internal X and cross. Three sides of rectangle outlined with three lines, fourth side has two lines. X pattern across rectangle formed by two sets of three lines; cross pattern composed of three vertical lines, two horizontal lines.

31 Man; star
 4181 ST 291
 Megaron 2, east wall
 Dim. of block: PL. 0.34, H. 0.19, Th. 0.52
 State of preservation: single block preserves portion of incised front face, lower and right surfaces; top surface and left side missing. Lower surface undercut towards front, probably to fit pre-existing block. All unfinished faces very rough, with visible marks of broad flat chisel. Drawing on right

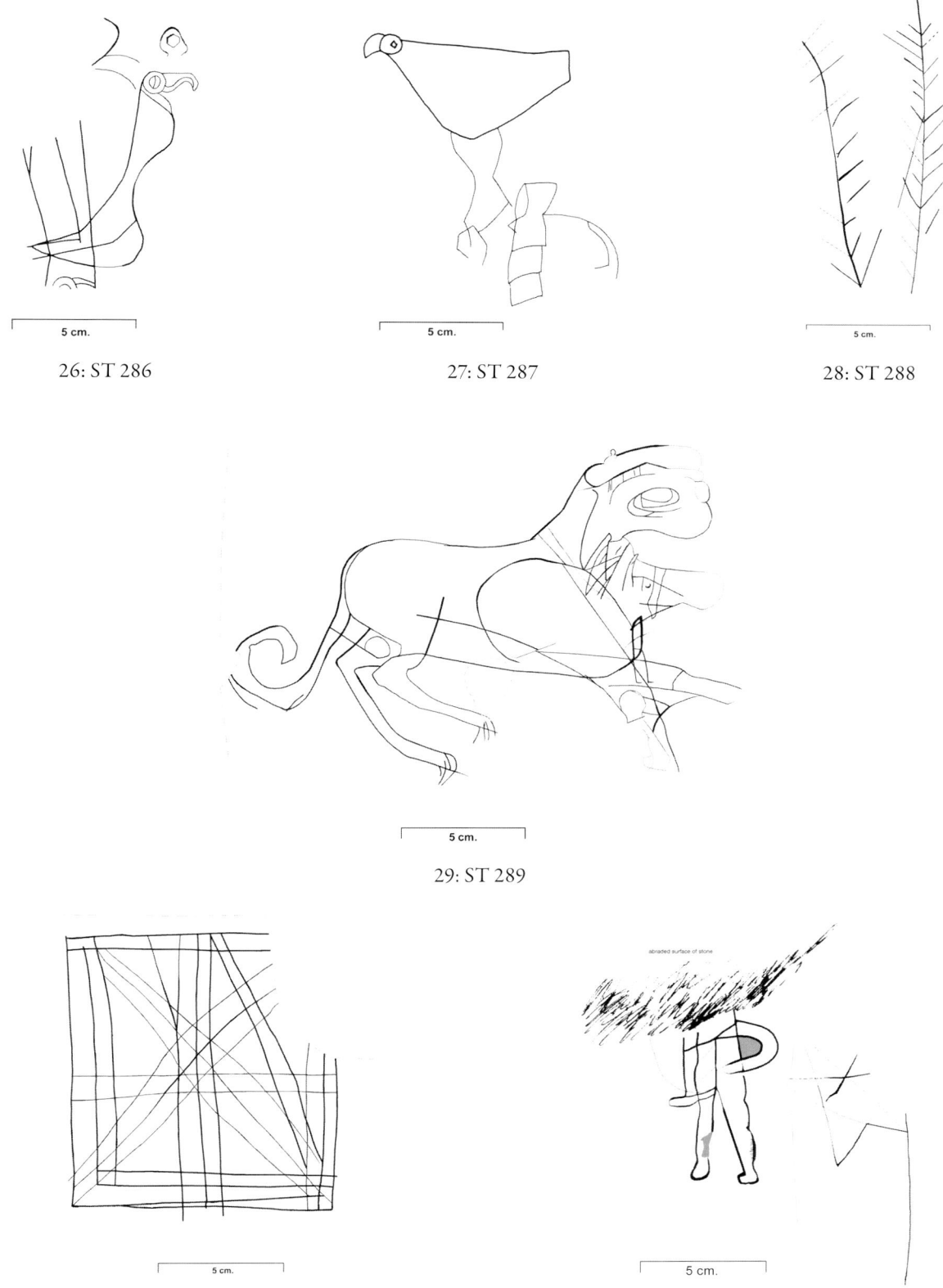

26: ST 286

27: ST 287

28: ST 288

29: ST 289

30: ST 290

31: ST 291

side of front surface, surface now much abraded, many gouges and chips so drawing only partially preserved.

Description: male figure, body shown full front, feet in left profile, has left hand on hip, right hand down by his side. Line at waist may indicate belt; otherwise no indication of clothing. Below figure's right hand, a horizontal projection may be intended to show weapon. At left of figure, curved line that may represent a bow held in figure's right hand, or may be a random line. Figure is deeply incised, almost as if intended as relief sculpture. At far right, a five-pointed star.

32 Formless marks; lion; symbols
4182 ST 292
Megaron 2, east wall
Dim. of block: PL. 0.46, PH. 0.13, Th. 0.27
State of preservation: block mended from several joining pieces, preserves upper part of block and right face, left face missing, top and bottom surfaces gone; no way to tell where drawing placed on original stone.

Description: at far left, carelessly drawn asterisk. In center, irregular two-pronged object, series of parallel lines radiating out from this; to the right, a large animal shown rampant, perhaps a lion. Two double-outlined zigzag shapes at right; several random lines and arcs in the field. Subject uncertain.

33 Man with spear; animal; symbols
4183 ST 293
Megaron 2, east wall
Dim. of block: PL. 0.42, H. 0.24, PTh. 0.41
State of preservation: single block, preserves top and bottom faces, part of incised front face, both sides missing. Front face very roughly finished, chisel marks visible over whole surface, large abrasion at left and in upper right corner.

Description: at left, standing human figure, wears long, belted garment; figure's head and body shown full front, legs in right profile; done in crude attempt to create low relief, note the deep cavities for eyes, nostrils, mouth, and legs and feet. Left arm of figure holds a long pointed object, perhaps a spear, together with an object that may be a shield drawn in profile, or alternatively a bow and arrow. At right side of stone, head of an animal with tongue sticking out, one eye visible, ribbon-like object which may be ear on top of head. Other marks, some partially destroyed by large abraded area, include forms like the head of a small animal, a human foot, a bird's tail, D form, and other random lines.

34 Formless marks; circles; perhaps bird head
4184 ST 294
Megaron 2, east wall
Dim. of block: L. 0.66, H. 0.19, Th. 0.32
Dim. of inscribed surface: 0.38 x 0.13
State of preservation: roughly two-thirds of finished face remains, lower edge and right side missing. Finished surface very rough, chisel marks visible.

Description: complicated set of graffiti, probably all formless marks. From left: latticing at upper left; below this, irregular lines extending to right. Next, arcs of compass-drawn circles; half of smaller compass-drawn circle; two irregular concentric circles with pointed object in the middle, perhaps bird head drawn at 90° right angle to bottom edge of stone. At far right, several triangles or flag designs, two roughly parallel lines form ribbon design (cf. **35**). Other random lines in the field.

35 Symbol
4186 ST 295
Megaron 2, east wall face
Dim. of block: PL. 0.27, PH. 0.08, PTh. 0.34
State of preservation: block mended from three joining pieces, preserves what appears to be top (or bottom) segment of larger block broken laterally; top and right surfaces present.

Description: series of two parallel lines forming bows and arcs, almost like tree or ribbon pattern. (Note similar lines in **89**.)

36 Formless marks
4186 ST 296
Megaron 2, east wall face

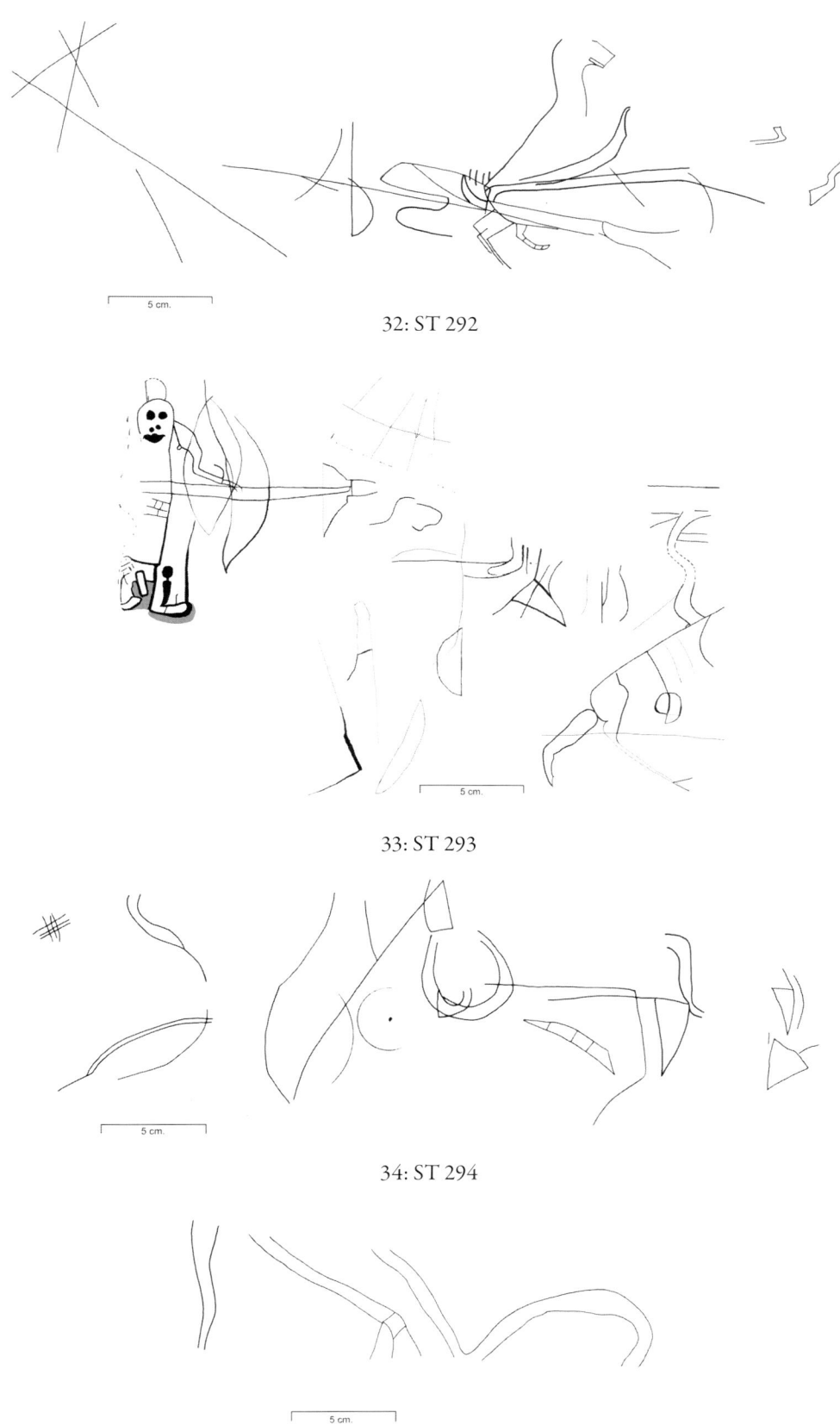

32: ST 292

33: ST 293

34: ST 294

35: ST 295

Dim. of block: L. 0.19, H. 0.18, PTh. 0.27
State of preservation: single block preserving part or all of top, bottom, both sides, and front surfaces. Upper left corner missing, large chip on right edge. Incised face rough and uneven.

Description: two lines that meet to form an acute angle. At left, half circle and smaller circle, very lightly incised.

37 Symbols; bow and arrow; hand-drawn circles
4187 ST 297
Megaron 2, east wall face
Dim. of block: PL. 0.18, H. 0.17, Th. 0.28
State of preservation: single block, broken on both sides; top and bottom surfaces and part of incised front face preserved. Finished front surface very rough, chisel marks visible.

Description: at left, arcs form a series of five hand-drawn concentric circles (note a similar pattern on **17, 60, 94,** and **104**). At bottom center, rectangular panel with central vertical line bisecting column of lozenges; single lozenge to the left, irregular circles to right of lozenges. Panel bounded by three vertical lines at right and one at left; two horizontal lines at the top and two at bottom; between the pair of horizontal lines at bottom is a row of short vertical lines. At upper right, arc of crudely drawn bow and horizontal shaft with sharp point on it, perhaps a bow and arrow held by a human figure, now missing. (Cf. **2, 5, 33**.)

38 Building; lion; bird
4188 ST 298
Megaron 2, east wall face
Dim. of block: L. 0.55, H. 0.22, PTh. 0.48
Dim. of incised face: 0.42 x 0.22
State of preservation: block mended from several joining pieces; joined whole appears to preserve entire wall block except for large chunk from lower left corner.

Description: at upper left, drawing of what appears to be an architectural structure; basic form is an irregular rectangle framed by single vertical line on each side, two parallel horizontal lines on top and bottom; in center are two parallel vertical lines with a pair of lines extending out diagonally from these to top corners of rectangle; irregular triangle above central vertical lines. The effect is very much like the front of an architectural structure made of wooden beams; double lines may indicate horizontal and diagonal bracing. Central triangular projection at top may either be a central tower or a decorative feature above the structure. Below this, series of parallel horizontal lines, all hand drawn and irregular (could indicate steps up to the structure). To the right of these, head of a large lion facing right, prominent eye, open mouth with tongue hanging out; series of irregular lines around lion's neck may indicate mane, but there is a large gap in stone in the middle of the lion's head, so some details not clear. To right of lion, elongated vertical profile of bird with long tail.
Previous bibliography: Roller, forthcoming: fig. 8-9.

39 Branch; formless marks
4189 ST 299
Megaron 2, east wall face
Dim. of block: L. 0.45, H. 0.20, Th. 0.47
Dim. of incised surface: 0.31 x 0.19
State of preservation: single block, preserves all original surfaces (top, bottom, both sides, and front). Incised front surface lacks edges, has several large chips.

Description: mostly random marks; at left, an inverted branch; to the right of branch, two parallel vertical lines, irregular hand-drawn circle below; at right, various horizontal, vertical, and diagonal lines in no discernible pattern.

40 Symbols; formless marks
4190 ST 300
Megaron 2, east wall face
Dim. of block: PL. 0.20, H. 0.23, Th. 0.30
State of preservation: single block, preserves original top and bottom surfaces and small part of incised front face. Both sides missing.

Description: at upper left, large irregular ellipse with random lines crossing it; below this, irregular shape,

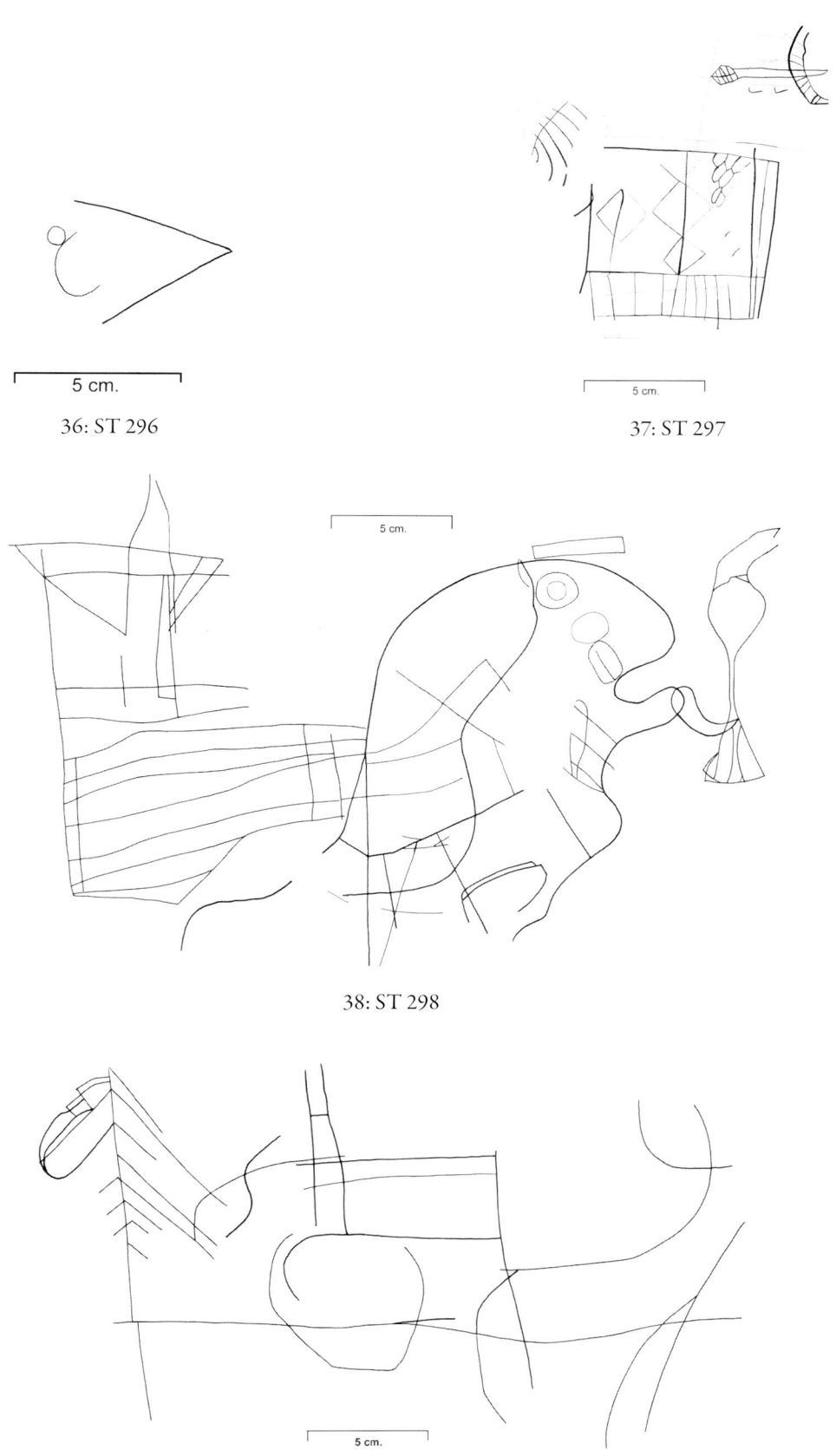

36: ST 296

37: ST 297

38: ST 298

39: ST 299

perhaps a bird's wing covered with cross-hatching (body of bird would be on missing section of stone), rectangle with internal cross-hatching below this. At right, large irregular ellipse, other random lines and arcs, no observable subject or pattern.

41 Bird; bird head; formless marks
   4191 ST 301
   Megaron 2, east wall
   Dim. of block: PL. 0.31, PH. 0.20, PTh. 0.30
   Dim. of inscribed surface: 0.18 x 0.16
   State of preservation: single piece, small part of face preserved and some evidence of roughly worked chisel marks on undersurface. All other surfaces broken. Incised front face of block very rough, many chisel marks still visible.

Description: in center, bird in right profile with long neck, like a swan, drawn at an angle of approximately 135° to base of block; to the left, part of a bird's head and beak along break of stone, drawn at 90° angle to base of block. Around them are what appears to be a random variety of shapes and lines, including a human foot and leg, triangles, and several straight and curved lines in no discernable pattern.

42 Latticing, circle
   4192 ST 302
   Megaron 2, east wall
   Dim. of block: PL. 0.18, H. 0.14, PTh. 0.085
   State of preservation: small fragment of block, preserves part of top and incised front face, otherwise broken all around.

Description: horizontal and vertical lines forming irregular latticing pattern; more heavily incised lines over latticing; arc of compass-drawn circle at right.

43 Symbols; formless marks
   4193 ST 303
   Megaron 2, east wall
   Dim. of block: PL. 0.23, H. 0.17, PTh. 0.17
   Dim. of inscribed surface: 0.18 x 0.13
   State of preservation: block mended from four large and several small joining pieces; top, bottom, right side surfaces and part of incised face preserved. Incised face has slightly orange tint to surface, perhaps the result of lichen.

Description: series of random lines and geometric patterns. In center, two roughly parallel vertical lines; two (and possibly more) vertical lozenges bisect left line and alternate with double triangles along right line that project left. To right of vertical pattern, a hand-drawn circle, deeply incised. Crudely drawn zigzag lines at left. Several lightly scored lines over whole surface.

44 Hunter and hare
   4403 ST 315
   Megaron 2, east wall
   Dim. of block: PL. 0.26, H. 0.20, PTh. 0.12
   Dim. of incised surface: 0.24 x 0.20
   State of preservation: single block, preserves top, bottom, and right faces, part of incised front surface.

Description: central scene depicts a standing male facing right, head and legs shown in profile, torso full front; figure's hair is drawn back into a pigtail at the nape of the neck; one eye visible. Figure is nude except for broad belt with geometric ornament and short kilt. Below kilt are three projections that curve down, forward, and then back, perhaps meant as fringe or tassels, shown as if blowing forward. Over the kilt is a horizontal object that projects forward, perhaps a weapon (cf. **31**, **59** right figure). Left arm of figure extends forward and bends at the elbow, fingers visible; hand holds end of a looped cord, frayed ends visible on other side of fist. Cord loops down to a bag containing a hare held upside down; two long ears, one eye, and front paw of animal visible. To the right of this is the outline of pair of hare ears, perhaps a trial sketch, later abandoned. Right arm of figure extends back behind figure's head, upper arm bent up at elbow, fingers visible; hand holds a weapon, perhaps a two-headed axe, that is turned inward towards the striding figure's head. Figure has prominent buttocks and thighs that taper to small pointed legs, no feet visible. Figure appears to be a hunter who is holding a weapon in his right hand, bagged hare in left hand, shown as if striding forward; the effect of the fringe on the kilt is to emphasize the figure's movement. Other random lines in the field at left of human figure. Much of the figured scene is covered by irregular chisel marks and heavy scoring that was done after the figured scene was incised, as if to obliterate scene.
Previous bibliography: Roller 1999a: fig. 4.

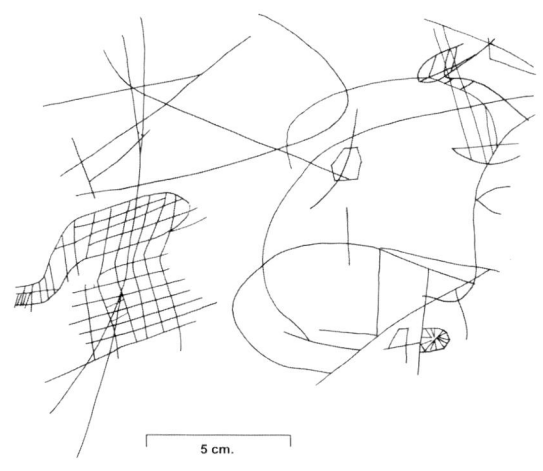

40: ST 300

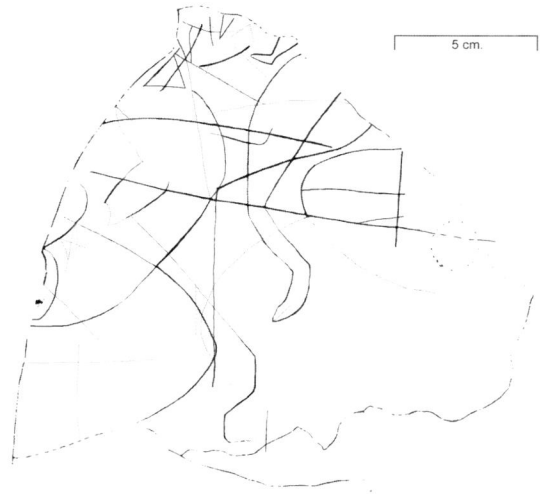

41: ST 301

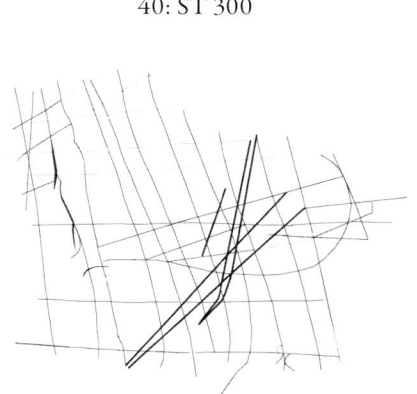

42: ST 302

43: ST 303

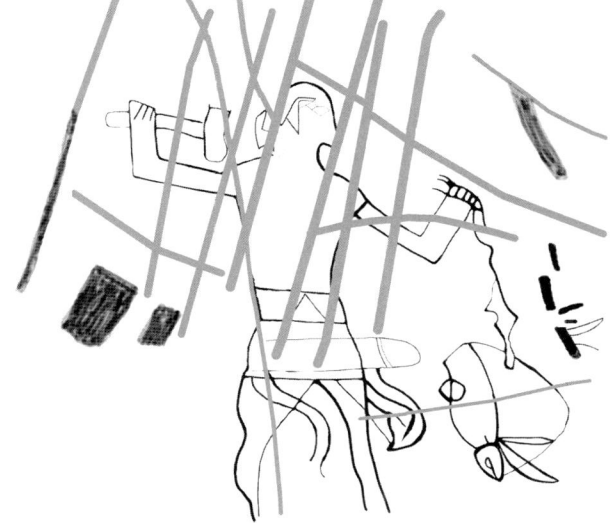

44: ST 315

44: ST 315
same scale, without lines

45 Lion
4422 ST 316
Megaron 2, fallen from east wall
Dim. of block: L. 0.19, H. 0.19, PTh. 0.22
State of preservation: single block, large chip missing from lower right corner. Top, bottom, and both side surfaces and most of incised face preserved.

Description: crudely drawn lion walking left, mouth open; below lion, several random lines.

46 Man; two birds; building; bird
4423 ST 317
Megaron 2, east wall, third buttress from south
Dim. of block: L. 0.64, H. 0.15, Th. 0.34
Dim. of inscribed surface: 0.24 x 0.15 (left); 0.22 x 0.12 (right)
State of preservation: large stone, mended from five (originally six) pieces. Mended together at time of discovery, but now two large separate pieces made up of two (left) and three (right) fragments; one piece from center front surface now missing.

Description, left section: bird in flight; next, a standing male figure, body full front, head in right profile; figure wears flat-topped headdress (cf. **71**, **77**), upper torso nude, lower torso has short kilt, on right side object tucked into belt, perhaps dagger or short sword. Figure stands with legs apart, right arm stretched back and bent up at elbow, left arm straight outstretched; at right, another bird in flight.

Description, right section: long curved line which may be the back of a lion; below this, a schematic bird in profile; above this, the body of a bird of prey in left profile, drawn at a 90° counterclockwise angle to the other objects on the stone. At far right, another schematic bird in profile; at the right end, the narrow end of building with gabled roof and akroterion, doorway in center; below building, horizontal line bisected by vertical line, perhaps to indicate step or entranceway (cf. **9b**).

Previous bibliography: Roller, forthcoming: fig. 5-6.

47 Animals; man; lion; bird; marks
4424 ST 318
Megaron 2, east wall, third buttress from south
Dim. of block: L. 0.73, H. 0.17, Th. 0.28
State of preservation: two joining pieces, mended to complete.

Description: at left, large irregular quadruped; next, irregular body, legs, and head of an animal walking right; head and left foreleg seem almost humanoid. Above this, an irregular hand-drawn circle and lines. Next right, a lion walking right, mouth open, muzzle and eye visible, one front leg with claws; next, back of another lion walking right, head and beak of bird of prey drawn over second lion's body. To right of break in stone: head of large lion; at far right, outline of lion body, diamond cross-hatching pattern overall. Along right edge of stone, series of irregular arcs. Several gouges and deeply incised lines over incised drawings; some of these appear to be ancient.

48 Two lions
Block uncovered in July 2004, left in situ, no inventory number
Megaron 2, east wall, 1.85 m from southeast corner, second course above ground level
Dim. of block: L. 0.51, H. 0.23
State of preservation: single block, still in place in the east wall of Megaron 2, surface intact

Description: two lions facing each other. Lion at left more lightly incised, only head and forepart of body present; head has squarish face, ridge indicated at base of neck, pronounced muzzle, tongue hanging from mouth. In lion at right the head, body, and part of rear leg are present; lion has rounded head, open mouth but no tongue. Above left lion, a few random scratches.
Previous bibliography: Roller 2007: fig. 2.

49 Patterns; human figures
5237 ST 344
Megaron 2, southeast corner (note location on drawing by D. H. Cox, fig. 10; see discussion below)
Dim. of block: PL. 0.21, H. 0.19, PTh. 0.09
State of preservation: block mended from many smaller pieces, rectangular chunk missing from lower left corner. Upper and lower surfaces and small part of left side present.

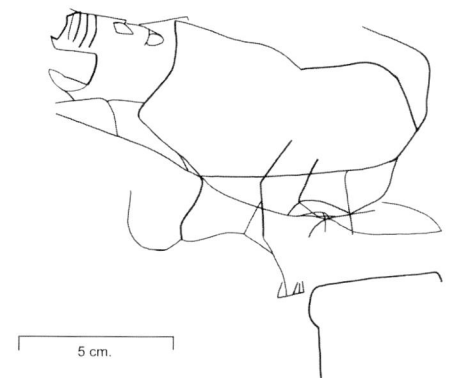

45: ST 316

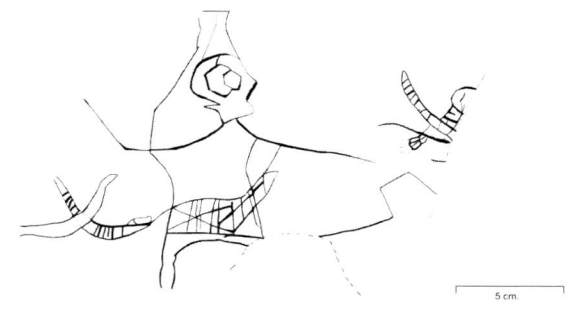
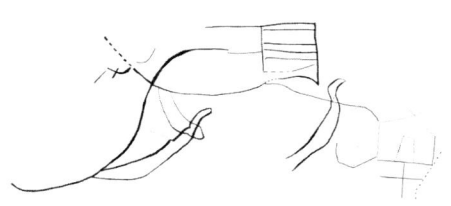

46: ST 317

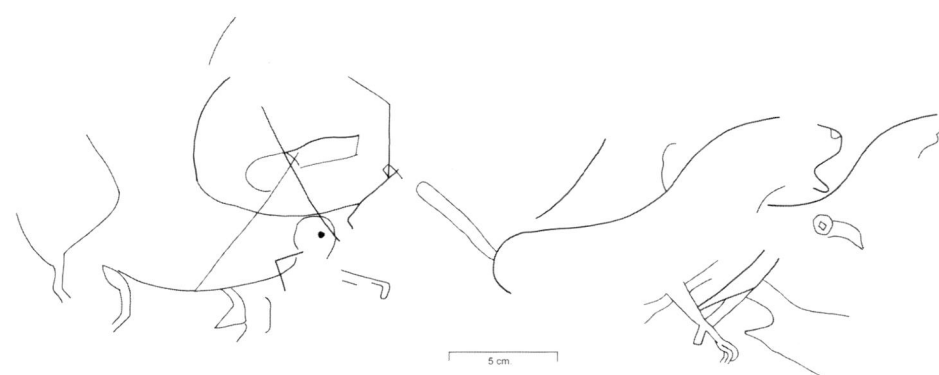

47: ST 318

48: no inventory
number

Description: at left, several parallel hand-drawn vertical lines, a few arcs and lozenges. In lower center, head and simple body of standing human figure, appears to be clad in a long gown, two lines at waist may indicate belt, stippled lines that curve up from upper body may be raised arms, horizontal projections on either side of figure's waist may indicate a weapon. Area above figure's head has lightly scored vertical lines. In upper right corner, rectangle outlined on left side with double lines, hooked rectangles in between them forming a meander pattern, double lines at right with horizontal divisions; this section appears to be a sketch of a complex geometric pattern such as might be found in furniture or textile design.

Note: The following eight drawings, **50–57**, were incised onto eight stones that formed two vertical piers in the east wall near the southeast corner of Megaron 2.[211] These piers were uncovered in 1956 and recorded in 1957 by Dorothy H. Cox, in a drawing that has since been reproduced several times; see Young 1958: pl. 21, fig. 3; Young 1969a:271; Prayon 1987:172, fig. 27a; Prayon 2004:619, fig. 1. The stones were apparently left in situ, although at some point the lower left block was removed to the Gordion depot and catalogued as ST 343 (**53** below). The remaining stones were covered with earth, except for the upper left stone, **50** (ST 839), which was left exposed. Because of its deteriorating condition, ST 839 was brought to the Gordion depot in 1983 and catalogued at that time.

In 2004 the earth was removed from the entire length of the east and west walls of Megaron 2, so that all stones remaining in situ, including the two southeast piers, were exposed. However, the surfaces of the stones in these piers had deteriorated so extensively that all traces of incised drawings that had been visible in 1957 were gone. The following catalogue descriptions and accompanying drawings were reconstructed from photographs taken at the time of excavation in 1956 and 1957. Every effort has been made to be accurate, but the drawings can no longer be verified by autopsy.

The numbering system follows the order of the stones as they appear in D. H. Cox's drawing (see references above): the four stones from the left pier are numbered from top to bottom, then the four stones in the right pier, top to bottom.

50 Bird; two quadrupeds; bird; man; hen; five birds
12537 ST 839a, b
Megaron 2, east wall, southeast corner, top left pier block
Dim. of extant portion of block: PL. 0.36, PH. 0.22, PTh. 0.15
State of preservation: two joining pieces, not fastened together, from larger block. Original block found almost intact (refer to *Archaeology* 22 [1969] for drawing [p. 271] and photo [p. 273] of complete stone). Stone found fallen from wall and brought to museum for inventory in 1983. Now very worn, surface pitted with a series of small holes. Right and left surfaces missing, top left corner and front surface worn away; much of the drawing that was visible at the time of excavation is now gone. The drawing of the whole incised stone has been partially taken from the incised surface now visible, and partially reconstructed from excavation photos made when the stone was first uncovered.

Description: at far left, an upright bird with curved beak facing right; next, hind quarters of two superimposed quadrupeds, perhaps lions; above these, what appears to be a bird facing left, although no beak visible. In center, man with pointed cap facing right, has big belly and fleshy buttocks, right arm drawn back with fingers extended, left arm reaches out, holds curved object that hangs down from his hand. To right of human figure, thirteen circular punch marks, apparently made with a drill, in an irregular vertical row, top to bottom in descending order of size; bottom punch in row at end of curved object held by figure. To right of punch row, a sitting hen facing right, below hen, a bird in flight, shown in right profile; at right of hen, long curved object which may be neck of another bird. At right, another bird, simply drawn, with long body and neck, then two smaller birds in right profile, one at rest, one in flight. Random lines in the field.
Previous bibliography: Young 1969a:273 top (actual stone).

---

211. For the excavation of this area, see Young 1958:142–43.

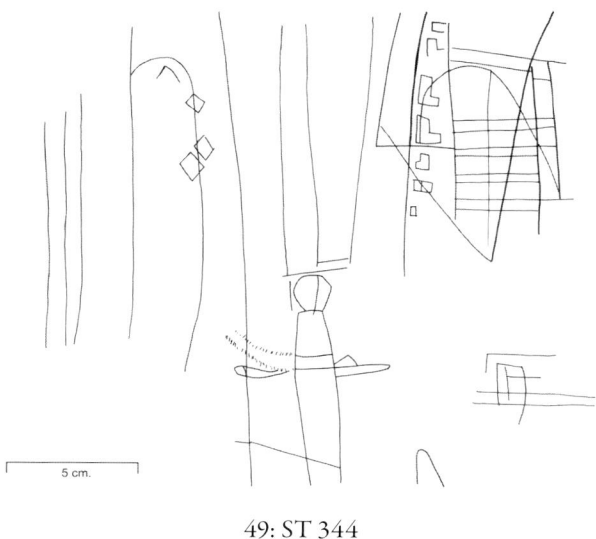

49: ST 344

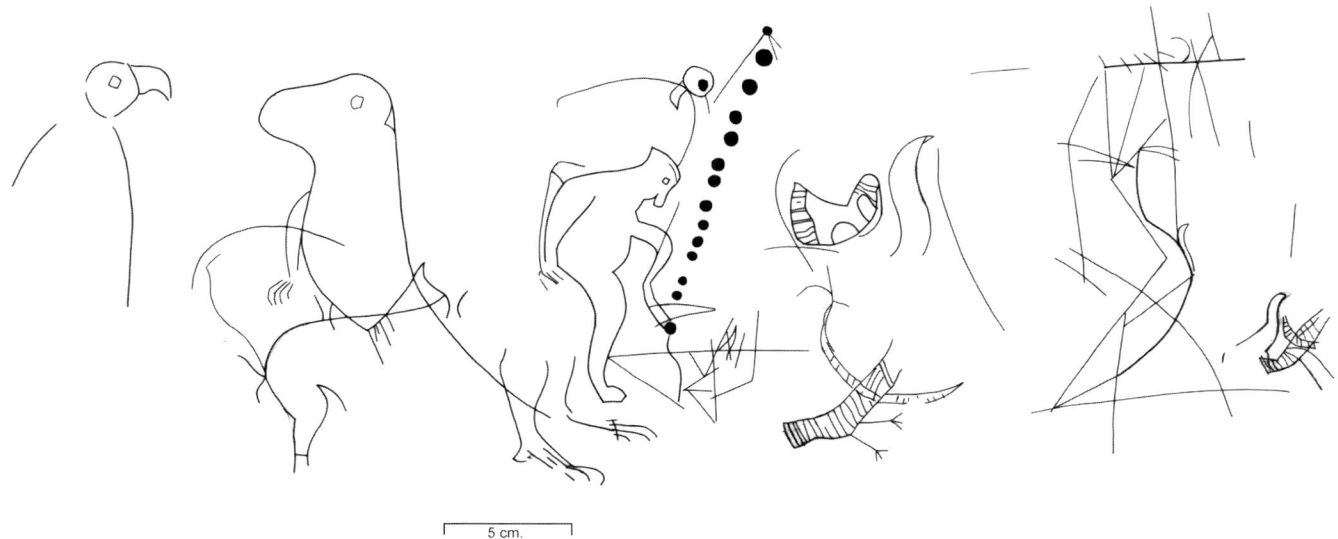

50: ST 839a, b

51 Quadruped; lion; cult idol; bird
No inventory number
Megaron 2, east wall, southeast corner, second stone in left pier
Dim.: unknown

Description: at left, indistinct form, may be quadruped. Next, lion facing right, body and head visible but no legs or tail; lion has squarish muzzle, double half-circle along neck line, perhaps crudely drawn cheek piece (cf. **1, 4, 6**). Next, irregular rectangle, partial circle above it with lines extending out on either side, perhaps intended as a Phrygian idol above a cult monument. At right, bird in right profile; bird has large beak, long tail feathers. Single wing of bird in flight above this.
Previous bibliography: Simpson 1998: pl. 181, fig. 17.

52 Animal; man; symbol
No inventory number
Megaron 2, east wall, southeast corner, third stone in left pier
Dim.: unknown

Description: at left, irregular lines, perhaps simplified drawing of a human being. Next, uncertain form, appears to be an animal (identity uncertain) drawn as if at 90° to base of stone. Next, simple drawing of a human figure, gender uncertain, wearing a long gown and striding right, arms outstretched. At far right, small circle with vertical line extending down; cross, random line.

53 Lion
5236 ST 343
Megaron 2, east wall, southeast corner, fourth stone in left pier
Dim. of block: PL. 0.35, H. 0.24, PTh. 0.24
Dim. of inscribed surface: 0.35 x 0.24
State of preservation: single block of stone, now dark gray and granular-looking. Part of lower surface, right side, and upper surface preserved. Left side probably broken, but block appears to have finely drafted left edge and corner, so left side may have been deliberately unfinished.

Description: lion walking left, has open mouth, tongue hanging out, pointed ears, collar-like ridge on neck, prominent shoulder muscles, long curved claws, circle visible on left rear thigh of animal. Two tails visible, one curves down between legs, the second, probably drawn later, extends up and over back.

54 Two birds; animal; two birds; man; symbol
No inventory number
Megaron 2, east wall, southeast corner, top stone in right pier
Dim.: unknown

Description: at left, bird in right profile, has prominent beak and claws of a bird of prey; tail of another bird visible at right. Next, a simple animal, perhaps a bird; below this, a large bird facing right, has long curved beak and prominent band on tail. Next, a bird in flight and another large bird in right profile; below this, outline of a human figure facing right, probably male, wears short kilt, hair drawn into a pigtail at back of head (cf. **1, 14, 44**). At far right, series of seven roughly parallel vertical lines, the left four of which are joined by a horizontal line at bottom; the central vertical line extends below the horizontal line to create a pattern like a pitchfork.

55 Two birds
No inventory number
Megaron 2, east wall, southeast corner, second stone in right pier
Dim.: unknown

Description: at right side of stone, bird facing left, only part of body, outstretched wing and tail visible. Below this, head and neck of bird facing left; bird has large curved beak.

56 Rectangle; arcs; lion; bird
No inventory number
Megaron 2, east wall, southeast corner, third stone in right pier
Dim.: unknown

Description: at left, irregular rectangle with projection at upper right corner, perhaps a schematic animal head. Next, irregular arc with semi-circle in the center; below this, series of parallel lines forming an

51: no inventory number or scale

52: no inventory number or scale

53: ST 343

54: no inventory number or scale

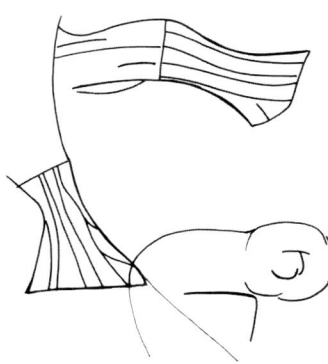

55: no inventory number or scale

irregular pattern of arcs and straight lines (cf. **89**). At right, standing lion facing right; at far right, bird in right profile, partially obscured by random lines scratched over the bird as if to erase it.

57 Rectangle; square; quadruped
No inventory number
Megaron 2, east wall, southeast corner, fourth stone in right pier
Dim.: unknown

Description: irregular rectangle at left, similar to the tail of a bird. Next, irregular square with large and small X patterns inside. At right, schematic quadruped with pointed nose, identity uncertain.

58 Lion; compass-drawn circle; formless marks
4698 ST 333
Found between Megaron 1 and Megaron 2, presumably fallen from Megaron 2, east wall
Dim. of block: PL. 0.15, PH. 0.14, PTh. 0.80
Dim. of inscribed surface: 0.15 x 0.11
State of preservation: single piece, part of finished left surface preserved, otherwise broken all around. Surface at upper right of stone heavily abraded, but lines of incised drawing still visible.

Description: lion walking right, tail, body, neck, and four legs with curved claws visible; head missing. Deep vertical line incised across surface of stone over drawing of lion, done after drawing was made. Above lion, random scratches, including arc of compass-drawn circle.

59 Latticing; two men fighting; bird; animal; two men fighting; ball/sun; formless marks
4401 ST 313
Megaron 2, south wall
Dim. of block: full length of three joining pieces 0.76
Dim. of each piece: (a) L. 0.30, H. 0.14, Th. 0.33; (b) L. 0.18, H. 0.18, Th. 0.30; (c) L. 0.28, H. 0.18, PTh. 0.26
Dim. of inscribed surface: (a) 0.30 x 0.14; (b) 0.18 x 0.18: (c) 0.28 x 0.18
State of preservation: large block, now broken into three joining pieces. Top and bottom surfaces, right and left sides, and incised face all preserve original dimensions. Several large pieces missing from incised surface along breaks in stone. Left third (now left piece of three) of stone 0.04 shorter than the rest of stone, probably cut back in order to fit irregular block below.

Description: at far left, light latticing with diagonal lines. At left, two male figures, shown in profile, facing each other; one has left arm up, right arm back, the other has right arm forward and left arm back; hands of both figures shown as rounded fists, as if in a gesture of fighting. Figures are deeply incised, extra stone cut away around right figure in pair as if relief sculpture was intended. Lightly scored latticing over lower part of left figure. To the right of this pair of figures, series of irregular lines which continue over break to next piece. In center, a carefully drawn bird in profile, perhaps a grouse or pheasant. To right of bird, crudely drawn animal facing left, unidentifiable; several random lines over animal. On right side, another pair of human figures, both deeply incised as if relief sculpture was intended. Scene shows two males facing each other; the left one has band with internal cross-hatching across waist, perhaps to indicate a broad belt; right one has horizontal projection below waist, perhaps to indicate a sword or bow case (cf. **31**, **44**). Both have outside arm drawn back, inside arm forward, in gesture of fighting, hands clenched into fists, similar to pair shown on left side of stone. Round object like a ball in mid-air between them (cf. **14**). Five-pointed star between figures. At right, what appears to be a sketch for another human head, abandoned. Series of irregular lines at far right.
Previous bibliography: Young 1956b:264, lower left; Young 1957: pl. 90, fig. 10 (photo of actual stone).

Note: The following catalogue entries describe blocks from the south/back wall of Megaron 2. Most of the incised blocks on the south wall of Megaron 2 were found in a series of vertical piers, placed between upright wooden posts, as can be seen in Figure 12. The piers were designated by letters, A–L, from left to right, and this information is given below in the catalogue entries when available; this also reflects the position of the blocks in the drawing by J. S. Last, here Figure 14a and b, although Last's drawing does not record the stones in pier L.

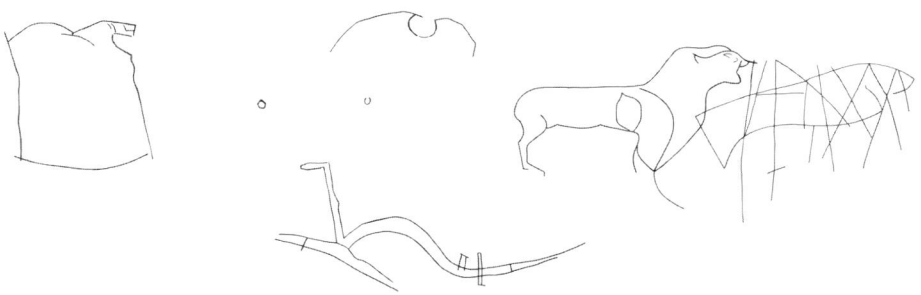

56: no inventory number or scale

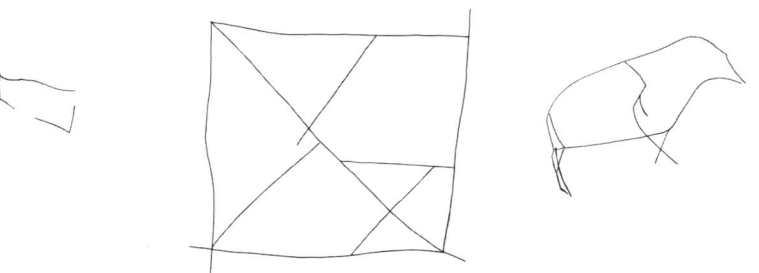

57: no inventory number or scale

5 cm.

58: ST 333

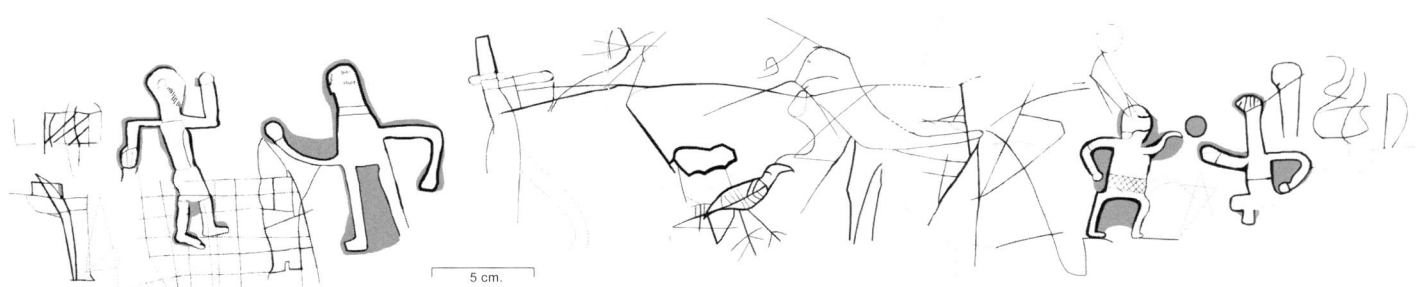

5 cm.

59: ST 313

60 Symbol; star
4402 ST 314
Megaron 2, south wall, pier and block unknown
Dim. of block: PL. 0.29, PH. 0.15, Th. 0.14
State of preservation: mended from several fragments; several chips in incised surface, section of lower center of incised face missing. Block preserves part of incised face, lower surface, and right edge; all other surfaces broken.

Description: central vertical line with arcs radiating out from it on both sides, forming irregular concentric circles (note similar pattern in **17**, **37**, **94**, and **104**). Central pattern resembles a type of maze, although design unclear because of damage to stone face. Five-pointed star at right.

61 Latticing; other random lines
5597 ST 382
Megaron 2, south wall face, pier A, block 2
Dim. of block: PL. 0.295, H. 0.21, Th. 0.22
State of preservation: single block, mended from several pieces, gaps in incised surface. Preserves upper and lower surfaces and part of left side; right side mended in plaster.

Description: irregular group of lines and latticing covers whole of incised surface. From left, vertical line, then vertical zigzag, then two groups of vertical lines, some lightly scratched and some heavily incised, then two parallel vertical lines with horizontal lines in between them. Two irregular rectangles with internal latticing in center of block, irregular arcs over all. Two more sets of vertical lines at right.

62 Bird; formless marks
5598 ST 383
Megaron 2, south wall, pier A, block 1
Dim. of block: L. 0.30, H. 0.215, PTh. 0.21
State of preservation: block mended from many smaller fragments, several gaps in incised surface. Top, bottom, and both side surfaces preserved.

Description: large bird in flight, outspread wings, body, legs, and large tail visible, head missing. Several random lines, arcs, and ellipses in the background.

63 Formless marks
5599 ST 384
Megaron 2, south wall face, pier A, block 3
Dim. of block: L. 0.30, H. 0.26, PTh. 0.10
State of preservation: block mended from two large and several smaller joining fragments. Top, bottom, and small parts of right and left side surfaces preserved. Incised face pitted with small holes.

Description: in lower left corner, pair of crescent-shaped lines with internal lines at right angle, perhaps partial rendition of wings for bird in flight depicted on missing section of stone (cf. **8**, **62**). Other random marks in the field, including two long horizontal boxes with internal diagonal lines. Whole is very lightly incised, hard to see.

64 Curved lines, perhaps quadruped
5600 ST 385
Megaron 2, south wall face, pier B, block 1
Dim. of block: L. 0.30, H. 0.20, Th. 0.27
State of preservation: block mended from several fragments, one fragment of lower right corner does not join with the rest. All surfaces roughly worked, but all original surfaces appear to be present. Numerous chips and one major gap in incised face.

Description: at far left, two parallel hooked lines, deeply incised; below this, small ellipse with central line and suspension thread, deeply incised. In center, irregular form, perhaps quadruped animal walking right; random marks across body, as if someone had started to make one animal form and then changed his mind. Front part of animal lost through break in stone, only tip of ear visible. Below, series of lines that may be part of irregular concentric circles.

65 Bird
5601 ST 386
Megaron 2, south wall face, pier A, block 4
Dim. of block: PL. 0.14, H. 0.23, Th. 0.19
State of preservation: single block, preserves left portion of stone, top, bottom, and left surfaces present. According to catalogue card, right two-thirds of block had two additional birds incised on it, one striped, one cross-

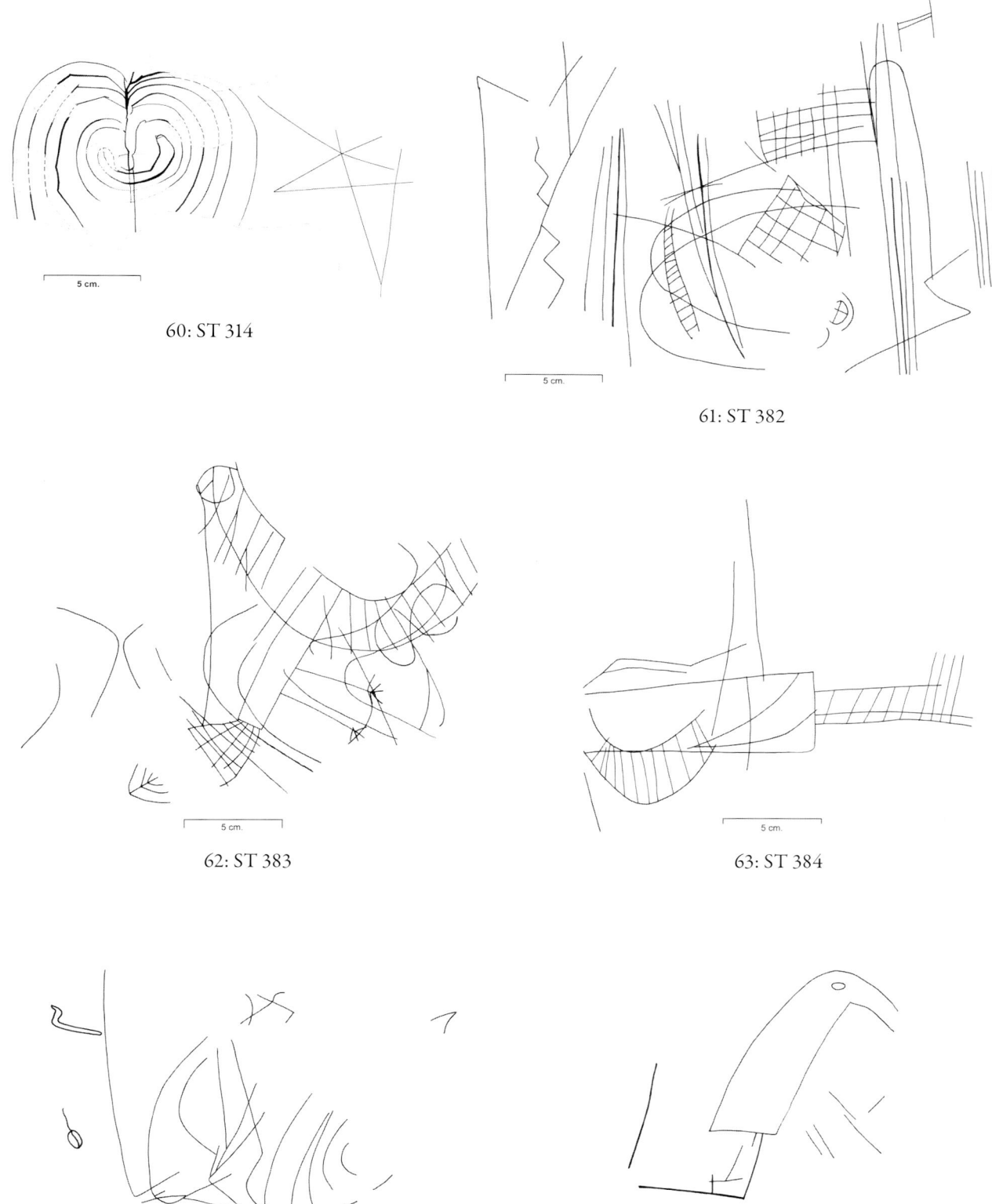

60: ST 314

61: ST 382

62: ST 383

63: ST 384

64: ST 385

65: ST 386

hatched; block was left in situ in Megaron 2 and is now lost.

Description: crudely drawn upright bird in right profile. Below bird, open-ended rectangle with central vertical line rising from base, perhaps the beginning of another larger bird.

66 Bird
5602 ST 387
Megaron 2, south wall face, pier H, block 5
Dim. of block: PL. 0.18, PH. 0.18, Th. 0.19
State of preservation: small part of block, preserves incised front, top, and left faces, other surfaces missing. Incised face pitted and abraded. Right half of block was incised with cross (per notebook information), but was left in situ in Megaron 2 back wall, and is now lost.

Description: at left, bird in right profile, bird's eye, pointed beak, and short tail shown; two legs with feet (not talons) visible.

67 Three birds; pattern; bird
5640 ST 394
Megaron 2, south wall, probably fallen from pier L, southwest corner
Dim. of block: L. 0.45, H. 0.21, PTh. 0.39
Dim. of inscribed surface: 0.45 x 0.21
State of preservation: single block, nearly complete, preserves original surfaces of top, bottom, both sides, and front face. Several chips and gouges on incised front surface.

Description: at left, large bird in right profile, wings outstretched. Light checkerboard pattern below this. In center, right profile of simply drawn bird with prominent crest; other random lines and ellipses drawn near and over bird. To right, perhaps beginning of another bird in right profile, form similar to bird in **65**. At far right, another bird in right profile, sitting upright; next to this bird, two horizontal lines which frame diamond cross-hatching and individually drawn diamonds; below this, diamond latticing with an individually drawn diamond. The effect is reminiscent of diamond patterning in pottery or diamond inlay in furniture. Several vertical lines drawn over right bird and diamond patterns.

68 Formless marks
5641 ST 395
Megaron 2, south wall, fallen from pier L in southwest corner
Dim. of block: PL. 0.38, H. 0.15, Th. 0.29
State of preservation: single block, preserves top, bottom, and left surfaces, right side broken. Incised front face heavily damaged; upper two-thirds of front surface missing except for small section at top right.

Description: irregular lines, most with no discernible pattern perhaps because of poor state of preservation of incised surface. At lower left, curved line which may be the back of an animal. To the right of this, irregular cross-hatching. At lower right, curved line and diamond, may be part of animal head with diamond eye; random lines above this.

69 Birds
5931 ST 407 + 6620 ST 449
Megaron 2, south wall, pier A, course 5
Dim. of block: PL. 0.41, H. 0.29, PTh. 0.19
State of preservation: block consists of two joining pieces, discovered and catalogued separately. Upper left section broken off from main block, now joins precisely except for one missing chip in center. Original top, bottom, and right surfaces preserved; left side missing. Lower left corner carefully cut away, probably to insert in wall around another block.

Description: four birds of prey, all facing right. Each has a diamond-shaped eye with pupil indicated, a prominent pointed beak, and talons. They are arranged on the left and right sides of the stone in two groups of two, separated by a series of vertical lines lightly incised on block. Part of tail on bird at far left missing because of break in stone. Each bird is internally scored to create an effect of diamond cross-hatching. Bird at lower right has more complicated internal markings formed by an X-in-square pattern, lightly incised legs and talons. Crude sketch of another bird above left pair of birds. At far right, possibly beginning of another bird of prey.
Previous bibliography: Roller 2005:126, fig. 1; Tsetskhladze 2007:297, fig. 1.

66: ST 387

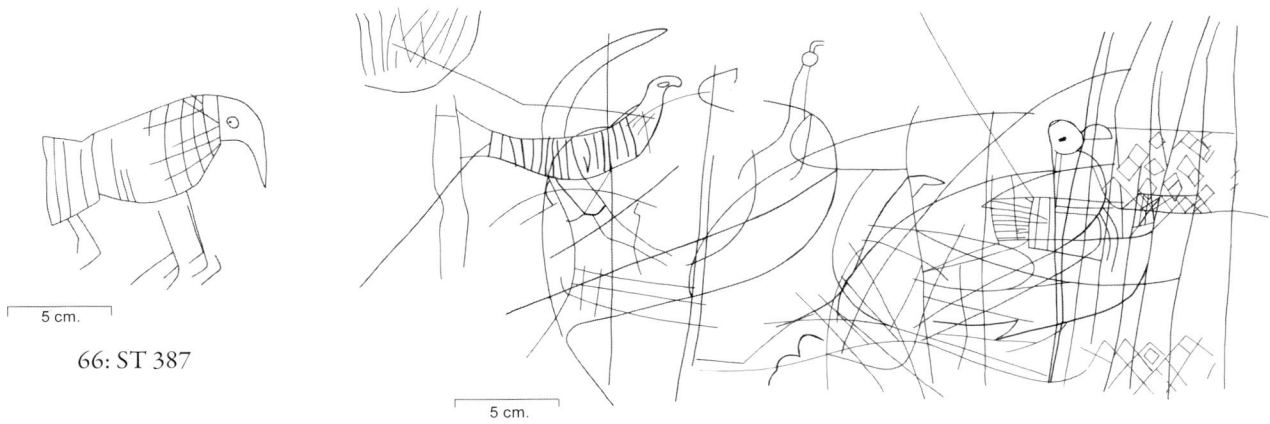

67: ST 394

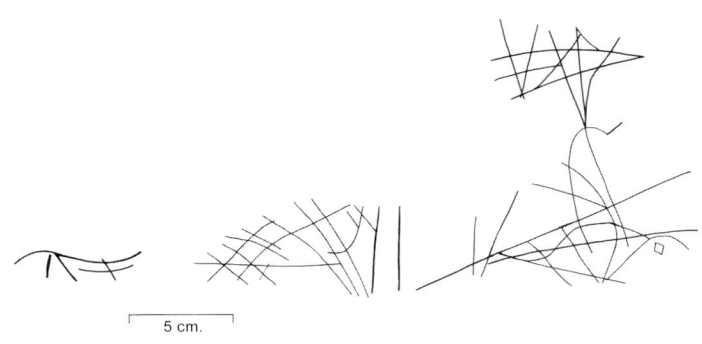

68: ST 395

69: ST 407 + ST 449

70 Rosette; bird; random lines
6605 ST 434
Megaron 2, south wall, pier D, course 2
Dim. of block: PL. 0.41, H. 0.24, PTh. 0.17
State of preservation: single block, preserves part of front (incised) and lower surfaces, all other surfaces broken and mended in plaster. Incised surface badly pitted, covered with plaster mend spots.

Description: along left edge, right half of compass-drawn circle, 0.078 diameter, with compass-drawn rosette inside; around this, a hand-drawn circle. To the right of these circles, random lines and arcs. On lower right area of incised face, beginning of outline of bird, sitting upright and facing right.

71 Stag; man; bird; symbols
6606 ST 435
Megaron 2, south wall, pier E, course 2
Dim. of block: L. 0.52, H. 0.23, Th. 0.17
Dim. of inscribed surface: 0.52 x 0.23
State of preservation: block mended from several joining pieces. Incised face complete except for lower left corner, which is mended in plaster. Upper surface and both sides of block preserved, bottom surface restored in plaster.

Description: at upper left, lightly incised bird with long neck, legs, and feet; to its left, upright oblong and two vertical lines. Central figure is a large stag, head tilted up, prominent antlers on head, four legs visible. Over lower left part of animal's body is a crudely drawn human figure in right profile, wearing a flat-topped funnel-shaped headdress (cf. **46**, **77**); eye, nose, open mouth, and chin visible. Figure shown wearing a long gown with a broad belt. Appears to have right arm drawn back and bent up; line may show extension of right arm in the air with elbow bent up, a gesture similar to figure in **46**. Above this figure are two flat-topped funnel-shaped objects similar to headdress of human figure, perhaps trial efforts for more human figures, later abandoned.
Previous bibliography: Roller 1999a: fig. 7.

72 Bird; rosette; horse; ibex
6607 ST 436
Megaron 2, south wall, pier F, course 2
Dim. of block: PL. 0.49, H. 0.12–0.14, Th. 0.18
State of preservation: two joining pieces, mended with plastered section in the middle to complete. Top, right, and front faces original; left end broken, bottom plastered.

Description: to left of plastered area, bird in flight, right profile; next to bird, a compass-drawn circle with six-petal rosette. To right of plastered area, horse running to right; horse has prominent mane and long tail, almost leonine legs; trace of second mane and second rump of horse, perhaps trial for another animal, abandoned. To right of horse and overlapping with it, another quadruped running right; set of large double antlers suggest a stag or elk.
Previous bibliography: Simpson 1998: pl. 181, fig. 18.

73 Ibex; snake; animal leg; random lines
6608 ST 437
Megaron 2, south wall, pier F, course 1
Dim. of block: L. 0.57, PH. 0.14–0.19, PTh. 0.18
Dim. of inscribed surface: 0.56 x 0.19
State of preservation: single block, mended in plaster from several smaller pieces. Incised face almost intact except for large chip on upper left surface, cracks and chips in areas where block was mended. Right and left side surfaces appear to be original, although both roughly finished. Part of original lower and upper surface preserved.

Description: at left, head and upper body of horned animal facing right, perhaps an ibex. Several random lines in central area, some lightly drawn and some lightly stippled. In center, animal which looks like long, flat snake with raised head; below and to the right, two legs, one pointed, one possible animal leg; on upper right, irregular circle with central lines.

74 Formless marks; bird; man with spear
6609 ST 438
Megaron 2, south wall, pier and course unknown
Dim. of block: L. 0.45, H. 0.13, PTh. 0.18
Dim. of inscribed surface: 0.45 x 0.13
State of preservation: single block, preserves almost all of incised face except for small section of left side and upper right corner.

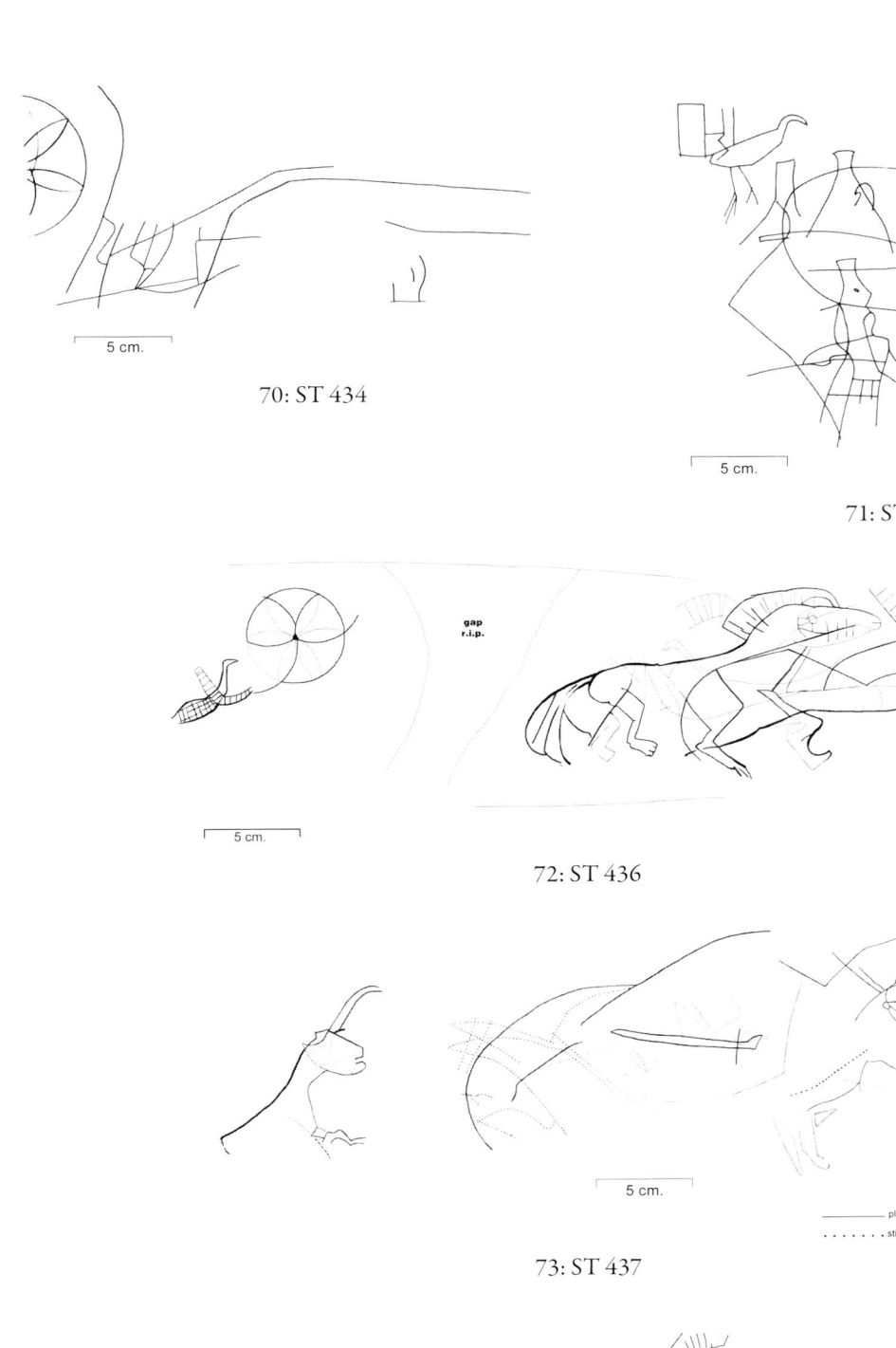

70: ST 434

71: ST 435

72: ST 436

73: ST 437

74: ST 438

Preserves bottom surface and both sides; top surface covered with plaster. Incised surface rough, many small pits and scratches in stone.

Description: drawing covers all of front surface. At far left, odd bottle-shaped form, perhaps attempt to draw a human figure, left unfinished; X above this. In center, random lines, form shaped like a boat; to right, a bird shown in flight. At far right, crudely drawn standing figure facing left; figure deeply incised, almost like relief sculpture (cf. **33**, **59**, **98**). Two human legs clearly shown, no other internal details present; head has a triangular left eye, face ends in almost beak-like point. Perhaps a composite human-animal creature is intended. Figure holds long pointed weapon, like a spear; weapon is too large for the size of the figure's body.

75 Bird head; figure; animal; rosette
6610 ST 439
Megaron 2, south wall, pier G, course 3
Dim. of block: L. 0.57, H. 0.18, PTh. 0.18
State of preservation: single block, preserves top, bottom, both sides, and incised front faces. Large chips in lower left face and upper right corner; upper right area of incised front face no longer extant.

Description: at left, random lines, some intersecting, some not; small bird's head below. In center, a figure that may be a simplified form of a human figure wearing a long gown and a flat-topped headdress (cf. **71**, **77**). At right below missing surface area are the head and neck of an animal; animal has snub nose, pointed object that extends back from its head; this may be a gazelle with a pointed horn. At far right, compass-drawn circle with partial six-petal rosette, incomplete.

76 Formless marks; animal legs; symbols
6611 ST 440
Megaron 2, south wall, pier C, course 2
Dim. of block: L. 0.37, H. 0.19, Th. 0.16
State of preservation: single block with two joining sections, mended; appears to be complete except for several cracks and chips and a large gap in center front mended in plaster. Top, bottom, both sides, and incised front faces present, front face very uneven.

Description: series of formless marks with no apparent pattern. At left, three vertical lines with diagonal cross lines; in center, three animal legs, unconnected to a body. At right, various lines, arcs, and triangles, all apparently random marks; at far right, three roughly parallel vertical lines with diagonal lines in between.

77 Man in long robe; birds
6612 ST 441
Megaron 2, south wall, pier J, fallen
Dim. of block: PL. 0.50, H. 0.23, PTh. 0.15
State of preservation: block mended in plaster from several pieces, surface very fragmentary and highly friable, several chips in incised front surface, large gap in lower part of center front. Top, bottom, left, and incised front faces preserved, right face missing.

Description: in lower left corner, two birds in flight; wavy horizontal band above. Main scene shows human figure wearing a flat-topped headdress (cf. **46**, **71**) and a long robe, belted, with ornamental belt buckle; lines of folds in lower part of robe delineated below belt buckle. Object protruding behind figure's gown may be sword. Figure may have arm extended to hold an object, although stone surface at right is heavily worn, making this unclear.
Previous bibliography: Roller 1999a: fig. 5.

78 Formless marks
6613 ST 442
Megaron 2, south wall, Pier J, fallen
Dim. of block: PL. 0.32, H. 0.21, Th. 0.18
State of preservation: single block, mended in plaster all around, preserves top, bottom, front, back, and left surfaces. Right side broken, lower right part of incised front surface covered in plaster.

Description: series of formless zigzag lines, curves, and arcs.

79 Lion; formless marks
6614 ST 443
Megaron 2, south wall, pier and course uncertain
Dim. of block: L. 0.54 W. 0.23, H. 0.15
Dim. of inscribed surface: L. 0.46, H. 0.15

75: ST 439

76: ST 440

77: ST 441

78: ST 442

State of preservation: left end of block gone, block mended from two large pieces, vertical join in center. Most of lower half of right front surface abraded away.

Description: formless lines at left, faint latticing and a haphazard crescent at right. In center, lion walking right, upper part of body and head with pointed ear, muzzle, nose, and mouth visible; underside of body and legs missing because of damage to stone. Irregular lines at right.

80 Two lions
6615 ST 444
Megaron 2, south wall, pier and course uncertain
Dim. of block: L. 0.56, H. 0.20, Th. 0.18
State of preservation: block mended from several broken pieces, complete except for chips on corners; entire incised face preserved.

Description: two lions walking right, a few extra lines in the field. Both lions have open mouths, blunt muzzles, upturned tails.
Previous bibliography: Roller 1999a: fig. 8.

81 Two men fighting; formless marks
6616 ST 445
Megaron 2, south wall, pier F, course 3
Dim. of block: PL. 0.54, H. 0.16-0.17, Th. 0.11
State of preservation: single block consisting of several fragments mended into two large non-joining pieces, restored in plaster in center to form complete block. Top, bottom, both sides, and incised front faces appear to be original. Several cracks and gaps in incised front surface of stone, large plastered area in center.

Description: two non-continuous scenes on right and left sections of stone, separated by plaster repair. At left, two human stick figures engaged in combat. Left figure has outline of square object around middle, perhaps a loincloth, kilt, or similar garment; note fleshy buttocks. Left figure faces right, extends both arms forward to grasp the hands of another stick figure at right; right figure's head missing, shown with large elliptical object on body, perhaps intended as a shield.

On right side of plaster repair, series of geometric patterns. Originally a grid pattern consisting of four horizontal lines and eight vertical lines; several diagonal and curved lines added over this. Right part of grid deliberately smoothed over as if to erase incised grid.

82 Bird; animals; symbol; bird; lion; rosette
6617 ST 446
Megaron 2, south wall, pier H, course 3
Dim. of block: PL. 0.52, H. 0.135, PTh. 0.16
Dim. of inscribed surface: 0.52 x 0.135
State of preservation: single block mended from four joining pieces, now encased in plaster. Several chips and gaps in incised front surface. Original left side preserved, all other surfaces now plastered.

Description: complex series of birds, animals, geometric patterns, and random lines, often overlapping. Several gaps interrupt drawing. At lower left, bird in flight, deeply incised, wings outstretched and legs extended. Above this, geometric pattern consisting of a vertical row of X-in-squares, lines defining X's and squares done in triplicate. To the right of break in stone, various random marks, then two vertical parallel lines with interior cross-hatching on a diamond grid; to right of this, two vertical parallel lines with column of small loops along left line, column of small compass-drawn circles along right line; two compass-drawn circles below this. To right of central break in stone, series of overlapping animals. Next to break, sitting bird in right profile, then very faint lion, compass-drawn circle behind lion; overlapping lion are three birds with outstretched wings, not all complete, and one deeply incised bird with long folded tail. At far right, another animal, probably a horse, mane visible; below this, compass-drawn circle with partially complete six-petal rosette pattern. Long horizontal line running across stones. Whole stone seems to have been incised on multiple occasions, creating an effect similar to that of an artist's sketch pad.

83 Lion; formless marks; bird
6618 ST 447
Megaron 2, south wall, pier C, course 1
Dim. of block: L. 0.56, H. 0.09-0.10, Th. 0.17
State of preservation: block mended in plaster from several joining pieces; full length of incised front surface preserved. A few cracks

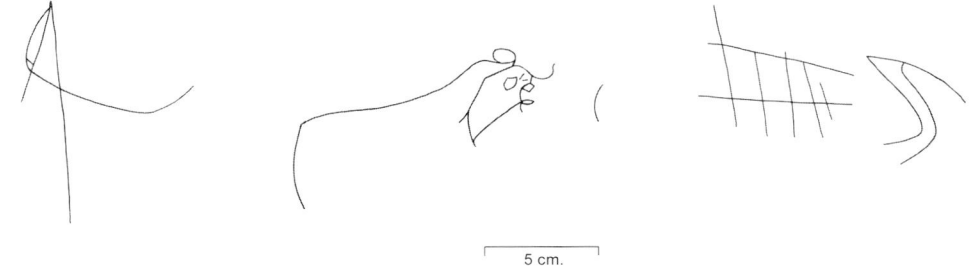

79: ST 443

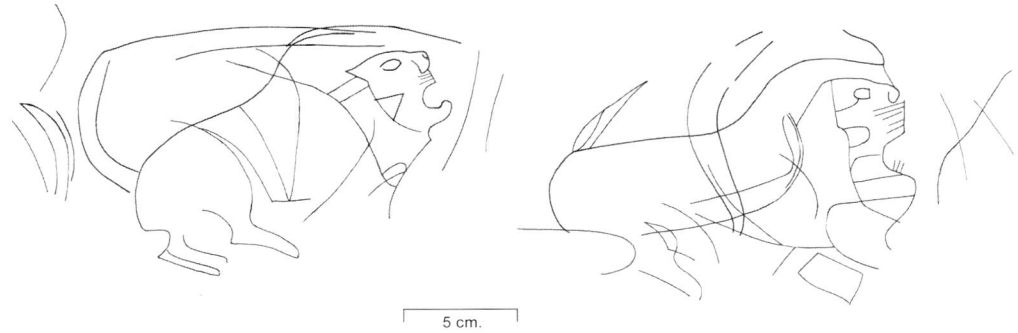

80: ST 444

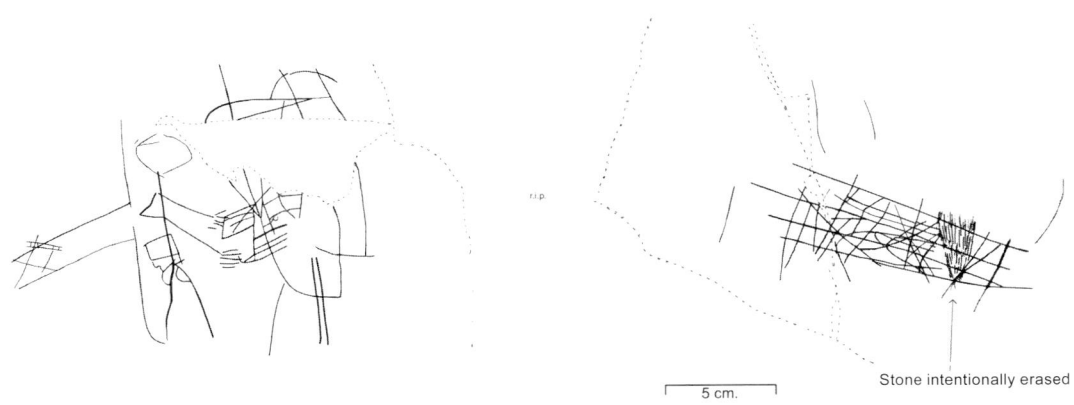

81: ST 445

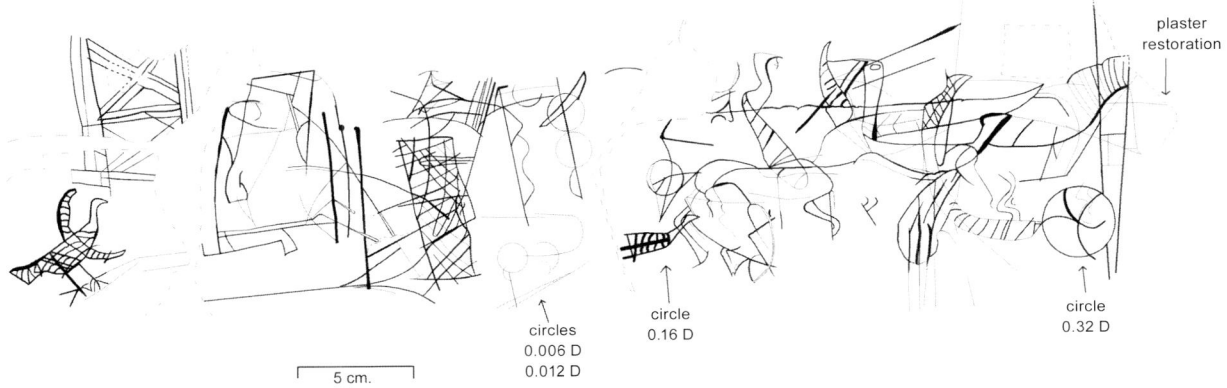

82: ST 446

and chips in incised surface. Right and left side surfaces preserved, top and bottom encased in plaster.

Description: at left, double curved lines, probably trial sketch for lion's tail; to right of this, outline of lion walking right, several random lines over front part of body. To right of lion, double curved line, uncertain function. Irregular horizontal line drawn across whole width of stone. At far right, a bird facing right, form above it may be a wing of another bird, abandoned.

84 Formless marks; two lions
6619 ST 448
Megaron 2, south wall, pier and course not recorded
Dim. of block: L. 0.61, H. 0.15, Th. 0.15
State of preservation: single block, mended in plaster from several small fragments; original top, bottom, and both side surfaces encased in plaster.

Description: at left, series of random vertical, horizontal, and diagonal lines; at right, two superimposed lions walking right; at far right, compass-drawn circle.

85 Lioness; rosette; bird
6621 ST 450
Megaron 2, south wall, pier B, course 3
Dim. of block: PL. 0.27, H. 0.25, PTh. 0.20
Dim. of incised face: 0.25 x 0.18
State of preservation: single block preserves top, bottom and left faces, broken at right. Left side of incised front surface abraded, surface gone.

Description: standing lioness facing right, head and front part of body missing, prominent teats on underside of body; compass-drawn circle with internal six-petal rosette on shoulder of lion. Above lion's back, simple bird facing right.
Previous bibliography: Simpson 1998: pl. 181, fig. 19.

86 Symbol; animal; formless marks
6622 ST 451
Megaron 2, south wall, pier E, course 4
Dim. of block: L. 0.253, H. 0.18, PTh. 0.11
State of preservation: block mended from several joining pieces; preserves top, bottom, both sides, and incised front surfaces. Back surface badly damaged, mended in plaster. Upper right and upper left areas of incised front surface abraded, lower right corner missing.

Description: at left, irregular oblong with knob on top, hooked projection at left, perhaps sketch of shield or helmet. At right, two overlapping elliptical shapes with knobs. At center top, a small animal; at center bottom, two joining circles.

87 Fish; bird
6623 ST 452
Megaron 2, south wall, pier and course not recorded
Dim. of block: PL. 0.38, H. 0.21, Th. 0.31
Dim. of inscribed surface: 0.36 x 0.15
State of preservation: single block, upper and lower surfaces partially preserved and mended in plaster, right side of stone broken off. Drawing near surviving right edge of stone.

Description: random lines at left; at right, fish, like a trout; below this, a small bird, drawn at a 90° counterclockwise angle to fish. Both figures covered with irregular lines.

88 Human figure
6624 ST 453
Megaron 2, south wall, pier G, course 3
Dim. of block: PL. 0.21, PH. 0.15, PTh. 0.18
State of preservation: small fragment of block, now encased in plaster except for small part of lower surface; surface of incised face very uneven, badly abraded.

Description: human figure walking right, head, two feet, and right arm shown in profile, body full front; figure wears long gown, has sword by side.
Previous bibliography: Roller 2005:127, fig. 4; Tsetskhladze 2007:296, fig. 1.

89 Formless marks; bird
6625 ST 454
Megaron 2, south wall, pier J, course 2

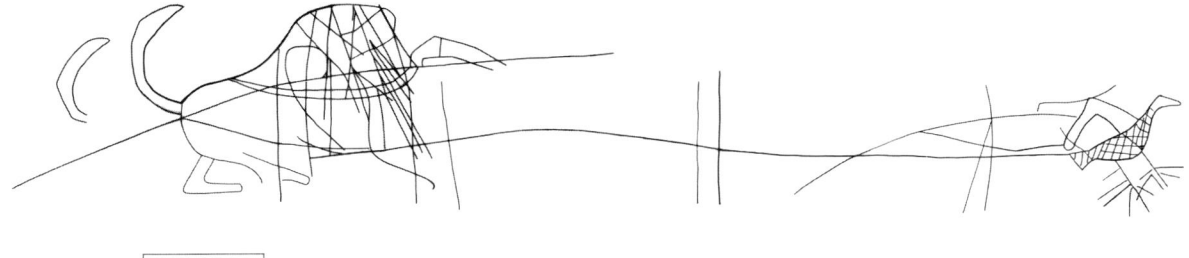

83: ST 447

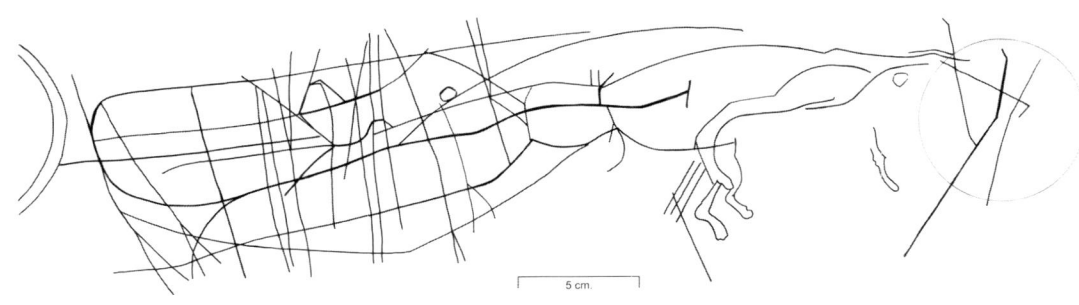

84: ST 448

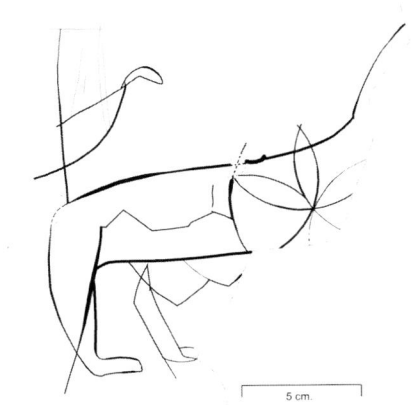

85: ST 450

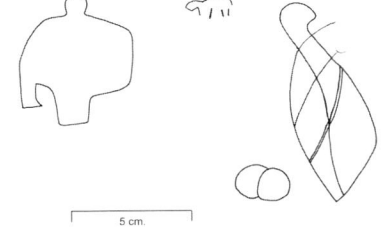

86: ST 451

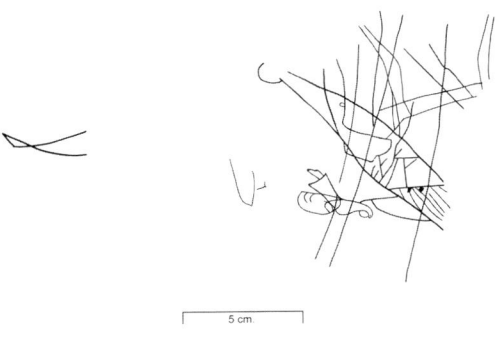

87: ST 452

88: ST 453

Dim. of block: PL. 0.20, PH. 0.21, PTh. 0.06
Dim. of incised face: 0.13 x 0.20
State of preservation: small fragment of block, mended in plaster, preserves small part of lower surface and section of incised face; all other surfaces broken. Incised surface badly pitted.

Description: series of parallel curved lines forming an irregular pattern of arcs; bird with long neck drawn at 135° counterclockwise angle to lower surface of stone; at lower right, what may be the hind quarters and leg of an animal.

90 Bird
6626 ST 455
Megaron 2, south wall, pier B, course 2B
Dim. of block: PL. 0.10, PH. 0.08, PTh. 0.08
Dim. of incised face: 0.08 x 0.05
State of preservation: single block, very small piece preserves small part of incised front face and upper surface. All other surfaces broken.

Description: may be bird of prey facing left. Very little is preserved so drawing is hard to interpret.

91 Animal
6627 ST 456
Megaron 2, south wall, pier G, course 4
Dim. of block: PL. 0.16, PH. 0.14, PTh. 0.08
Dim. of incised surface: 0.11 x 0.10
State of preservation: single block, broken on all sides except for one finished surface; orientation uncertain. Small part of incised front face preserved.

Description: subject uncertain, may be the head of an animal facing right, perhaps a horse or cow.

92 Two Birds
6628 ST 457
Megaron 2, south wall, pier and course unknown
Dim. of block: PL. 0.19, H. 0.18, PTh. 0.19
Dim. of incised face: 0.18 x 0.14
State of preservation: piece mended from several fragments, restored in plaster. Appears to be the right end of a horizontal ashlar block; top, bottom, and right surfaces original, left side now partially encased in plaster. Incised front face has several cracks and chips.

Description: at top, sitting bird facing right, looks like a hen or duck; below this, what appears to be the outstretched wings of a bird in flight. Two parallel arcs of a circle below.

Note: The following six catalogue entries, **93–98**, present incised stones that were removed from the south (back) wall of Megaron 2 in 1961.[212] All were in very poor condition, with exterior surfaces that were crumbling badly; to preserve them, they were encased in plaster, but they were not inventoried or otherwise entered into the Gordion records at that time. In 1996 the stones in the six plaster cases were given inventory numbers. Although there was no record of their original provenience, their position on the vertical piers forming the south wall of Megaron 2 can be verified by their presence in the drawing of this wall by J. Last (Fig. 14).[213] The stones in the six plaster cases were inventoried as six individual items, but in fact four of the plaster cases—**94, 95, 96,** and **97**—actually contain two separate stones, placed one on top of another and fused together by the fire that destroyed Megaron 2. Thus the next six catalogue entries actually comprise a record of ten incised stones.

93 Formless marks; perhaps a lion
12976 ST 840
Megaron 2, south wall, pier unknown
Dim. of block: H. 0.245, PL: 0.52
State of preservation: single rectangular block, now encased in plaster. Incised face mended from many small pieces, several sections missing. Parts of original surfaces preserved on top, bottom, and left side; right side completely missing.

Description: irregular patterns and random lines

---

212. Young 1962:160 describes the excavation and removal of the incised stones from the south wall of Megaron 2.
213. These circumstances have been confirmed by Ellen Kohler, the Gordion Registrar at the time of the incised stones' excavation.

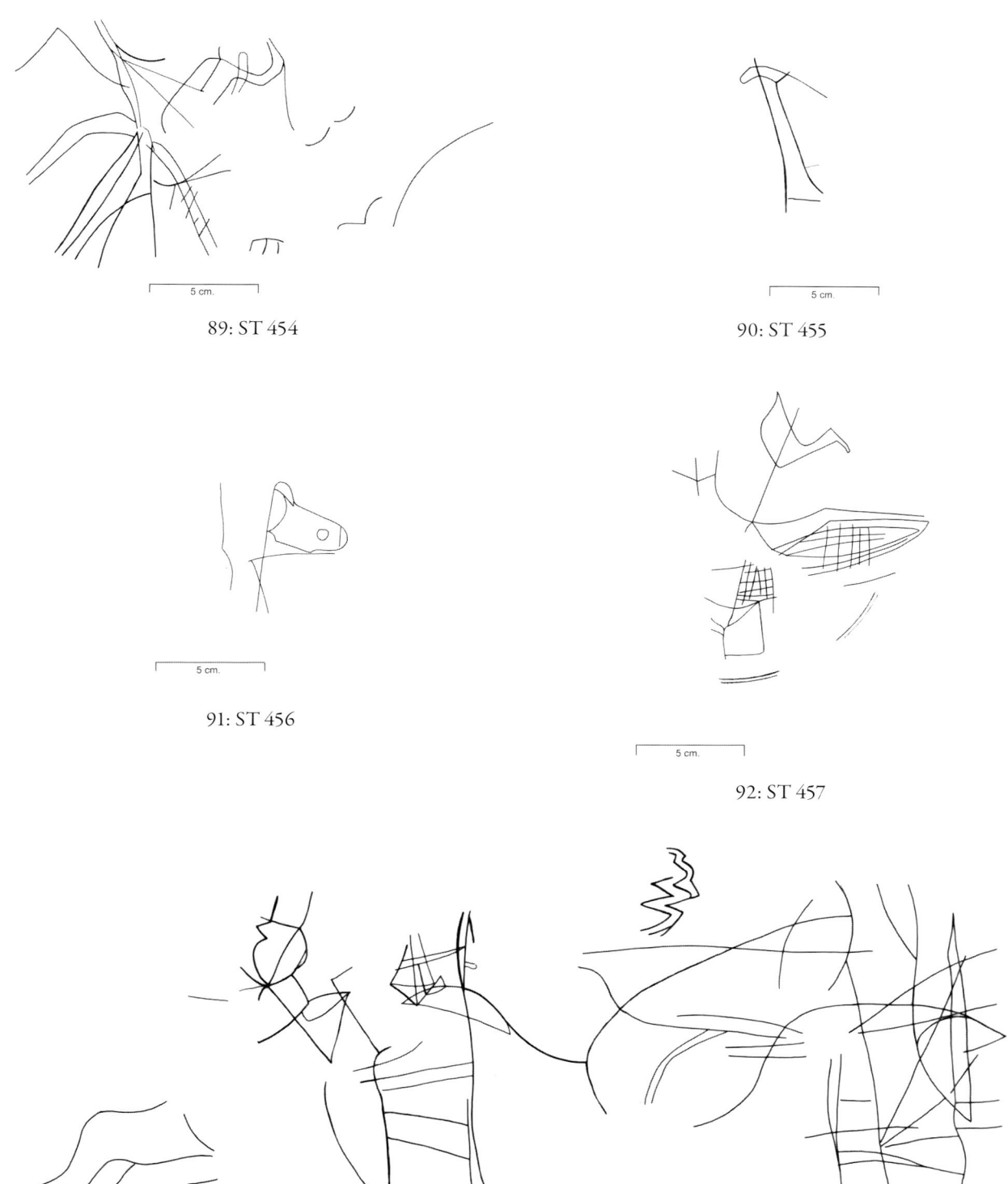

89: ST 454

90: ST 455

91: ST 456

92: ST 457

93: ST 840

across whole surface of stone. At lower left, three curved lines, roughly parallel. At left center, several irregular shapes and two vertical wavy lines, roughly parallel, with horizontal lines between. To right of this, irregular shape crossed by random lines; two parallel zigzag lines above. In center, two more vertical parallel lines with random horizontal lines across them; a series of curved and zigzag lines above.

94 Animal; mazes; idol; man; wheel; bird
12977 ST 841
Megaron 2, south wall, pier E
Dim. of joined block: L. 0.61, H. 0.48
Dim. of upper block: L. 0.61, H. 0.24
Dim. of lower block: L. 0.61, H. 0.23
State of preservation: originally two blocks, one on top of the other, fused together by the fire and now encased in single plaster block. Parts of original surfaces preserved on all outer edges. Incised face cracked in several places; break running the height of the stone on the top block; much of the bottom surface of the lower block severely abraded.

Description, upper stone: at left, crudely drawn quadruped animal, one hind leg and one front leg visible but head gone, so animal cannot be identified. Over this, very lightly incised human figure in right profile, head, neck, and part of bent right arm visible. Below human figure, a compass-drawn circle, light scoring over it. At right: two sets of hand-drawn concentric circles side by side, perhaps a maze pattern. Only the lower part of circle patterns is now preserved, but excavation photos taken at the time of the stone's discovery indicate that these were originally circles that came together in a pattern somewhat like a heart; the whole is reminiscent of pattern seen on **17, 37, 60,** and **104**. Trace of another similar design at lower left. In between circle groups, upright bird in right profile; lower part of body and legs/talons visible, head missing.

Description, lower stone: at left, several random lines, circle with curved lines extending down; form is reminiscent of an aniconic Phrygian idol, although the surface is now so heavily abraded that this remains uncertain. In center, human figure facing right; has crude face, wears high headdress (cf. **46, 71, 77,** and **96**) and long gown with decorative belt; pointed object at belt, perhaps sword. At figure's right, a wheel, outer rim compass-drawn, inner rim partly compass-, partly hand-drawn, six spokes visible. Human figure appears to extend hand to hub of wheel. To right of this, a large bird in right profile, has long neck and beak. Overlapping with this, a large duck or goose facing right. Another smaller bird in right profile below duck/goose; to its right, a small animal with a curved tail. Various random lines and compass-drawn circles over whole area.

95 Lion; branch; bird
12978 ST 842
Megaron 2, south wall, pier F
Dim. of joined block: L. 0.56, H. 0.33
Dim. of upper block: L. 0.56, H. 0.14
Dim. of lower block: L. 0.56, H. 0.18
State of preservation: originally two separate blocks, fused together by fire and now encased together in plaster. Several cracks and chips in front surface, but otherwise intact. Incised surface much abraded, drawings faint and often hard to see.

Description, top block: bird facing right, wing span outstretched, has long elaborate tail almost like a peacock. Bottom block: at left, a standing lion facing right, body elongated and crudely drawn, tail curved upright over back; neck band visible. Hind quarters, two hind legs and tail deeply incised and carved as if shallow relief was intended. To right of lion, various lines, perhaps an upright tree and branches. At far right, what may be a human stick figure (or simply a circle and series of lines).

96 Symbols; formless marks; bird; bird; human head; bird; goat; bird
12979 ST 843
Megaron 2, south wall, pier G
Dim. of joined block: PL. 0.55, H. 0.28
Dim. of upper block: L. 0.55, H. 0.15
Dim. of lower block: L. 0.55, H. 0.13
State of preservation: originally two separate blocks, both blocks now encased together in plaster. Incised surface of both blocks now split in the middle, right side of upper

94: ST 841

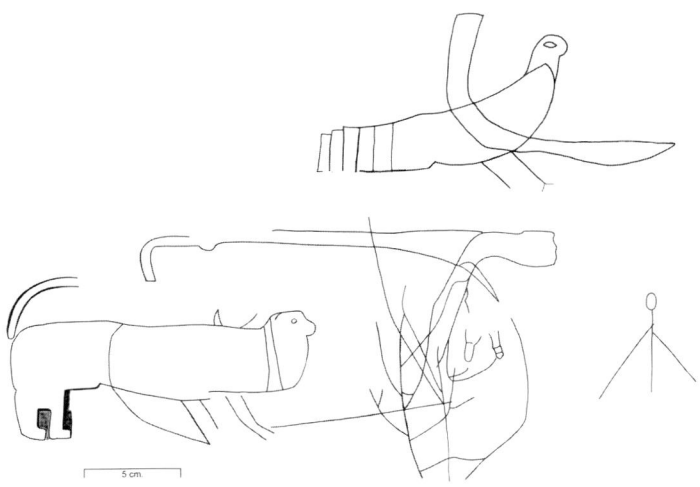

95: ST 842

block badly abraded, remaining surface has several cracks and chips. Some smaller chips present in incised surface of lower block.

Description, top block: on left side, series of roughly parallel lines curving down and left, perhaps body of bird, although no head visible. To right of this, several curved projections extending left, no particular pattern or shape obvious. Right surface is almost gone, but one bird can be seen, sitting upright and facing right; beak, eye, curved talons all visible.

Description, bottom block: at left side, large bird facing right with long curved beak and legs, talons visible, very lightly incised. To right of this, several curved and straight lines, apparently random. In the center, design which looks like sketch for human head facing right, has funnel-shaped headdress and crude face (cf. **46, 71, 77,** and **94**), no body present. To right of this, sitting bird facing right has outstretched wings and long elaborate tail (cf. **95**). Next, a small goat facing right, details include long ears, blunt nose, and beard. To right of goat, a bird facing left, beak, eye, legs, talons, and internal cross-hatching all visible. Irregular ellipse below bird.

97 Formless marks; animal; man
12980 ST 844
Megaron 2, south wall, Pier J
Dim. of joined block: L. 0.59, H. 0.23
Dim. of upper block: L. 0.58, H. 0.11
Dim. of lower block: L. 0.59, H. 0.12
State of preservation: originally two separate blocks, now fused together and encased together in plaster. Surface of both blocks badly fractured into several pieces, large sections of upper right and upper left corners of top block missing. Top, bottom, and both side surfaces of bottom block preserved. Incised surface of both blocks poorly preserved, with many cracks and gaps.

Description, top block: left surface missing; at center, series of vertical and diagonal lines. At right, two legs of human figure facing right, body missing, legs and feet deeply incised; more lightly incised lines between legs, perhaps an indication of a garment, such as a kilt.

Description, lower block: at left, zigzag lines, head of a quadruped (perhaps lion) lightly incised. Remaining surface covered with zigzag lines, a few straight lines, and one arrow.

98 Formless marks; lion; man
12981 ST 845a, b
Megaron 2, south wall, pier I
Dim. of whole block: L. 0.69, H. 0.24
Dim. of ST 845a: L. 0.26, H. 0.23
Dim. of ST 845b: L. 0.34, H. 0.23
State of preservation: originally one large block; during removal from the wall of Megaron 2, the block fractured into two pieces with a gap in the center and was subsequently restored in plaster. In 1996 the plaster repair was no longer effective, and so the two sections of the stone were separated into two non-joining pieces, a (left) and b (right).

Description, ST 845a: several curved and straight lines, probably formless marks. At right, deeply incised oval; two curved lines below.

Description, ST 845b: main figure is a lion walking right, head, front legs, and back so deeply incised that the scene almost appears to be relief sculpture; internal whorls mark muscles of lion's legs, especially forelegs; light cross-hatching on lion's neck perhaps indicates fur. Over rear haunches of lion is a standing male, more lightly incised. Head and legs of figure shown in right profile, torso full front; upper torso nude, wears short kilt on lower torso. Hairline and ear visible on head, but no eye. Both arms are extended out from body, left arm bent up, fingers visible; hand holds a double axe or other weapon that is turned towards figure's head in an awkward position for striking (cf. similar gesture in **44**). To left of human figure, deeply incised funnel-shaped object, similar to headdress found in other drawings (cf. **46, 71, 77, 94, 96**), no body present. Random lines, cross-hatching, lightly incised, over whole figure.

Previous bibliography: Roller 1999a: fig. 2.

96: ST 843

97: ST 844

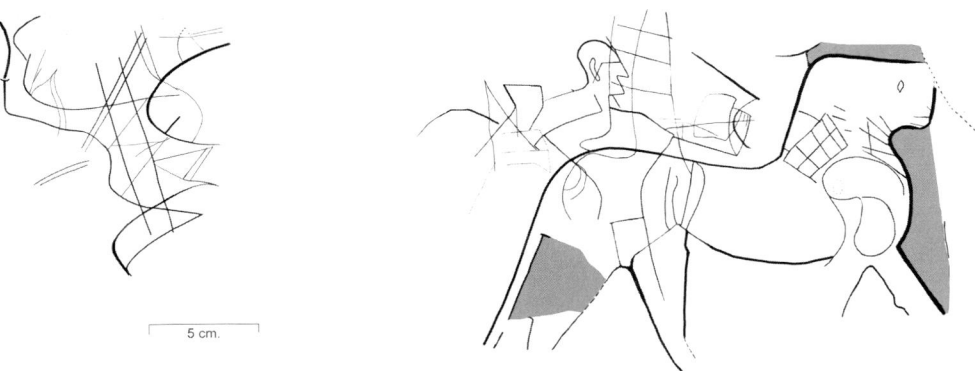

98: ST 845a, b

Drawings on House Y, behind Megaron 2

99 Lion; formless marks
5238 ST 345
House Y, behind Megaron 2
Dim. of block: L. 0.26, H. 0.20
State of preservation: single block, appears to be nearly complete, with top, bottom, and both side faces preserved. Upper and lower edges of incised front surface missing, two large and several small chips in center front.

Description: lion walking left, has open mouth, wrinkled muzzle, whiskers, pronounced ridge on neck. In lower left corner, another small figure, now unidentifiable; curved lines at right.

100 Animal; bird
5239 ST 346
House Y, behind Megaron 2
Dim. of block: L. 0.26, H. 0.19
State of preservation: single block mended from two joining pieces, upper right corner broken. Top, bottom, and both sides surfaces preserved. Crack across center of incised face where two pieces join, upper right section of incised face missing.

Description: in lower left corner, small bird with long neck and long pointed beak, perhaps a bird in flight. To the right, head and body of a cow or ibex, head slightly raised, eye, nose, mouth, and one horn visible; animal drawn as if parallel to the right side of the stone block.

Drawings on Stones from Clay Fill above Destruction Level

101 Human figure, shown frontally
4425 ST 319
Rubble fill of Building G, over Megaron 1
Dim. of block: PL. 0.19, PH. 0.13, PTh. 0.17
Dim. of incised face: 0.12 x 0.10
State of preservation: single fragment, preserves part of upper surface and small part of incised face; all other surfaces broken.

Description: standing human figure (gender uncertain), head and torso frontal, legs in right profile, right leg down, left leg extends out as if to indicate movement; left arm extended out with elbow bent up, hand missing; right arm extended out with elbow bent down, hand clenched in fist. Figure's hair shown as if parted in the middle, braids hanging down on each side. No indication of clothing except five horizontal lines across waist that may indicate a belt. On figure's left side is a long object with one curved side, perhaps a sword, shown as if hanging from body.
Previous bibliography: Roller 1999a: fig. 1.

102 Lion
3493 S 33
Deep Cut 4, Persian Wall bedding (Middle Phrygian fill over Megaron 2)
Dim. of block: PL. 0.17, H. 0.20
State of preservation: Fragment from left portion of block, two joining pieces, mended. Preserves upper and lower surface and left side; right side missing.

Description: lion walking right; lion has open mouth and bared teeth, ridge on neck, articulated shoulder muscle. Chisel mark visible under chin and below neck of lion, as if beginning of relief sculpture was attempted.
Previous bibliography: Roller 2008: fig. 2.

103 Symbol
6196 ST 418
WML-4 trench, clay fill
Dim. of block: PL. 0.15, PH. 0.14
State of preservation: single piece, broken all around except for lower surface. Surface on which incised drawing appears is badly damaged, shows signs of burning. Drawing may have been incised after surface was burned (perhaps after destruction of Megaron 2).

Description: X in square.

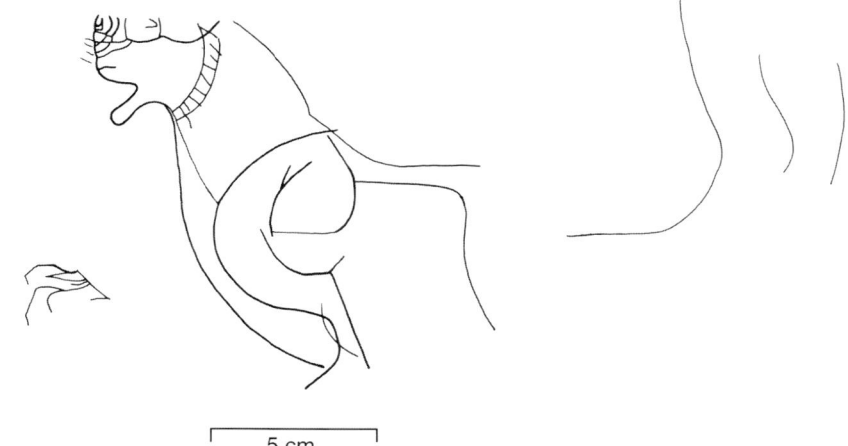

99: ST 345

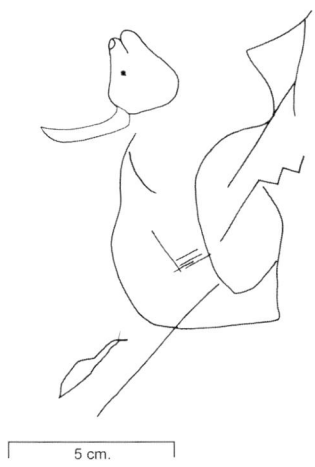

100: ST 346

101: ST 319

102: S 33

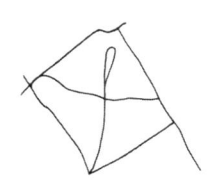

103: ST 418

Drawings on Stones in City Gate

104 Horse; bird; perhaps a maze; bird; formless marks

Gate stone 1

Stone still in situ, not inventoried

Location: interior east wall of the north courtyard room of the Early Phrygian Gate building, approximately ten courses above current ground level

Dim. of incised face: L. 0.54, H. 0.32

State of preservation: block is complete in wall; upper part of incised surface very worn.

Description: near left side, horse walking left, placed on horizontal ground line; above this, faint traces of the body and tail of a large bird in right profile, head no longer visible. Central part of the stone has banana-shaped object in the center with a series of irregular hand-drawn concentric circles around it, perhaps a type of maze pattern (note the same pattern found on **17**, **37**, **60**, and **94**). Overlapping right side of the maze pattern, a bird in right profile, has long curved beak and crest on head; right edge of stone covered with various random lines and circles, no discernible pattern. Upper surface of block covered with chisel marks that obscure part of drawing, suggesting that chisel marks were applied after drawing finished.

105 Straight and zigzag lines

Gate stone 2

Stone still in situ, not inventoried

Location: incised onto one block in the south tower of the Early Phrygian Gate, facing the entrance into the city. The block is the third course above the present ground level.

Dim.: unknown

State of preservation: upper surface of block has crumbled away. The block shows no sign of weathering or lichens, so it may have been covered with mud plaster until fairly recently.

Description: two straight vertical lines, roughly parallel, two vertical zigzag lines near or on top of straight line at right; horizontal line with loop at base of zigzag. Both the vertical and the zigzag lines may have extended higher on the stone, now missing because of damage to stone's surface. (No drawing; see photograph, Fig. 123.)

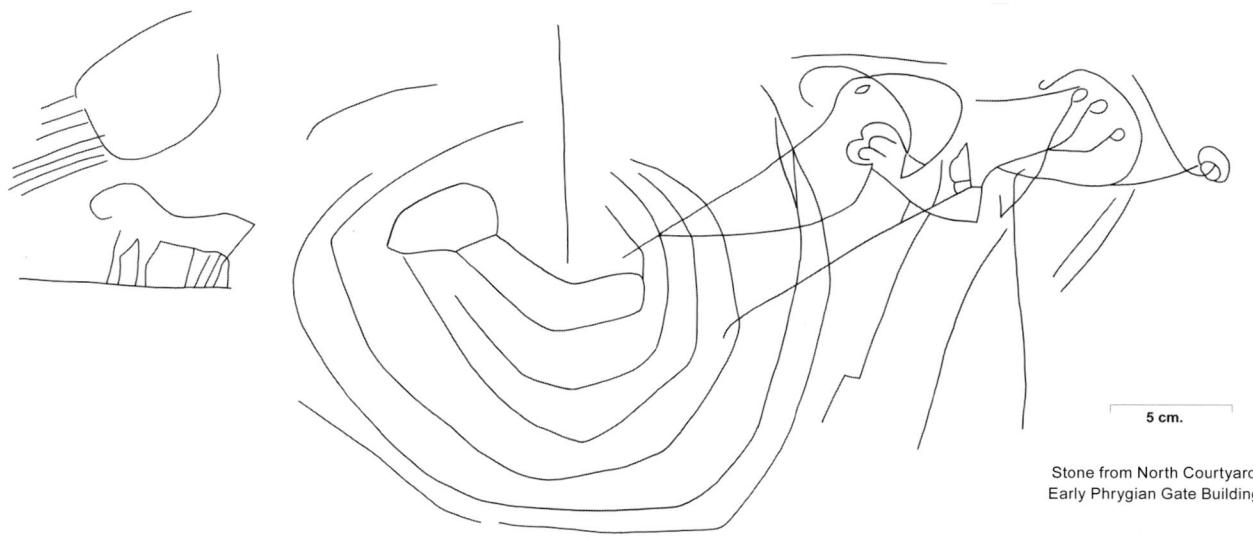

Stone from North Courtyard
Early Phrygian Gate Building

104: Gate Stone 1

III

Figures, Including Photographs of Stones 1–105

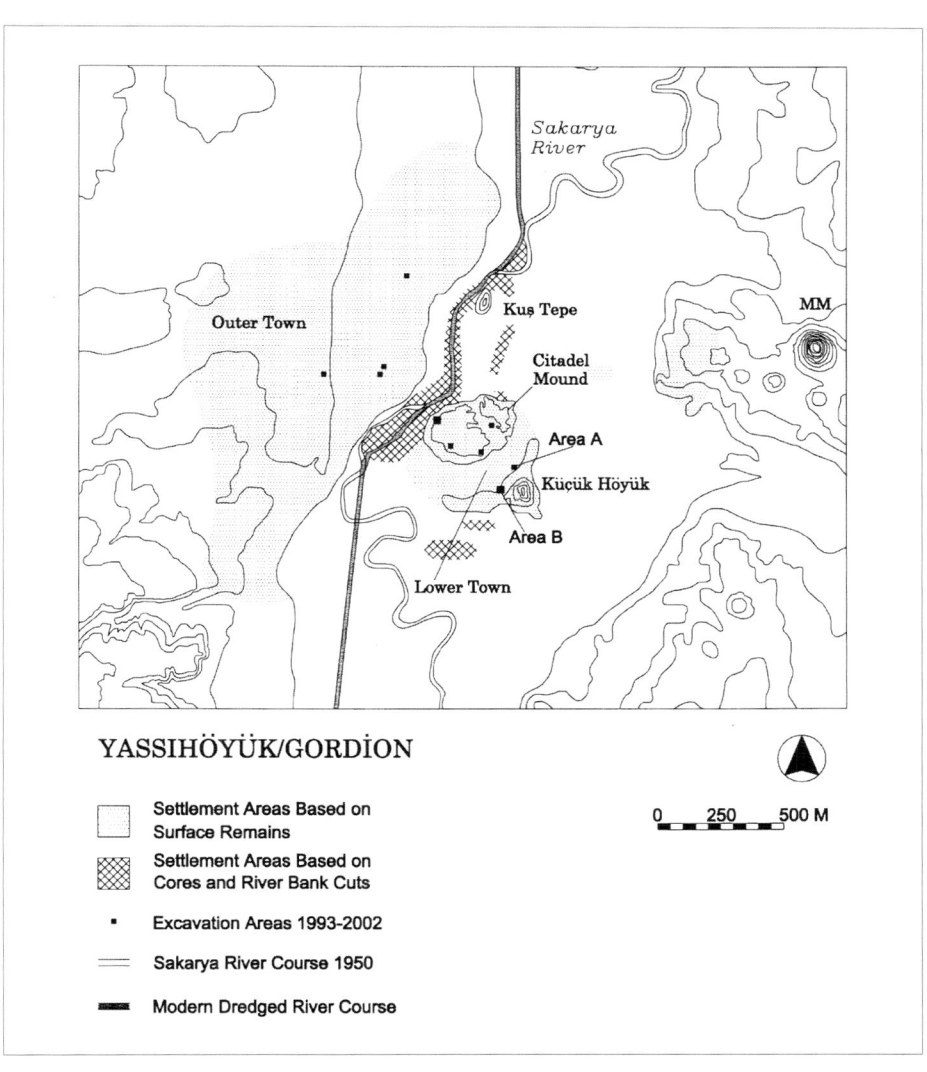

Figure 1. General view of Gordion settlement showing location of Citadel Mound (from Kealhofer 2005: fig. 3-1).

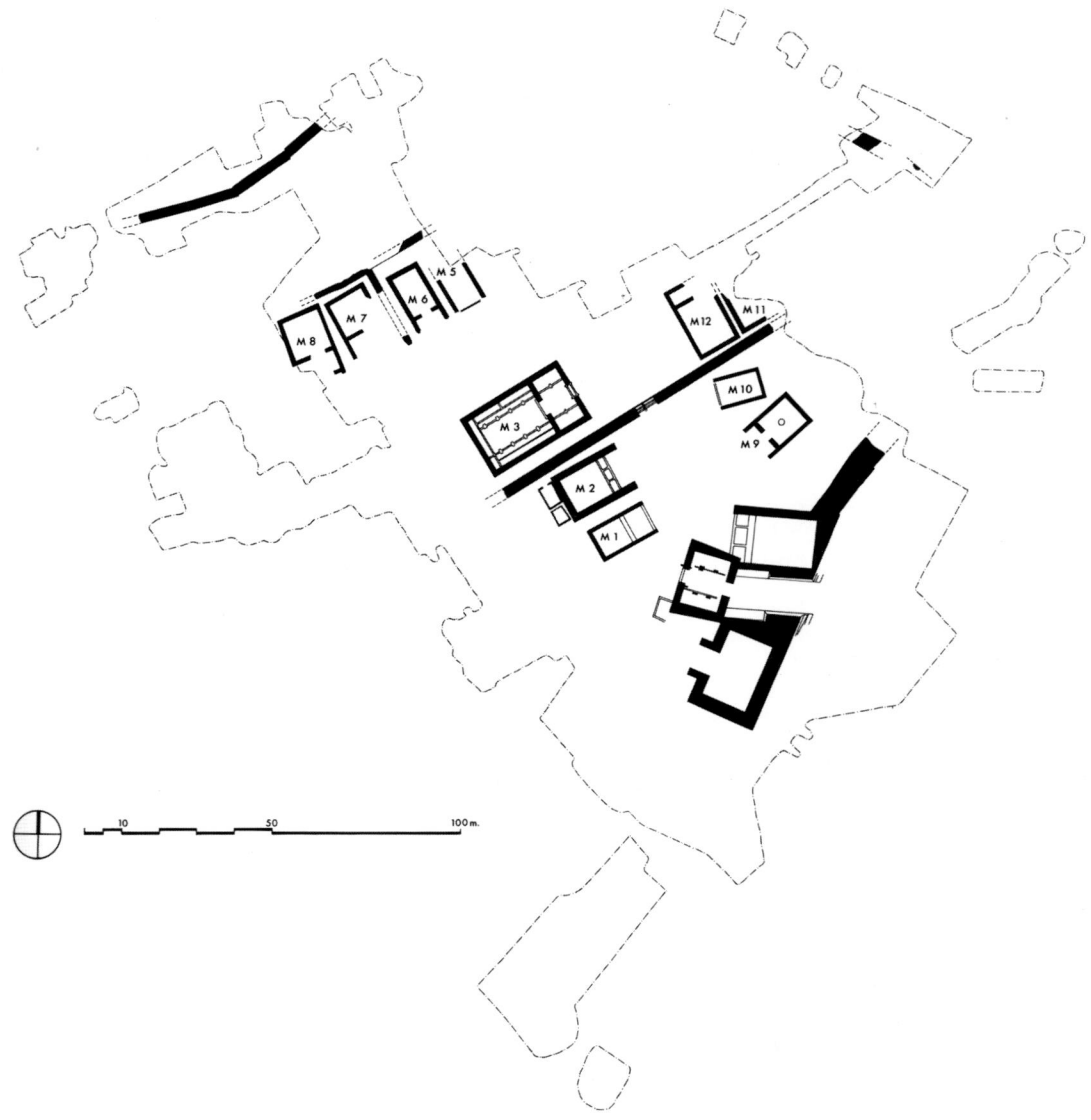

Figure 2. Plan of the Early Phrygian Pre-Terrace Level, Gordion. (Courtesy, Gordion Archives)

FIGURES 1–20

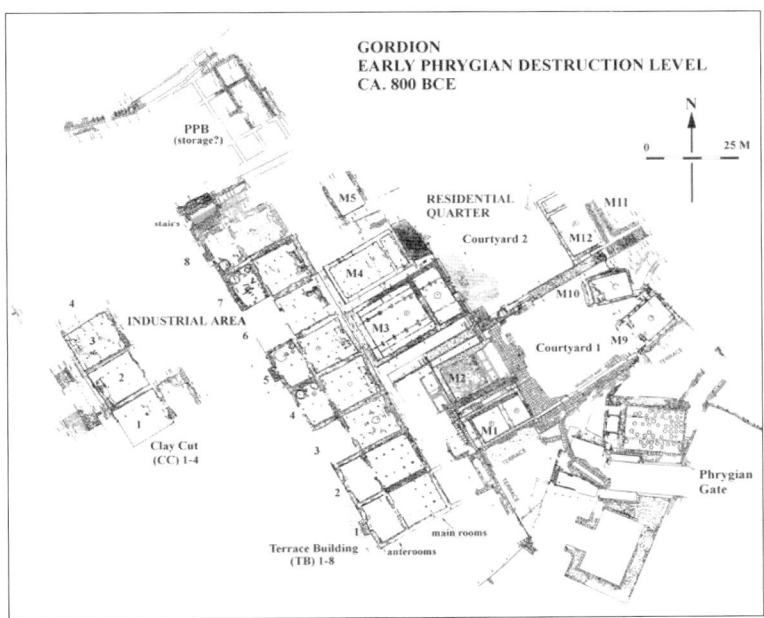

Figure 3. Plan of the Early Phrygian Destruction Level, Gordion (from Kealhofer 2005: fig. 6-1).

Figure 4. Megaron 2 and enclosure wall to its west; Megaron 1 and Early Phrygian Gate Complex in the background. (Courtesy, Gordion Archives)

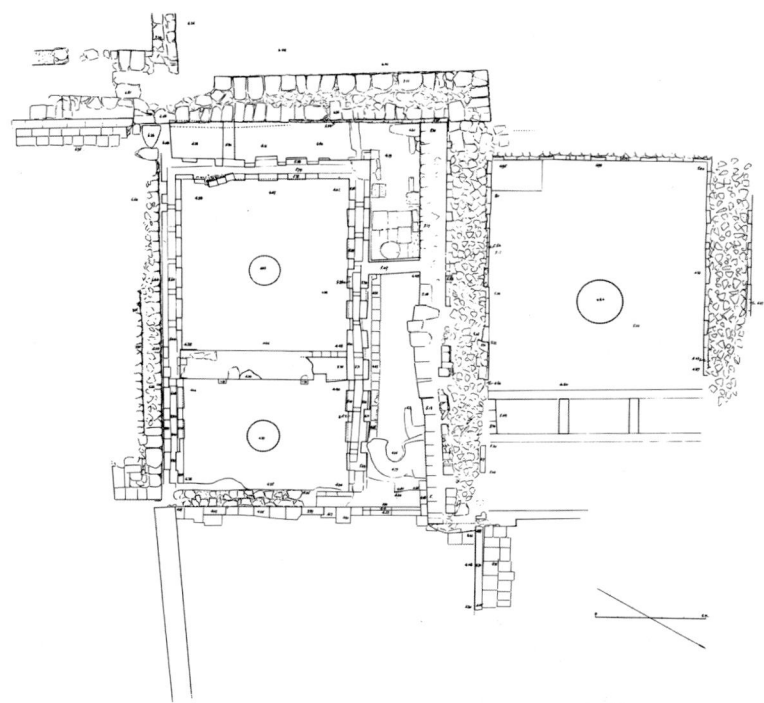

Figure 5. Plan of Megarons 1 and 2 by J. S. Last, in 1956. (Courtesy, Gordion Archives)

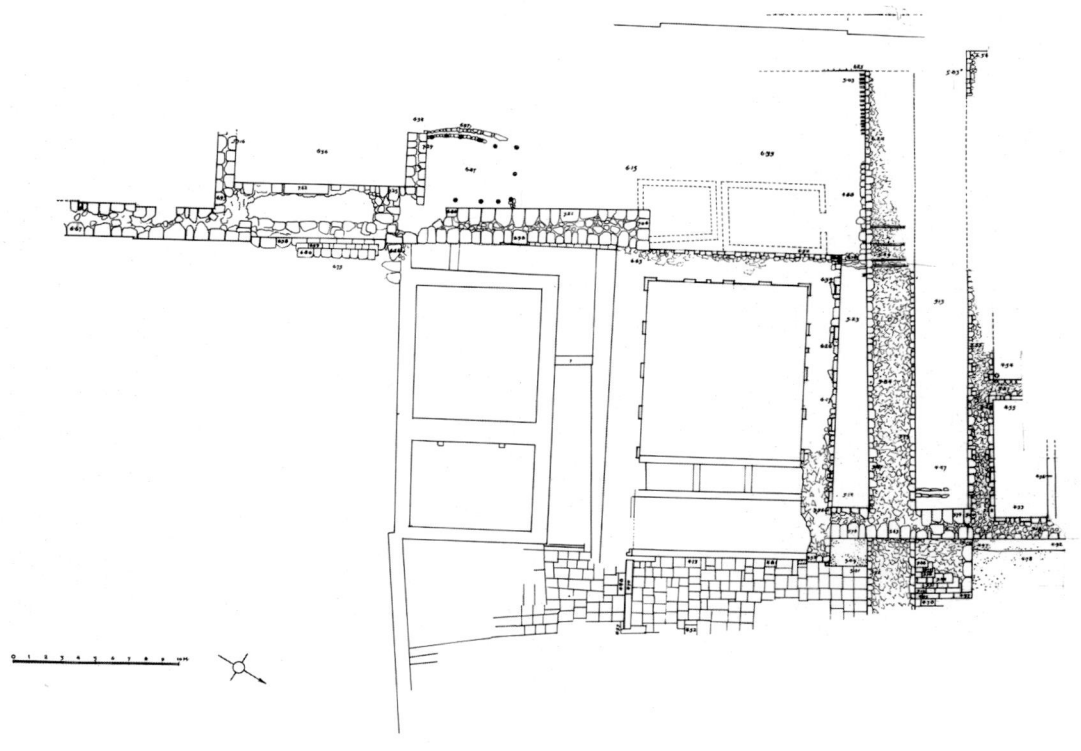

Figure 6. Plan of Megarons 1 and 2 by J. S. Last, in 1957. (Courtesy, Gordion Archives)

Figure 7. Megaron 2 from north. (Courtesy, Gordion Archives)

Figure 8. Drawing of the pebble mosaic in the main room, Megaron 2, by J. S. Last. (Courtesy, Gordion Archives)

Figure 9. Actual state photograph of two piers of incised stones from the southeast corner of Megaron 2. (Courtesy, Gordion Archives)

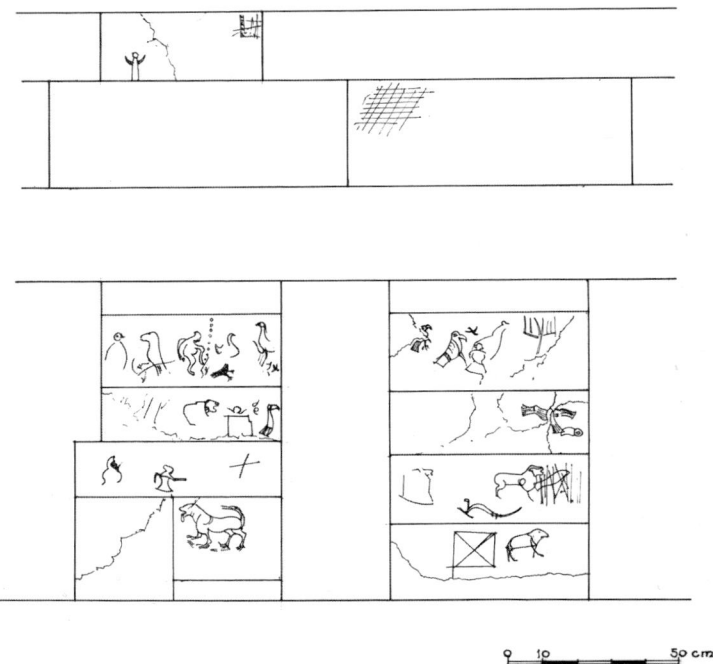

Figure 10. Drawing of two piers of incised stones from the southeast corner of Megaron 2, by Dorothy H. Cox, 1956. (Courtesy, Gordion Archives)

Figure 11. Houses X and Y, behind Megaron 2. (Courtesy, Gordion Archives)

Figure 12. General view of rear or south wall of Megaron 2, showing stone piers with incised drawings in situ. (Courtesy, Gordion Archives)

Figure 13. Detail of incised blocks in situ, from south wall of Megaron 2. (Courtesy, Gordion Archives)

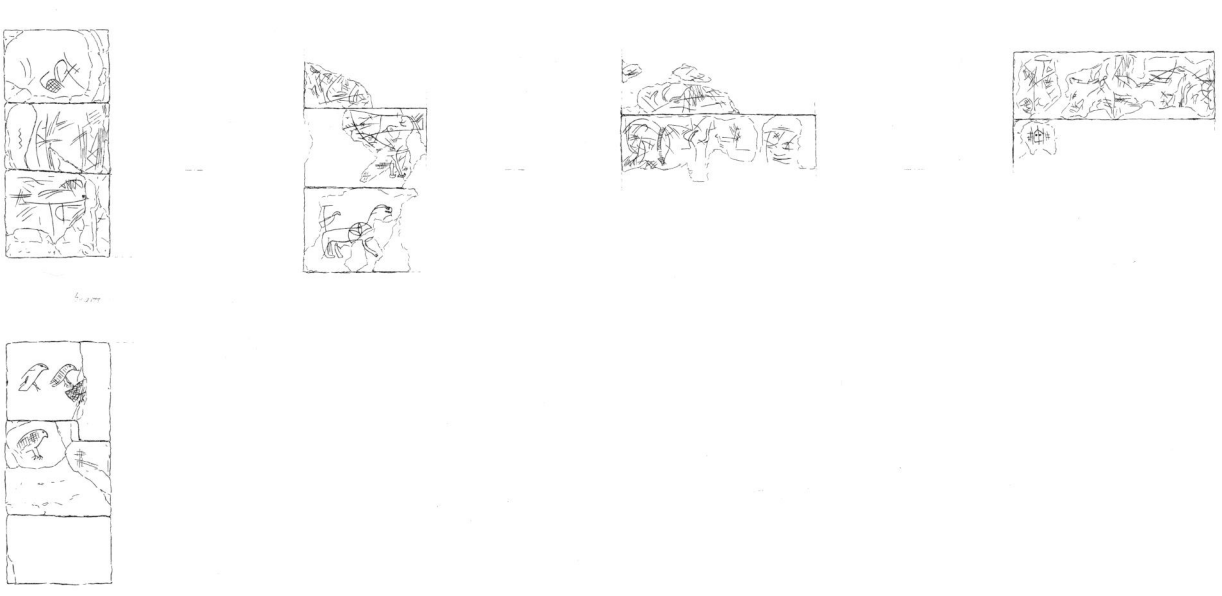

Figure 14. Drawing of incised stone piers from the south wall of Megaron 2, by J. S. Last; left section above. (Courtesy, Gordion Archives)

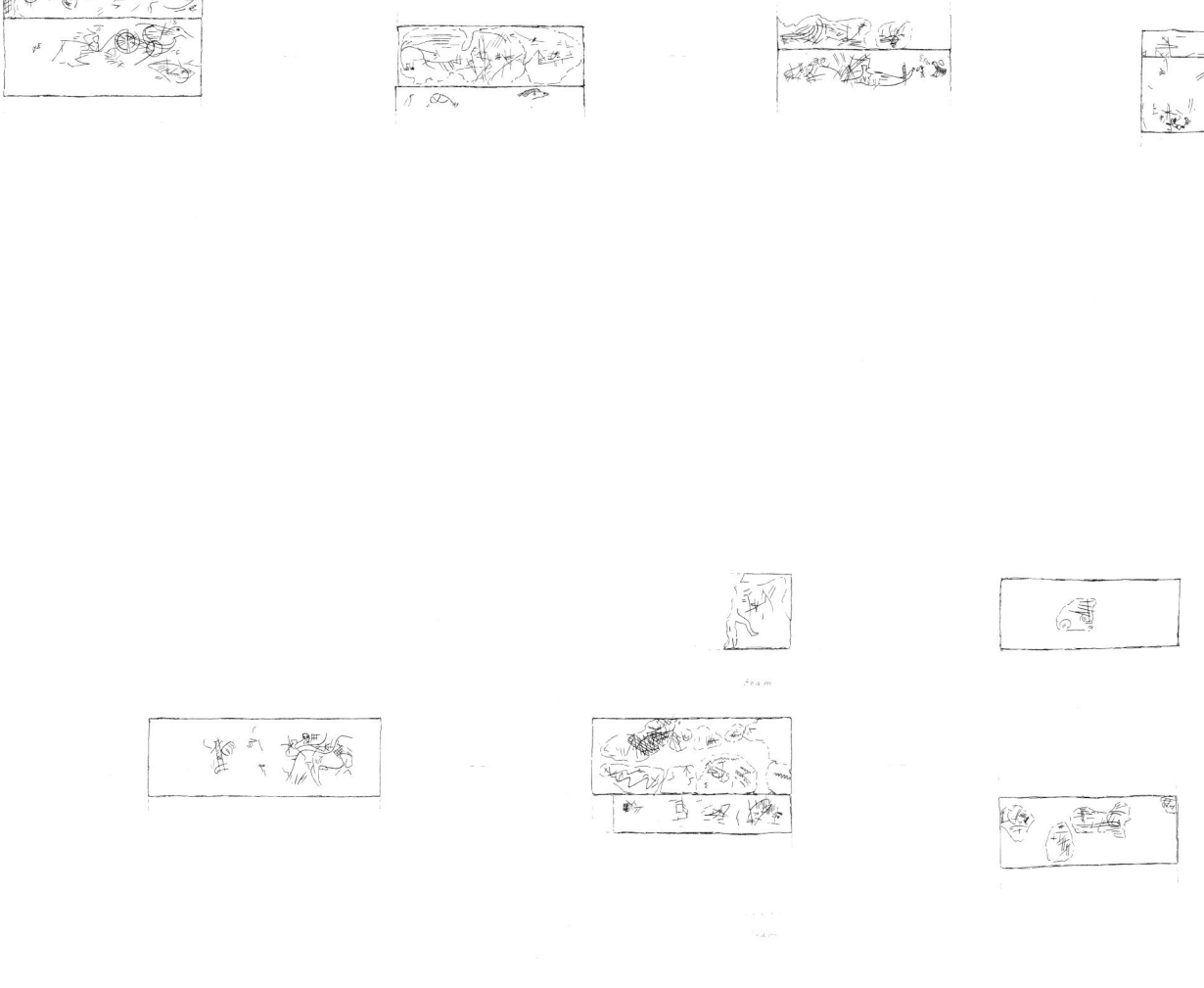

Figure 14 (cont'd.). Top, middle section; bottom: right section.

Figure 15. Incised stones in situ on west wall of Megaron 2. (Courtesy, Gordion Archives)

 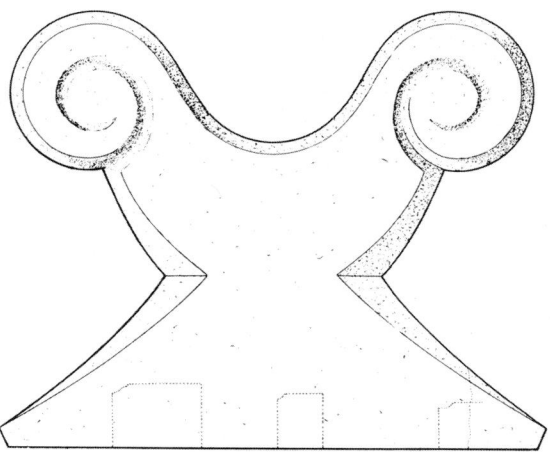

Figure 16. Photograph and drawing of poros akroterion found above Megaron 2. (Courtesy, Gordion Archives)

Figure 17. Poros lion found above Megaron 2. (Courtesy, Gordion Archives)

Figure 18. Poros lions found above Megaron 2. (Courtesy, Gordion Archives)

Figure 19. Comparison: **48** and lion from Yılantaş monument.

Figure 20. Comparison: **80** and lion from Arslantaş monument.

Figure 21: Stone 1

Figure 22: Stone 2

Figure 23: Stone 3

Figure 24: Stone 4

Figure 25: Stone 5

Figure 26: Stone 6

Figure 27: Stone 7

Figure 28: Stone 8

Figure 29a: Stone 9a

Figure 29b: Stone 9b

Figure 30: Stone 10

Figure 31: Stone 11

Figure 32: Stone 12

Figure 33: Stone 13

Figure 34: Stone 14

Figure 35: Stone 15

Figure 36: Stone 16

Figure 37: Stone 17

Figure 38: Stone 18

Figure 39: Stone 19

Figure 40: Stone 20

Figure 41: Stone 21

Figure 42: Stone 22

Figure 43: Stone 23

Figure 44: Stone 24

Figure 45: Stone 25

Figure 46: Stone 26

Figure 47: Stone 27

Figure 48: Stone 28

Figure 49: Stone 29

Figure 50: Stone 30

Figure 51: Stone 31

Figure 52: Stone 32

Figure 53: Stone 33

Figure 54: Stone 34

Figure 55: Stone 35

Figure 56: Stone 36

Figure 57: Stone 37

Figure 58: Stone 38

Figure 59: Stone 39

Figure 60: Stone 40

Figure 61: Stone 41

Figure 62: Stone 42

Figure 63: Stone 43

Figure 64: Stone 44

Figure 65: Stone 45

Figure 66: Stone 46

Figure 67: Stone 47

Figure 68: Stone 48

Figure 69: Stone 49

Figure 70: Stone 50

Figure 71: Stone 51

Figure 72: Stone 52

Figure 73: Stone 53

Figure 74: Stone 54 (top) and Stone 55 (bottom)

Figure 75: Stones 56 and 57

Figure 76: Stone 58

Figure 77: Stone 59

Figure 78: Stone 60

Figure 79: Stone 61

Figure 80: Stone 62

Figure 81: Stone 63

Figure 82: Stone 64

Figure 83: Stone 65

Figure 84: Stone 66

Figure 85: Stone 67

Figure 86: Stone 68

Figure 87: Stone 69

Figure 88: Stone 70

Figure 89: Stone 71

Figure 90: Stone 72

Figure 91: Stone 73

Figure 92: Stone 74

Figure 93: Stone 75

Figure 94: Stone 76

Figure 95: Stone 77

Figure 96: Stone 78

Figure 97: Stone 79

Figure 98: Stone 80

Figure 99: Stone 81

Figure 100: Stone 82

Figure 101: Stone 83

Figure 102: Stone 84

Figure 103: Stone 85

Figure 104: Stone 86

Figure 105: Stone 87

Figure 106: Stone 88

Figure 107: Stone 89

Figure 108: Stone 90

Figure 109: Stone 91

Figure 110: Stone 92

Figure 111: Stone 93

Figure 112: Stone 94

Figure 113: Stone 95

Figure 114: Stone 96

Figure 115: Stone 97

Figure 116: Stone 98

Figure 117: Stone 99

Figure 118: Stone 100

Figure 119: Stone 101

Figure 120: Stone 102

Figure 121: Stone 103

Figure 122: Stone 104

Figure 123: Stone 105

IV

Concordances

1. Catalogue Number to Gordion Inventory Number

Catalogue No.	Gordion Inventory No.	Catalogue No.	Gordion Inventory No.
1	4014 ST 255	32	4182 ST 292
2	4016 ST 256	33	4183 ST 293
3	4017 ST 257	34	4184 ST 294
4	4018 ST 258	35	4186 ST 295
5	4019 ST 259	36	4186 ST 296
6	4020 ST 260	37	4187 ST 297
7	4021 ST 261	38	4188 ST 298
8	4022 ST 262	39	4189 ST 299
9	4023 ST 263	40	4190 ST 300
10	4024 ST 264	41	4191 ST 301
11	4025 ST 265	42	4192 ST 302
12	4026 ST 266	43	4193 ST 303
13	4027 ST 267	44	4403 ST 315
14	4028 ST 268	45	4422 ST 316
15	4045 ST 269	46	4423 ST 317
16	4046 ST 270	47	4424 ST 318
17	4047 ST 271	48	No inventory no.
18	4048 ST 272	49	5237 ST 344
19	4049 ST 273	50	12537 ST 839
20	4050 ST 274	51	No inventory no.
21	4171 ST 281	52	No inventory no.
22	4172 ST 282	53	5236 ST 343
23	4173 ST 283	54	No inventory no.
24	4174 ST 284	55	No inventory no.
25	4175 ST 285	56	No inventory no.
26	4176 ST 286	57	No inventory no.
27	4177 ST 287	58	4698 ST 333
28	4178 ST 288	59	4401 ST 313
29	4179 ST 289	60	4402 ST 314
30	4180 ST 290	61	5597 ST 382
31	4181 ST 291	62	5598 ST 383

Catalogue No.	Gordion Inventory No.	Catalogue No.	Gordion Inventory No.
63	5599 ST 384	84	6619 ST 448
64	5600 ST 385	85	6621 ST 450
65	5601 ST 386	86	6622 ST 451
66	5602 ST 387	87	6623 ST 452
67	5640 ST 394	88	6624 ST 453
68	5641 ST 395	89	6625 ST 454
69	5931 ST 407 + 6620 ST 449	90	6626 ST 455
		91	6627 ST 456
70	6605 ST 434	92	6628 ST 457
71	6606 ST 435	93	12976 ST 840
72	6607 ST 436	94	12977 ST 841
73	6608 ST 437	95	12978 ST 842
74	6609 ST 438	96	12979 ST 843
75	6610 ST 439	97	12980 ST 844
76	6611 ST 440	98	12981 ST 845
77	6612 ST 441	99	5238 ST 345
78	6613 ST 442	100	5239 ST 346
79	6614 ST 443	101	4425 ST 319
80	6615 ST 444	102	3493 S 33
81	6616 ST 445	103	6196 ST 418
82	6617 ST 446	104	Gate Stone 1
83	6618 ST 447	105	Gate Stone 2

2. Gordion Inventory Number to Catalogue Number

Gordion Inventory No.	Catalogue No.	Gordion Inventory No.	Catalogue No.
3493 S 33	102	4188 ST 298	38
4014 ST 255	1	4189 ST 299	39
4016 ST 256	2	4190 ST 300	40
4017 ST 257	3	4191 ST 301	41
4018 ST 258	4	4192 ST 302	42
4019 ST 259	5	4193 ST 303	43
4020 ST 260	6	4401 ST 313	59
4021 ST 261	7	4402 ST 314	60
4022 ST 262	8	4403 ST 315	44
4023 ST 263	9	4422 ST 316	45
4024 ST 264	10	4423 ST 317	46
4025 ST 265	11	4424 ST 318	47
4026 ST 266	12	4425 ST 319	101
4027 ST 267	13	4698 ST 333	58
4028 ST 268	14	5236 ST 343	53
4045 ST 269	15	5237 ST 344	49
4046 ST 270	16	5238 ST 345	99
4047 ST 271	17	5239 ST 346	100
4048 ST 272	18	5597 ST 382	61
4049 ST 273	19	5598 ST 383	62
4050 ST 274	20	5599 ST 384	63
4171 ST 281	21	5600 ST 385	64
4172 ST 282	22	5601 ST 386	65
4173 ST 283	23	5602 ST 387	66
4174 ST 284	24	5640 ST 394	67
4175 ST 285	25	5641 ST 395	68
4176 ST 286	26	5931 ST 407 + 6620 ST 449	69
4177 ST 287	27	6196 ST 418	103
4178 ST 288	28	6605 ST 434	70
4179 ST 289	29	6606 ST 435	71
4180 ST 290	30	6607 ST 436	72
4181 ST 291	31	6608 ST 437	73
4182 ST 292	32	6609 ST 438	74
4183 ST 293	33	6610 ST 439	75
4184 ST 294	34	6611 ST 440	76
4186 ST 295	35	6612 ST 441	77
4186 ST 296	36	6613 ST 442	78
4187 ST 297	37	6614 ST 443	79

Gordion Inventory No.	Catalogue No.	Gordion Inventory No.	Catalogue No.
6615 ST 444	80	12977 ST 841	94
6616 ST 445	81	12978 ST 842	95
6617 ST 446	82	12979 ST 843	96
6618 ST 447	83	12980 ST 844	97
6619 ST 448	84	12981 ST 845	98
6621 ST 450	85	Gate Stone 1	104
6622 ST 451	86	Gate Stone 2	105
6623 ST 452	87	New Stone, 7/2004	48
6624 ST 453	88	No inventory no.	51
6625 ST 454	89	No inventory no.	52
6626 ST 455	90	No inventory no.	54
6627 ST 456	91	No inventory no.	55
6628 ST 457	92	No inventory no.	56
12537 ST 839	50	No inventory no.	57
12976 ST 840	93		

3. Incised Stone Drawings: Subjects

CAT. NO.	GORDION INV. NO.	1st SUBJECT	2nd SUBJECT	3rd SUBJECT	4th SUBJECT	5th SUBJECT	6th SUBJECT	7th SUBJECT
1	ST 255	star	man	lion	man	flag		
2	ST 256	armed warrior	bird	formless marks				
3	ST 257	bird	bird	animal	bird, marks	flag		
4	ST 258	lion	bird head					
5	ST 259	3 birds	man	3 birds				
6	ST 260	lion	random lines					
7	ST 261	lion						
8	ST 262	lion	birds	pattern	bird	man		
9a	ST 263a	2 buildings	bird	animal				
9b	ST 263b	building	lion	lines				
10	ST 264	lion	horse	bird	goat	symbols		
11	ST 265	bird	star	bird				
12	ST 266	symbols	bird head	horse	lion			
13	ST 267	animal	animal	formless marks				
14	ST 268	2 men fighting	man	ball/sun	bird	lion		
15	ST 269	symbol: diamond						
16	ST 270	3 birds	formless marks					
17	ST 271	hand-drawn circles						
18	ST 272	symbols						
19	ST 273	2 birds	human arm?					
20	ST 274	3 birds	symbols					
21	ST 275	bird						
22	ST 282	latticing						
23	ST 283	maze						
24	ST 284	symbol						
25	ST 285	asterisk	lion					

164 CONCORDANCE 3. INCISED STONE DRAWINGS: SUBJECTS

CAT. NO.	GORDION INV. NO.	1st SUBJECT	2nd SUBJECT	3rd SUBJECT	4th SUBJECT	5th SUBJECT	6th SUBJECT	7th SUBJECT
26	ST 286	bird	2 bird heads					
27	ST 287	bird	symbol					
28	ST 288	2 branches						
29	ST 289	lion						
30	ST 290	symbol						
31	ST 291	man	star					
32	ST 292	formless marks	lion	symbols				
33	ST 293	man with weapons	animal	symbols	human foot/leg			
34	ST 294	formless marks	compass-drawn circles	flag				
35	ST 295	symbol						
36	ST 296	formless marks						
37	ST 297	symbols	bow & arrow probably held by man	hand-drawn circles				
38	ST 298	building	lion	bird				
39	ST 299	branch	formless marks					
40	ST 300	symbols	formless marks					
41	ST 301	bird	bird	formless marks				
42	ST 302	latticing	compass-drawn circles					
43	ST 303	symbols	formless marks					
44	ST 315	hunter & hare						
45	ST 316	lion						
46	ST 317	man	2 birds	building	bird			
47	ST 318	animals	man	lion	bird	marks		
48	new stone 2004–no inv. no.	2 lions						
49	ST 344	patterns	human figure					
50	ST 839	bird	2 quadrupeds	bird	man	hen	5 birds	
51	L 2–no inv. no.	quadruped	lion	cult idol	bird			

CONCORDANCE 3. INCISED STONE DRAWINGS: SUBJECTS

CAT. NO.	GORDION INV. NO.	1st SUBJECT	2nd SUBJECT	3rd SUBJECT	4th SUBJECT	5th SUBJECT	6th SUBJECT	7th SUBJECT
52	L 3–no inv. no.	animal	man	symbols				
53	ST 343	lion						
54	R 1–no inv. no.	4 birds	man	bird	symbol			
55	R 2–no inv. no.	2 birds						
56	R 3–no inv. no.	rectangle	arcs	lion	bird			
57	R 4–no inv. no.	rectangle	square	quadruped				
58	ST 333	lion	compass-drawn circle	formless marks				
59	ST 313	2 men fighting	2 men fighting	ball/sun	bird	animal	formless marks	
60	ST 314	symbol	star					
61	ST 382	latticing						
62	ST 383	bird	formless marks					
63	ST 384	formless marks						
64	ST 385	animal	lines					
65	ST 386	bird						
66	ST 387	bird						
67	ST 394	3 birds	pattern	bird				
68	ST 395	formless marks						
69	ST 407 + ST 449	4 birds						
70	ST 434	rosette	bird	random lines				
71	ST 435	stag	man	bird	symbols			
72	ST 436	bird	rosette	horse	ibex			
73	ST 437	ibex	snake	animal leg				
74	ST 438	formless marks	bird	man with spear				
75	ST 439	bird head	figure	animal	rosette			
76	ST 440	formless marks	animal legs	symbols				
77	ST 441	man in long robe	birds					
78	ST 442	formless marks						

CONCORDANCE 3. INCISED STONE DRAWINGS: SUBJECTS

CAT. NO.	GORDION INV. NO.	1st SUBJECT	2nd SUBJECT	3rd SUBJECT	4th SUBJECT	5th SUBJECT	6th SUBJECT	7th SUBJECT
79	ST 443	lion	formless marks					
80	ST 444	2 lions						
81	ST 445	2 men fighting	formless marks					
82	ST 446	bird	symbol	birds	lion	rosette		
83	ST 447	lion	formless marks	bird				
84	ST 448	formless marks	2 lions			rosette		
85	ST 450	lioness	rosette	bird				
86	ST 451	symbol	animal	formless marks				
87	ST 452	fish	bird					
88	ST 453	human figure						
89	ST 454	formless marks	bird					
90	ST 455	bird						
91	ST 456	animal						
92	ST 457	bird	bird					
93	ST 840	formless marks	lion					
94	ST 841	animal	maze	idol	man	wheel		birds
95	ST 842	lion	branch	bird				
96	ST 843	symbols	bird	bird	human face	bird	goat	bird
97	ST 844	formless marks	animal	man				
98	ST 845	formless marks	lion	man				
99	ST 345	lion	formless marks					
100	ST 346	animal	bird?					
101	ST 319	man, shown frontally						
102	S 33	lion						
103	ST 418	symbol						
104	Gate Bldg. stone 1	horse	bird	maze	bird	formless marks		
105	Gate Bldg. stone 2	straight & zigzag lines						

4. Subjects Found in the Incised Stone Drawings

Human Figures

Men standing, no activity: 1, 8, 14, 31, 52, 54, 97
Two men fighting: 14, 59 (two pairs, no weapons), 81 (cartoon-like, no weapons)
Man standing, holding weapons: 2, 5, 33, 37 (only weapon visible)
Man holding hare in bag, weapon: 44
Man striding right, weapon: 98
Man with raised arm, falconry (?): 46
Man standing frontally: 101
Man with large spear: 74
Man in long gown, belt: 71, 77, 94
Man in long gown, unbelted: 88
Dancer: 50
Simple human figure with upraised arms: 49
Human foot/leg: 33

Animals

Lion: 1, 4, 6, 7, 8, 9b, 10, 12, 14, 25, 29, 38, 45, 47, 48 (two), 53, 58, 79, 80 (two), 83, 84 (two), 85 (nursing lioness), 93, 95, 98, 99, 102
Bird: 2, 3, 4, 5 (six birds), 8 (several, exact number uncertain), 9a, 10, 11 (three), 14, 16 (three), 19 (two, on arm?), 20 (three), 21, 26 (also two bird heads), 33 (tail), 38, 40 (one wing only), 41, 46 (three), 47, 50 (seven), 51, 54 (five), 55 (two), 56, 59, 62, 65, 66, 67 (three), 69 (four), 70, 71, 72, 74, 77 (two), 82 (three), 83, 85, 90 (?), 92 (two), 94 (duck or goose, two others), 95, 96 (four), 100 (?), 104
Goat: 10, 96
Horse: 10, 12, 72, 82, 104
Stag: 71
Gazelle: 75
Fish: 87
Ibex or wild cattle: 72, 73, 100
Snake: 73
Unknown quadruped: 3, 9a, 13 (two), 32, 59, 91, 94
Animal leg: 73, 76, 89
Animal head: 91

Architecture

Phrygian megaron: 9a, 9b, 46
Steps, walls, and tower: 38

Geometric Patterns and Symbols

Star: 1, 11, 31, 60
Flag: 1, 3, 34

Wall meander: 8
Framed triangles: 43, 82
Framed horizontal lines: 46
Framed crosshatching: 82
Inlaid diamonds, squares: 49, 67
Hook meander: 8, 23, 49
Latticing: 12, 14, 22, 40, 42, 59, 61, 67, 92
X in parallel lines: 10, 20
X-in-square or X-in-lozenge designs: 10, 20, 30, 57, 82, 103
Concentric squares/rectangles: 12
Diamonds and lozenge rows: 15, 37, 49, 67
Asterisk: 25
Hand-drawn circle: 10, 34, 43
Circle or arc of a circle: 34, 42, 82
Rosette: 10, 70, 72, 75, 82, 85
Wheel: 94
Sun/ball: 14, 59
Branch: 28 (two), 39, 95
Row of punch marks: 50
Zigzag lines: 97, 105
Unknown symbols: 35, 36, 86
Phrygian cult idol: 10, 51, 94
Maze or cult symbol: 17, 37, 60, 94 (two examples), 104

Formless Marks
13, 18, 24, 32, 33, 34, 39, 40, 41, 49, 59, 61, 63, 64, 67, 68, 70, 73, 74, 75, 76, 78, 79, 82, 84, 87, 89, 93, 97, 98

Bibliography

Akurgal, E. 1962. *The Art of the Hittites*. New York: Thames and Hudson.

Anadolu Medeniyetleri. 1983. *Catalogue of the Eighteenth European Art Exhibition, Istanbul, 22 May–30 October 1983*. Istanbul.

Aro, S. 1998. *Tabal. Zur Geschichte und materiellen Kultur des zentralanatolischen Hochplateaus von 1200 bis 600 v. Chr.* Ph.D. diss., Humanities Faculty, University of Helsinki. Helsinki.

—— 2003. Art and Architecture. In *The Luwians,* ed. H. C. Melchert, pp. 281–337. Leiden: Brill.

Beran, T. 1963. Eine Kultstätte phrygischer Zeit in Boğazköy. *Mitteilungen der deutschen Orient-Gesellschaft* 94:35–52.

Berndt-Ersöz, S. 2003. Phrygian Rock-Cut Shrines and Other Religious Monuments. A Study of Structure, Function and Cult Practice. Ph.D. diss., Dept. of Classical Archaeology and Ancient History, Stockholm University. Stockholm.

—— 2004. In Search of a Phrygian Male Superior God. *Offizielle Religion, lokale Kulte und individuelle Religiosität. Akten des religionsgeschichtlichen Symposiums "Kleinasien und angrenzende Gebiete vom Beginn des 2. bis zur Mitte des 1. Jahrtausends v. Chr." (Bonn, 20.22. Februar 2003),* ed. M. Hutter and S. Hutter-Braunsar, pp. 47–56. Alter Orient und Altes Testament 318. Münster: Ugarit-Verlag.

—— 2006. *Phrygian Rock-Cut Shrines. Structure, Function, and Cult Practice.* Leiden: Brill.

—— 2008. The Chronology and Historical Context of Midas. *Historia* 57:1–37.

Boardman, J. 1978. *Greek Sculpture: The Archaic Period.* New York: Oxford University Press.

Boehmer, R. M. 1973. Phrygische Prunkgewänder des 8. Jahrhunderts. *Archäologischer Anzeiger* 2:149–72.

Bonatz, D. 2000a. Syro-Hittite Funerary Monuments. A Phenomenon of Tradition or Innovation? *Essays on Syria in the Iron Age,* ed. G. Bunnens, pp. 189–210. Ancient Near Eastern Studies Supplement 7. Louvain: Peeters Press.

—— 2000b. *Das syro-hethitische Grabdenkmal. Untersuchungen zur Entstehung einer neuen Bildgattung in der Eisenzeit im nordsyrisch-südostanatolischen Raum.* Mainz: P. von Zabern.

Brixhe, C. 2002. Corpus des inscriptions paléo-phrygiennes. Supplément I. *Kadmos* 41:1–102.

Brixhe, C., and M. Lejeune. 1984. *Corpus des inscriptions paléo-phrygiennes.* Editions Recherches sur les civilisations Mémoire 45. Paris.

Bunnens, G. 2004. The Storm God in Northern Syria and Southern Anatolia from Hadad of Aleppo to Jupiter Dolichenus. *Offizielle Religion, lokale Kulte und individuelle Religiosität. Akten des religionsgeschichtlichen Symposiums "Kleinasien und angrenzende Gebiete vom Beginn des 2. bis zur Mitte des 1. Jahrtausends v. Chr." (Bonn, 20.22. Februar 2003),* ed. M. Hutter and S. Hutter-Braunsar, pp. 57–81. Alter Orient und Altes Testament 318. Münster: Ugarit-Verlag.

Burke, B. 2005. Textile Production at Gordion and the Phrygian Economy. *The Archaeology of Midas and the Phrygians: Recent Work at Gordion,* ed. L. Kealhofer, pp. 69–81. Philadelphia: University of Pennsylvania Museum.

Canby, J. V. 2002. Falconry (Hawking) in Hittite Lands. *Journal of Near Eastern Studies* 61:161–201.

Collins, B. J. 2002. Animals in the Religions of Ancient Anatolia. *A History of the Animal World in the Ancient Near East,* ed. B. J. Collins, pp. 309–34. Handbook of Oriental Studies 64. Leiden: Brill.

—— 2004. The Politics of Hittite Religious Iconography. *Offizielle Religion, lokale Kulte und individuelle Religiosität. Akten des religionsgeschichtlichen Symposiums "Kleinasien und angrenzende Gebiete vom Beginn des 2. bis zur Mitte des 1. Jahrtausends v. Chr." (Bonn, 20.22. Februar 2003),* ed. M. Hutter and S. Hutter-Braunsar, pp. 83–115. Alter Orient und Altes Testament 318. Münster: Ugarit-Verlag.

Collon, D. 1972. The Smiting God. A Study of a Bronze in the Pomerance Collection in New York. *Levant* 4:111–34.

Denel, E. 2007. Ceremony and Kingship at Carchemish. *Ancient Near Eastern Art in Context. Studies in Honor of Irene J. Winter by Her Students,* ed. J. Cheng and M. H. Feldman, pp. 179–204. Leiden: Brill.

DeVries, K. 1980. Greeks and Phrygians in the Early Iron Age. *From Athens to Gordion. Papers of a Memorial Symposium for Rodney S. Young,* ed. K. DeVries, pp. 33–49. Philadelphia: University Museum, University of Pennsylvania.

—— 1990. The Gordion Excavation Seasons of 1969–1973 and Subsequent Research. *American Journal of Archaeology* 94:371–406.

—— 2007. The Date of the Destruction Level at Gordion: Imports and the Local Sequence. *Anatolian Iron Ages 6. The Proceedings of the Sixth Anatolian Iron Ages Colloquium Held at Eskişehir, 16–20 August 2004,* ed. A. Çilingiroğlu and A. Sagona, pp. 79–101. Ancient Near Eastern Studies Supplement 20. Leuven: Peeters.

DeVries, K., P. I. Kuniholm, G. K. Sams, and M. M. Voigt. 2003. New Dates for Iron Age Gordion. *Antiquity* 77(296): http://antiquity.ac.uk/ProjGall/devries/devries.html.

DeVries, K., G. K. Sams, and M. M. Voigt. 2005. Gordion Re-dating. *Anatolian Iron Ages 5: Proceedings of the Fifth Anatolian Iron Ages Colloquium Held at Van, 6–10 August 2001,* ed. A. Çilingiroğlu and G. Darbyshire, pp. 45–46. British Institute of Archaeology at Ankara Monograph 31. London.

Dusinberre, E. R. M. 2005. *Gordion Seals and Sealings: Individuals and Society.* Gordion Special Studies III. Philadelphia: University of Pennsylvania Museum.

Genge, H. 1979. *Nordsyrisch-südanatolische Reliefs: eine archäologisch-historische Untersuchung, Datierung unde Bestimmung.* Det Kongelige Danske Videnskabernes Selskab. Historisk-filosofiske Meddelelser 49(1). Copenhagen.

Grave, P., L. Kealhofer, and B. Marsh. 2005. Ceramic Compositional Analysis and the Phrygian Sanctuary at Dümrek. *The Archaeology of Midas and the Phrygians: Recent Work at Gordion,* ed. L. Kealhofer, pp. 149–60. Philadephia: University of Pennsylvania Museum.

Güterbock, H. 1980. Seals and Sealing in Hittite Lands. *From Athens to Gordion. Papers of a Memorial Symposium for Rodney S. Young,* ed. K. DeVries, pp. 51–63. Philadelphia: University Museum, University of Pennsylvania.

Haspels, C. H. E. 1971. *The Highlands of Phrygia.* Princeton: Princeton University Press.

Hawkins, J. D. 1981. Kubaba at Karkamiš and Elsewhere. *Anatolian Studies* 31:147–76.

—— 1982. The Neo-Hittite States in Syria and Anatolia. In *Cambridge Ancient History* 3, Pt. 1, *History of the Middle East and the Aegean Region c. 1800–1380 B.C.,* ed. I. E. S. Edwards, J. Boardman, N. G. L. Hammond, and E. Sollberger, pp. 372–441. 2nd ed. Cambridge: Cambridge University Press:.

—— 2000. *Corpus of Hieroglyphic Luwian Inscriptions.* 4 vols. Berlin: W. de Gruyter.

—— 2003. Scripts and Texts. In *The Luwians,* ed. H. C. Melchert, pp. 128–69. Leiden: Brill.

Kealhofer, L., ed. 2005. *The Archaeology of Midas and the Phrygians. Recent Work at Gordion.* Philadelphia: University of Pennsylvania Museum.

Kohler, E. L. 1995. *The Lesser Phrygian Tumuli, Part I. The Inhumations.* The Gordion Excavations. Final Reports Vol. II. Philadelphia: University of Pennsylvania Museum of Archaeology and Anthropology.

Körte, G., and A. Körte. 1904. *Gordion. Ergebnisse der Ausgrabung im Jahre 1900.* Jahrbuch des kaiserlich deutschen archäologischen Instituts. Ergänzungsheft 5. Berlin: G. Reimer.

Melchert, H. C., ed. 2003. *The Luwians.* Handbuch der Orientalistik, Sec. 1, Vol. 68. Leiden: Brill.

Mellink, M. J. 1962. A Votive Bird from Anatolia. *Expedition* 6(2): 28–32.

—— 1983. Comments on a Cult Relief of Kybele from Gordion. In *Beiträge zur Altertumskunde*

Kleinasiens: Festschrift für Kurt Bittel, ed. R. M. Boehmer and H. Hauptmann, pp. 349–60. Mainz am Rhein: P. von Zabern.

Miller, M. C. 1988. Midas as the Great King in Attic Fifth-Century Vase Painting. *Antike Kunst* 31:79–88.

Naumann, F. 1983. *Die Ikonographie der Kybele in der phrygischen und der griechischen Kunst.* Istanbuler Mitteilungen Beiheft 28. Tübingen: E. Wasmuth.

Neumann, G. 1975. Bruchstücke alphabetischer Schriftdenkmäler aus Boğazköy. *Boğazköy* 5, ed. K. Bittel, pp. 76–84. Abhandlungen der deutschen Orient-Gesellschaft 18. Berlin: Mann.

——— 1997. Die zwei Inschriften auf der Stele von Vezirhan. In *Frigi e Frigio. Atti del 1º Simposio internazionale, Roma, 16–17 ottobre 1995,* ed. R. Gusmani, M. Salvini, and P. Vannicelli, pp. 13–32. Rome: Consiglio nazionale delle ricerche.

Nylander, C. 1970. *Ionians in Pasargadae. Studies in Old Persian Architecture.* Uppsala: Universitetet.

Orthmann, W. 1971. *Untersuchungen zur späthethitischen Kunst.* Saarbrücker Beiträge zur Altertumskunde 8. Bonn: R. Habelt.

Osten, H. H. von der. 1927–1929. *Explorations in Hittite Asia Minor.* Chicago: University of Chicago Press. Reprint, Westport, CT: Greenwood Press, 1971.

Özgüç, T. 1971. *Kültepe and Its Vicinity in the Iron Age.* Turkish Historical Society Publications, 5th series, no. 29. Ankara.

Porada, E. 1981. The Cylinder Seals Found at Thebes in Boeotia. *Archiv für Orientforschung* 28:1–70.

Prayon, F. 1987. *Phrygische Plastik. Die früheisenzeitliche Bildkunst Zentral-Anatoliens und ihre Beziehungen zu Griechenland und zum Alten Orient.* Tübinger Studien zur Archäologie und Kunstgeschichte 7. Tübingen: E. Wasmuth.

——— 2004. Zum Problem von Kultstätten und Kultbildern der anatolischen Muttergöttin im 8. Jh. v. Chr. In *60. Yaşında Fahri Işık'a Armağan: Anadolu'da Doğdu. Festschrift für Fahri Işık zum 60. Geburtstag,* ed. T. Korkut, pp. 611–22. Istanbul: Ege Yayınları.

Richter, G. M. A. 1946. Greeks in Persia. *American Journal of Archaeology* 50:15–30.

Roaf, M., and J. Boardman. 1980. A Greek Painting at Persepolis. *Journal of Hellenic Studies* 100:204–6.

Roller, L. E. 1983. The Legend of Midas. *Classical Antiquity* 2:299–313.

——— 1987. *Nonverbal Graffiti, Dipinti, and Stamps.* Gordion Special Studies I. Philadelphia: University Museum, University of Pennsylvania.

——— 1988. Phrygian Myth and Cult. *Source* 7:43–50.

——— 1991. The Great Mother at Gordion: The Hellenization of an Anatolian Cult. *Journal of Hellenic Studies* 111:128–43.

——— 1994. The Phrygian Character of Kybele: The Formation of an Iconography and Cult Ethos in the Iron Age. *Anatolian Iron Ages 3: The Proceedings of the Third Anatolian Iron Ages Colloquium,* ed. A. Çilingiroğlu and D. H. French, pp. 189–98. British Institute of Archaeology at Ankara Monograph 16. London.

——— 1999a. Early Phrygian Drawings from Gordion and the Elements of Phrygian Artistic Style. *Anatolian Studies* 49:143–51.

——— 1999b. *In Search of God the Mother: The Cult of Anatolian Cybele.* Berkeley: University of California Press.

——— 2005. A Phrygian Sculptural Identity? Evidence from Early Phrygian Drawings in Iron Age Gordion. *Anatolian Iron Ages 5: Proceedings of the Fifth Anatolian Iron Ages Colloquium,* ed. A. Çilingiroğlu and G. Darbyshire, pp. 125–30. British Institute of Archaeology at Ankara Monograph 31. London.

——— 2007. Towards the Formation of a Phrygian Iconography in the Iron Age. *Anatolian Iron Ages 6. The Proceedings of the Sixth Anatolian Iron Ages Colloquium Held at Eskişehir, 16–20 August 2004,* ed. A. Çilingiroğlu and A. Sagona, pp. 205–21. Ancient Near Eastern Studies Supplement 20. Leuven: Peeters.

——— 2008. Early Phrygian Sculpture: Refining the Chronology. *Ancient Near Eastern Studies* 45:187–98.

——— Forthcoming. Early Phrygian Incised Drawings from Gordion. In "The Archaeology of Phrygian Gordion," ed. B. Rose. Philadelphia: University of Pennsylvania Museum. In preparation.

Salzmann, D. 1982. *Untersuchungen zu den antiken Kieselmosaiken.* Berlin: Gebr. Mann Verlag.

Sams, G. K. 1974. Phrygian Painted Animals: Anatolian Orientalizing Art. *Anatolian Studies* 24:169–96.

——— 1989. Sculpted Orthostates at Gordion. In *Anatolia and the Ancient Near East. Studies in Honor of Tahsin Özgüç,* ed. K. Emre, B. Hrouda, M. Mellink, and N. Özgüç, pp. 447–54. Ankara: Türk Tarih Kurumu Basımevi.

——— 1993. Gordion and the Near East in the Early Phrygian Period. In *Aspects of Art and Iconography. Anatolia and Its Neighbors. Studies in Honor of Nimet Özgüç,* ed. K. Emre, B. Hrouda, M. Mellink, and T. Özgüç, pp. 549–55. Ankara.

——— 1994a. *The Gordion Excavations, 1950–1973: Final Reports.* 2 vols. Vol. IV, *The Early Phrygian Pottery.* Philadelphia: University Museum, University of Pennsylvania.

——— 1994b. Aspects of Early Phrygian Architecture at Gordion. In *Anatolian Iron Ages 3: The Proceedings of the Third Anatolian Iron Ages Colloquium Held at Van, 6–12 August 1990,* ed. A. Çilingiroğlu and D. H. French, pp. 211–20. British Institute of Archaeology at Ankara Monograph 16. London.

——— 1995. Midas of Gordion and the Anatolian Kingdom of Phrygia. In *Civilizations of the Ancient Near East* II, ed. J. Sasson, pp. 1147–59. New York: Scribner.

——— 1997. Gordion and the Kingdom of Phrygia. In *Frigi e Frigio. Atti del 1° Simposio internazionale, Roma, 16–17 ottobre 1995,* ed. R. Gusmani, M. Salvini, and P. Vannicelli, pp. 239–48. Rome: Consiglio nazionale delle ricerche.

Seidl, U. 1972. *Gefässmarken von Boğazköy. Boğazköy-Hattuša* 8, ed. K. Bittel. Wissenschaftliche Veröffentlichungen der deutschen Orient-Gesellschaft 88. Berlin: Gebr. Mann.

Simpson, E. 1988. The Phrygian Artistic Intellect. *Source* 7:24–42.

——— 1998. Symbols on the Gordion Screens. *XXXIVème Rencontre Assyriologique Internationale: 6–10 VII 1987 Istanbul: kongreye sunulan bildiriler:* 630–39. Ankara: Türk Tarih Kurumu Basımevi.

Simpson, E., and K. Spirydowicz. 1999. *Gordion Wooden Furniture.* Ankara: Museum of Anatolian Civilizations.

Summers, G. D. 2006. Phrygian Expansion to the East. Evidence of Cult from Kerkenes Dağ. *Bagdader Mitteilungen* 37:647–56.

Tsetskhladze, G. R. 2007. Thracians versus Phrygians: About the Origin of the Phrygians Once Again. *Anatolian Iron Ages 6: The Proceedings of the Sixth Anatolian Iron Ages Colloquium Held at Eskişehir, 16–20 August 2004,* ed. A. Çilingiroğlu and A. Sagona, pp. 283–310. Ancient Near Eastern Studies Supplement 20. Leuven: Peeters.

Voigt, M. M. 1994. Excavations at Gordion 1988–89: The Yassıhöyük Stratigraphic Sequence. In *Anatolian Iron Ages 3: The Proceedings of the Third Anatolian Iron Ages Colloquium Held at Van, 6–12 August 1990,* ed. A. Çilingiroğlu and D. H. French, pp. 265–82. British Institute of Archaeology at Ankara Monograph 16. London.

——— 2005. Old Problems and New Solutions. Recent Excavations at Gordion. In *The Archaeology of Midas and the Phrygians. Recent Work at Gordion,* ed. Lisa Kealhofer, pp. 22–35. Philadelphia: University of Pennsylvania Museum.

——— 2007. The Middle Phrygian Occupation at Gordion. *Anatolian Iron Ages 6. The Proceedings of the Sixth Anatolian Iron Ages Colloquium Held at Eskişehir, 16–20 August 2004,* ed. A. Çilingiroğlu and A. Sagona, pp. 311–33. Ancient Near Eastern Studies Supplement 20. Leuven: Peeters.

Voigt, M. M., and R. C. Henrickson. 2000. Formation of the Phrygian State: The Early Iron Age at Gordion. *Anatolian Studies* 50:37–54.

Winter, I. J. 1983. Carchemish *ša kišad puratti. Anatolian Studies* 33:177–97.

——— 1987. Art as Evidence for Interaction: Relations between the Assyrian Empire and North Syria. *Mesopotamien und seine Nachbarn. Politische und kulturelle Wechselbeziehungen im alten Vorderasien vom 4. bis 1. Jahrtausend v. Chr.,* ed. H. Nissen and J. Renger, pp. 355–82. Berliner Beiträge zum Vorderen Orient 1. Berlin:D. Reimer.

——— 1989. North Syrian Ivories and Tell Halaf Reliefs: The Impact of Luxury Goods upon

"Major" Arts. *Essays in Ancient Civilization Presented to Helene J. Kantor*, ed. A. Leonard Jr. and B. Williams, pp. 321–32. Studies in Ancient Oriental Civilization 47. Chicago: Oriental Institute of the University of Chicago.

Young, R. S. 1953. Progress at Gordion, 1951–1952. *University Museum Bulletin* 17(4): 3–39.

—— 1955. Gordion: Preliminary Report 1953. *American Journal of Archaeology* 59:1–18.

—— 1956a. The Campaign of 1955 at Gordion: Preliminary Report. *American Journal of Archaeology* 60:249–66.

—— 1956b. Discoveries at Gordion 1956. *Archaeology* 9(4): 263–267.

—— 1957. Gordion 1956: Preliminary Report. *American Journal of Archaeology* 61:319–31.

—— 1958. The Gordion Campaign of 1957: Preliminary Report. *American Journal of Archaeology* 62:139–54.

—— 1960. The Gordion Campaign of 1959: Preliminary Report. *American Journal of Archaeology* 64:227–43.

—— 1962. The 1961 Campaign at Gordion. *American Journal of Archaeology* 66:153–68.

—— 1963. Gordion on the Royal Road. *Proceedings of the American Philosophical Society* 107:348–64.

—— 1965a. Gordion: Problems of Western Phrygia. *Le rayonnement des civilisations grecque et romaine sur les cultures périphériques,* pp. 481–85. Paris: E. de Boccard.

—— 1965b. Early Mosaics at Gordion. *Expedition* 7(3): 4–13.

—— 1969a. Doodling at Gordion. *Archaeology* 22:270–75.

—— 1969b. Old Phrygian Inscriptions from Gordion: Toward a History of the Phrygian Alphabet. *Hesperia* 38:252–96.

—— 1981. *Three Great Early Tumuli*. With contributions by K. DeVries, E. L. Kohler, J. F. McClellan, M. J. Mellink, and G. K. Sams. The Gordion Excavations. Final Reports Vol. I. Philadelphia: University Museum, University of Pennsylvania.

Index

Achaemenian, 45, 46n197
Ain Dara, 23, 24n89, 26n103
Aleppo, 20
Alişar, 25
alphabet
    Greek, 35, 37
    Lycian, 34
    Lydian, 34
    Phrygian, 33–34, 35, 37
Ankara, 31n131, 48
Apollo, 45
Aramaean, Aramaic, 19n54, 20, 41
Arslankaya, 30, 36. *See also* Phrygian Highlands
Arslan Taş (Neo-Hittite site), 20
Arslantaş (Phrygian site), 24n90, 25, 48, Fig. 20. *See also* Phrygian Highlands
Athens, 46n197
Ayaş, 31n131

Babylon, 20
Boğazköy, 33, 34, 35n157, 36n159
Boiotia, 21
Büyük Kapıkaya, 36. *See also* Phrygian Highlands

Carchemish, 19n53, 20, 22, 23, 24, 25, 26, 28, 35, 44

Darius, 45
Delos, 24n87
drawing subjects
    akroterion, 15–16, 30, 31
    animals, 2, 13–15, 23–29, 37–38, 41, 43, 44, 46
    architecture, 2, 9–10, 15–16, 29–32, 38, 43, 46
    beard, 10, 11, 12, 19, 22
    belt, 10, 11, 12, 13, 22
    birds, 8, 10, 12, 13–14, 15, 23, 26–29, 37–38, 40, 43, 48–49
        birds in flight, 10, 12, 13, 14, 27
        bird of prey. *See* raptor
        crane, 26, 27
        crested bird, 26, 27
        ducks, 26, 27
        geese, 26, 27
        grouse, 13, 26
        hen, 13, 26, 27
        peacock, 13, 27
        pheasant, 13, 27
        raptor, 13, 14, 15, 21n69, 26–29, 31, 34, 37, 38, 40, 43, 48, 49
        stork, 13, 26, 27
    branch, 33–34
    cattle, 14, 26
    combat scenes, 10, 11, 13, 20, 43, 46
    composite figure, 10, 13, 23, 29
    costume, 10, 11, 12, 13, 20, 22, 23
    cult idol, 17–18, 35–36, 43
    dancing, 12
    falconry, 12, 13, 14, 23, 28, 29, 31, 34, 38, 48
    fish, 14, 26
    gate, 16, 31–32
    gazelle, 14, 26
    geometric patterns, 10, 16–17, 30, 32–35, 38, 46
    goat, 14, 25, 29
    hairstyle, 10, 12, 19, 21, 22
    hare, 12, 13, 14, 21, 45, 47
    headdress, 10, 11, 12, 13, 22, 37, 41
    helmet, 10, 11, 20
    horse, 8, 10, 14, 23, 25, 29, 49
    human figures, 2, 9, 10–13, 14, 19–23, 28, 37, 41, 43, 44, 46, 47
    hunter, 12, 13, 14, 20–21, 45
    ibex, 14, 26, 40
    lines, circles, zigzags, 8, 10, 18, 21, 39, 41, 44, 46
    lion, 8, 9, 10, 13, 14, 15, 16, 21, 23–25, 29, 30, 38, 40, 41, 43, 46, 48, 49
    lioness, 14, 25, 36–37
    maze, 8, 18, 37
    megaron, 15–16, 29–31
    quadruped, 14, 26
    rosette, 17, 30, 32, 35–37, 41
    snake, 26
    stag, 14, 23, 25, 29, 38, 46
    stick figures, 10, 11, 43

weapons, 10, 11, 12, 20–21, 23
Dümrek, 36

Eusebios, 6

falconry, 12, 13, 14, 23, 26, 28, 29, 31, 34, 38, 48

Göllüdağ, 23, 45
Gordion
    Burnt Phrygian Building, 3. *See also* Megaron 1
    Early Phrygian Citadel, 3, 4, 6, 15, 25, 28, 29, 31, 37, 38, 41, 42, 45, 46, 47
    Early Phrygian Citadel Gateway, 1, 2, 8, 39, 40, 42, 100
    Early Phrygian Destruction Level, 1, 2, 3, 4, 6, 7n32, 22, 24n81, 25, 27, 28, 29–30, 32, 33n145, 42, 43, 45, 46, 49
    fill above Megaron 2, 8, 25, 29, 98–99
    House X, 5, 6n29, 7, 44
    House Y, 1, 3, 5, 6n29, 7, 44, 98–99
    Megaron 1, 3, 4, 5, 6, 40n174, 42
    Megaron 2, 1, 2, 3–9, 15, 16n48, 17, 18, 19, 25, 27, 29, 32n133, 33, 36, 38, 39, 40, 42, 43, 44, 45, 49, 51–97
    Megaron 3, 4, 5, 6, 25, 26n99, 29n123, 30, 32n133, 42, 49
    Megaron 4, 6
    Megaron 10, 35n154
    Middle Phrygian Level (post-Destruction Level), 6, 24n81, 25n98, 26n99, 27, 28, 49
    orthostates, 26, 28n115, 29, 37, 41, 42, 47n199, 49
    Pre-Destruction Level, 26n99, 29, 37, 41, 47
    Pre-Terrace phase, 5
    storage sheds, 1, 3, 5. *See also* Houses X and Y
    Terrace Buildings, 5, 6, 7, 8, 29n123, 30, 32n133, 44, 45
    tumuli, 13, 25, 29n123, 32, 37
    Tumulus K-III, 25n98
    Tumulus MM, 1, 13n41, 29n123, 32, 33n141, 33n145, 35n155, 36
    Tumulus P, 1, 13n41, 24n88, 25, 26n99, 27, 29n123, 32, 33n140, 33n141, 36
    Tumulus W, 13n41
    West Phrygian House, 3. *See also* Megaron 2
Greece, 3, 21, 24n87, 45
    art, 45, 46n107
    script, 35, 37

Havuz, 45

Hittites, 19n53, 19n54, 21, 27, 33, 45

Julius Africanus, 6

Karatepe, 20
Kerkenes Dağ, 35n156, 44
Kimmerians, 6
Köhnüş Valley, 48. *See also* Phrygian Highlands
Körkün, 20
Kubaba, 26, 28, 34
Kültepe, 21, 45
Kululu, 45

Luwian, 19n54, 21, 26, 34–35, 37, 38, 41, 45, 47. *See also* the entries under Neo-Hittite
Lycia, 34
Lydia, 34

Malatya, 20, 21, 23, 24n89
Maltaş, 36. *See also* Phrygian Highlands
Maraş, 24, 26n104, 28n181
Matar, Phrygian Mother goddess, 26n99, 27–28, 30–31, 34, 35, 36, 37n165, 48
Mellink, Machteld J., 2n9, 49
Midas, 6
Midas City, 30, 31n128, 36. *See also* Phrygian Highlands
Mycenae, 3

Neo-Hittite
    cities, 2, 20–24, 45, 47
    cult, 26
    funerary stelae, 26, 28n121
    ivories, 45
    sculpture, 12, 19–26, 37–38, 40, 41, 43, 44, 47–48

Pancarlı, 20, 21
Persepolis, 45
Phrygian
    akroteria, 5, 16, 31
    art, 2, 17, 48, 49
    bronzes, 19, 27, 29n123
    cult symbols, 2, 5, 6, 17–18, 27–28, 30–31, 34, 35–37, 43, 44
    figurines of birds, 27
    furniture, 17, 32, 33, 36, 38
    idols, 17–18, 28n118, 35–36, 43, 44
    iron tools, 5
    ivories, 25, 26n99, 29n123, 45, 49
    language, 37

megaron, 3, 4, 15, 29–31. *See also* individual Megarons under "Gordion"
mosaic, 3n12, 5, 32–33, 36, 43
owners' marks, 33–34, 38, 43
pottery, 5, 17, 19, 25, 26n99, 27, 29n123, 32–34, 36, 38, 49
sculpture, 5, 9, 10, 16, 19, 25, 26, 28n115, 29, 37, 38, 40, 41, 48, 49n206
seals and sealings, 45–46
temple, 5–6, 30
textiles, 5n18, 17, 30, 32, 33n145, 38
wooden objects, 19, 25, 26n99, 27, 29n123, 32, 33, 36
writing, 2, 33–35, 37
Phrygian Highlands, 24, 30, 31, 35n157. *See also* Arslankaya, Arslantaş, Büyük Kapıkaya, Köhnüş Valley, Maltaş, Midas City, Yılantaş

Sakçagözü, 22, 26

Sam'al. *See* Zincirli
Sams, G. Kenneth, 40
"Smiting God", 21
Storm God, 21
Strabo, 6
sun disk, 22, 26
Syria, 2, 19, 29, 37, 45n194

Tabal, 21, 44–45, 47
Tell Halaf, 20, 22, 25, 26n100, 45
Thebes (Boiotia), 21

Vezirhan, 37

Yılantaş, 24n90, 48, Fig. 19. *See also* Phrygian Highlands
Young, Rodney S., 1, 2, 3, 6, 39

Zincirli, 20, 21, 22, 23, 24, 25, 26n103